Sociology

Sociology
Essays on Approach and Method

ANDRÉ BÉTEILLE

OXFORD
UNIVERSITY PRESS

Sociology

Essays on Approach and Method

ANDRÉ BÉTEILLE

OXFORD
UNIVERSITY PRESS

OXFORD
UNIVERSITY PRESS

YMCA Library Building, Jai Singh Road, New Delhi 110 001

Oxford University Press is a department of the University of Oxford. It furthers the
University's objective of excellence in research, scholarship, and education
by publishing worldwide in

Oxford   New York

Athens   Auckland   Bangkok   Bogota   Buenos Aires   Cape Town
Chennai   Dar es Salaam   Delhi   Florence   Hong Kong   Istanbul   Karachi
Kolkata   Kuala Lumpur   Madrid   Melbourne   Mexico City   Mumbai   Nairobi
Paris   São Paolo   Shanghai   Singapore   Taipei   Tokyo   Toronto   Warsaw

with associated companies in   Berlin   Ibadan

Oxford is a registered trade mark of Oxford University Press
in the UK and in certain other countries

Published in India
By Oxford University Press, New Delhi

ISBN 019 565 5540

Typeset in Sabon
By Eleven Arts, Keshavpuram, Delhi 110 035
Printed in India by Roopak Printer, Noida
Published by Manzar Khan, Oxford University Press
YMCA Library Building, Jai Singh Road, New Delhi 110 001

For

Radha and Tara

The intellect of man is forced to choose
Perfection of the life, or of the work,
And if it take the second must refuse
A heavenly mansion, raging in the dark.

Acknowledgements

Although most of the papers in this collection have been published previously, a few of them, notably 'Politics as a Subject for Sociology' (chapter 8) and 'Economics and Sociology' (chapter 9), were written while the volume was being prepared and with a view to their inclusion in it. Like other academics, I have been dependent on professional journals for opportunities for scholarly publication. There are three in particular from which I have received much support and sustenance: *Economic and Political Weekly* (EPW), *Sociological Bulletin* (SB) and *Contributions to Indian Sociology* (CIS), and it gives me great satisfaction to acknowledge my debt to them.

The following chapters were published earlier in *Economic and Political Weekly*: chapter 1, 'Sociology and Common Sense' (EPW, vol. xxxi, nos. 35, 36 & 37, pp. 2361–5, 1996); chapter 7, 'Religion as a Subject for Sociology' (EPW, vol. xxvii, no. 35, pp. 1865–70, 1992); chapter 9, 'Economics and Sociology' (EPW, vol. xxxv, no. 18, pp. 1531–8, 2000); and chapter 11, 'Science and Tradition' (EPW, vol. xxxiii, no. 10, pp. 529–32, 1998). Two chapters appeared previously in *Sociological Bulletin*: chapter 5, 'The Comparative Method and the Standpoint of the Investigator' (SB, vol. 47, no. 2, pp. 137–54, 1998); and chapter 12, 'Newness in Sociological Enquiry' (SB, vol. 46, no. 1, pp. 97–110, 1997). Chapter 3, 'Sociology and Anthropology: Their Relationship in One Person's Career' appeared first in *Contributions to Indian Sociology* (CIS, vol. 27, no. 2, pp. 291–304, 1993).

Chapter 6, 'Sociology and Area Study' was published originally in *Journal of the Japanese Association for South Asian Studies*, vol. 11, pp. 124–37, 1999. Chapter 4, 'Some Observations on the Comparative Method' was published by the Centre for Asian Studies Amsterdam in 1990 as the first Wertheim Lecture, and chapter 10, 'The Place of Tradition in Sociological Enquiry' by the Indian Institute of Advanced Study, Shimla in 1997 as the fifth Radhakrishnan Memorial Lecture.

Chapter 2, 'Sociology and Social Anthropology' was written for an encyclopedia to be published by Oxford University Press and, like chapter 8, 'Politics as a Subject for Sociology', is being published here for the first time.

Appendix I, which is an interview conducted by Stefan Molund at Stockholm, was published in *Anthropologiska Studier*, no. 48, pp. 31–47, 1991. Appendix II is being reproduced from my *Essays in Comparative Sociology*, Oxford University Press, Delhi, 1987, pp. 141–66.

I am deeply indebted to Professor Vinay Srivastava for his many contributions towards the preparation of this volume, and particularly for preparing the Index.

A.B.

Contents

Introduction

This is not a text-book of sociology but it has the basic ingredients for the making of one. It comprises a set of essays, written in the last ten years of my career as a professor of sociology in the Delhi School of Economics, in which I have tried to examine the nature and significance of sociology as a distinctive body of knowledge. The essays were not written in pursuance of a plan formulated in advance of their writing; in that sense they do not, when put together, make up a text-book. But they were all written in response to the need to clarify to myself and others what is distinctive of sociological understanding and explanation. The essays are addressed primarily to fellow sociologists and to students of sociology, but they may also be read by others with a more general interest in society and its institutions. Although, as I have explained in the very first chapter, sociology is not the same thing as common sense, it has a great deal to offer to the general reader with an interest in the nature and forms of social life.

It is difficult, if not impossible, to give a short answer to the question: 'what is sociology?' This is probably just as true of other disciplines such as economics, politics or law. No intellectual discipline is to be found in a finished state with its subject matter fully formed, its concepts and methods defined once and for all, and its boundaries with other disciplines finally closed. It is difficult to say briefly what sociology is because it is still in the process of formation; perhaps it will be easier to say what it was after it has ceased to be a living subject.

There is no dearth of formal definitions of sociology. Indeed, it is the number and variety of such definitions that is the main source of confusion. Unfortunately, a formal definition is of use only to someone who already has some sense of the basic contours of the subject. It conveys very little meaning to the neophyte, although it often serves as a useful point of departure in debates between scholars whose approaches to the subject are not the same.

Instead of trying to define the subject in a formal way, one may simply say that sociology is what sociologists do. The subject is no longer in its inception but has been cultivated for more than a hundred years in the west and since the 1920s in India. Several generations have studied, taught and done research in sociology. It has its own professional associations and its own periodicals. But as one would expect, the practice of sociology has not been the same either in all places or at all times. Therefore, to say that sociology is what sociologists do is merely to open up the question rather than to provide an answer.

What sociologists actually do is not quite the same thing as what they believe or say they ought to do. The divergence between the two is often quite large. But there is a dialectical relationship between them, for our practice, as sociologists, is shaped by what we ourselves and our fellow professionals think sociology to be, just as our conception of what the subject is or ought to be shaped in some measure by our practice. Therefore, in seeking to explain what sociology is, one oscillates inevitably between general discussions on the scope, aims and methods of the discipline, and specific accounts of the topics, problems and issues whose study constitutes the everyday practice of sociologists.

In the essays put together here, I have tried to approach the question of what sociology is from both ends, moving frequently and sometimes without notice from the one to the other. There are general discussions on the scope and method of sociology, and on its distinctive features in relation to other disciplines such as anthropology, economics and politics. But there are also specific accounts of what sociologists actually do when they undertake studies of religion, politics or inequality. The two types of accounts are interwoven with each other. This interweaving has come about in part because the essays were not all written in accordance with a preconceived plan. But a preconceived plan to maintain a strict separation between the general and the specific would almost certainly result in an artificial and unconvincing product.

The oscillation between the general and the specific—or the abstract and the concrete—reflects my long-standing concerns as a teacher of sociology in the Delhi School of Economics. Over a period of forty years, I have taught a whole range of courses from sociological theories to the sociology of India through social stratification, political sociology and the sociology of religion, mainly to post-graduate students but for some time also to undergraduates. It is impossible to teach any course to post-graduate students without having to address the question as to what is distinctively sociological about the approach to the topic under discussion. My own view of what sociology is and ought to be has grown mainly from discussions of this kind.

If one is serious about teaching and research, one cannot simply articulate one's own point of view and leave it at that. One must seek to relate it to other points of view, those of one's contemporaries and one's predecessors. How far afield in space and time should one venture in doing that?

* * *

If what sociology is cannot be understood in isolation from what sociologists do, then one should be prepared to find different conceptions of it because what sociologists do itself differs a great deal. Sociology is an empirical discipline whose growth has been dependent not only on the formulation of new concepts and theories but also on the investigation and analysis of new data. It has been driven as much by the engagement with facts as by the engagement with ideas. Sociological arguments become fruitful only when they throw new light on social relations, social processes and social institutions in particular places at particular times.

As an intellectual discipline, sociology was a latecomer in India as compared to the west, though not by a very wide margin. In the west, the subject developed first outside the universities and then made inroads into them by the end of the nineteenth and the beginning of the twentieth centuries. It found a place for itself in the Indian universities within a couple of decades, but its real growth as an academic discipline occurred largely after independence. There were no counterparts in India of Auguste Comte or Herbert Spencer, writers who had laid the foundations of sociology in the west from outside the universities. There were of course Indians who had contributed to social thought before sociology began to be studied and taught in Indian universities, but it is doubtful that thinkers such as Tagore and Gandhi can be properly described as sociologists or even proto-sociologists.

Because they were the first in the field, European sociologists such as Weber and Durkheim felt free to write about all societies, from the simplest to the most complex, and not just about their own society. It is this interest in and attention to the entire range of human societies the world over that gave to sociology in its formative phase its distinctive orientation as a comparative and not just an empirical discipline. Sociologists in India have been much more confined in their interests, and in the early decades of independence their work ran the risk of being absorbed into Indian studies. It is true that India offers enormous scope for comparative studies within its own boundaries but the development of the subject has undoubtedly suffered from the absence of sound empirical work by Indian sociologists on societies other than their own. New entrants into the profession feel discouraged when they find that western sociologists write freely about all societies whereas the leaders of the profession in their own country have very little to say about societies outside India.

If we consider sociology separately from anthropology, we will find that the principal focus of interest among the majority of the practitioners of the former in the west has been western society. A leading western sociologist of the previous generation had put it thus: 'Most sociologists study contemporary Western societies' (Shils 1997: 225). This rather bald statement has to be read in the context of a broader formulation by the same author: 'The societies studied by sociologists have mainly been their own; they have given most of their attention to their own contemporary societies and in the quite recent past' (Shils 1985: 801). If we accept this as a fair statement of the case, the difference between the practices of western and Indian sociologists may turn out to be only one of degree. At the same time, the difference cannot be easily ignored.

It is undeniable that, despite its comparatist orientation, the theory and practice of sociology as we know it today carries a certain western or Eurocentric bias. This is to some extent inevitable since the discipline has, as of now, attained its most developed form in the west. Not only the data but also the concepts and categories of sociology bear to some extent the imprint of the societies in which they were first formulated and used. But all sociological concepts and categories do not bear that imprint to the same extent. Concepts such as structure, process, institution, and even status and power can be detached to a very large extent from the historical forms taken by them in particular societies; other concepts such as tradition, modernity and even rationality have proved more resistant to such detachment. Sociology would amount to little as an intellectual discipline if its ablest practitioners failed completely to detach their basic concepts from the sites of their origin. There is indeed a western bias in contemporary sociology, but it serves little purpose to exaggerate it or to remain obsessed with it.

With regard to theory and method, Indian sociologists have had the advantages as well as the disadvantages of latecomers. In their teaching and research, they did not have to struggle from the very beginning to formulate all the basic concepts and categories essential for their work. Above all, they did not have to struggle, as their predecessors in nineteenth century Europe had to do, to establish the legitimacy of sociology itself as a serious intellectual discipline. By the 1920s when it came to India, sociology had already established its legitimacy; it had found a place for itself in some, though not in all, western universities, and it was relatively easy for Indian sociologists to claim a place for it in their universities.

Concepts and methods take time and effort to create and refine. When sociologists began their work in India, they found that many of the basic tools of their craft had already been fashioned, hence they were spared the time and effort needed for their fashioning. In their research, and even more in their teaching, Indian sociologists have been inclined to use, somewhat mechanically, the tools of enquiry and analysis developed first in the west and now available worldwide. In this, they have not acted very differently from sociologists in other non-western countries, for instance Mexico or Japan.

But in mental work what is too easy can also become a snare. Not all the tools available worldwide are well suited for use in every social and historical context. Their mechanical application in inappropriate settings leads to findings that are trivial and even misleading. The ready availability of the tools of their trade has discouraged innovation in concepts and methods, and made Indian sociologists shy about writing on issues relating to general sociology.

The essays presented here adopt the view that there is and can be only one general sociology, although it admits variant forms arising from different traditions of sociological practice existing within the same broad framework of aims and objectives. It is neither possible nor desirable to have different sociologies attuned to different nationalities, civilizations, religions or ideologies although, naturally, national, religious and other differences are bound to be reflected in sociological practice in different places at different times. As an intellectual discipline, sociology seeks to minimize rather than maximize such differences. Whether in the west or in India, sociology as I understand it is not an ideology, its basic aim being to treat all societies, irrespective of national, religious or ideological differences, on the same plane of enquiry and analysis.

The search for an alternative sociology for India has not led to any tangible results and is not likely to do so in the future. It has been in any case a somewhat half-hearted pursuit, and it has not seriously undermined the practice of standard sociology in the country. This practice has grown enormously in the last fifty years and is now extremely diverse. Its empirical focus, as I have already indicated, is almost entirely on Indian society although it freely utilizes the various tools employed by sociologists worldwide.

It is difficult to make a balanced assessment of the work being done by sociologists in contemporary India, and this is not the place to attempt such a task. Much of the work is of very poor quality—dull, repetitive and imitative—although in this respect Indian sociologists are not unique. At the same time, if we consider the work as a whole and over a sufficiently long period of time, we will be struck by the variety and the vitality of Indian sociology. It is doubtful that we will find such variety and vitality in any country outside the west where, as I have already said, the subject has had its longest continuous development.

It is often said that Indian sociology has not yet acquired a distinctive character, comparable to American, or even French or German sociology. There are, as I have indicated, several reasons for this. But if something distinctive in general approach and orientation emerges in Indian sociology in course of time, it is more likely to come from empirical studies relating to religion, politics and inequality in their concrete settings than from any pre-determined programme for an alternative approach and method rooted in the Indian soil.

* * *

The pursuit of sociology as a serious intellectual discipline presupposes the assignment of some value—not necessarily a uniformly positive one—to society and its institutions. There are some who say that only the individual is of value and others who maintain that the idea of society itself has become obsolete (Ingold 1990). It is difficult to see how such views can be reconciled with the sociological approach to human conduct. To extend the definition by Shils, sociology is a modern and not a post-modern discipline.

Post-modernism makes light of the institutions of society, whereas in my view, the study of institutions is at the core of sociology. In the sociological perspective adopted here, human action is at the same time both constrained and free. It is a truism that not all human action is social action, but social action is nonetheless a distinctive form of it. This means that human action takes place within a social framework which from the standpoint of the actor or agent is both a facility and a constraint. No doubt the actor enjoys some freedom in defining his social situation, but he does not create *ex nihilo* the social framework within which he situates himself.

The sociological perspective, or at least the one adopted in the essays presented here, is antithetical to the utopian. The utopian perspective has a very strong appeal for Indians, including Indian intellectuals. This is not surprising in a society in which fatalism has prevailed for so long, for utopianism and fatalism are in a fundamental sense two sides of the same coin. Indians, including Indian social scientists, often argue as if inequality, class, patriarchy, casteism and communalism can all be removed from society if only social scientists give up their self-serving ways and act strenuously and sincerely for their removal. Doing serious sociology is an uphill task in such an intellectual climate.

The sociologist who points to the many constraints against sweeping and radical changes is put on the defensive by being labelled as a conservative and a nochanger. This of course is absurd, for it is the fatalist or the utopian, and not the sociologist, who does not take change seriously. If the sociologist is first and foremost the student of modern or at least contemporary societies, then the understanding and analysis of social change is central to his subject matter.

Societies not only change, but the only way in which they can change—or resist change—is through human action. But while it is true that men make their own history, it is also true that they 'do not make it just as they please; they do not make it under circumstances chosen by themselves, but under circumstances directly encountered, given and transmitted from the past' (Marx n.d.: 15). It is these 'circumstances directly encountered', particularly in their contemporary forms, and their structures and antinomies and that constitute the starting point of sociological enquiry, whether the specific subject of that enquiry is religion or politics or class.

Moreover, and without prejudice to the case for human agency, the work of the sociologist rests on the presumption that human action has unintended and unforeseen consequences. Here I would like to draw attention to a difference of orientation between economists and sociologists by which I have been greatly struck. The main interest of the economist is in action that meets its aim, whereas for the sociologist what is striking about human action, including what is presumed to be rational action, is that it so often fails to meet its aim. In the sixties, when I was studying land reforms, my experience was that economists generally expected the reforms, provided they were well-formulated, to achieve their objectives, while sociologists were less surprised when they found that the consequences of the reforms were sometimes the opposite of what was intended.

The standpoint from which these essays were written distinguishes sociology from social engineering on one hand and from social activism on the other. My view of sociology is that it serves a larger social purpose through neither social engineering nor social activism but by advancing man's critical understanding of his social circumstances. This is not a very dramatic or heroic view of the subject, but one which corresponds fairly well with the actual aims and objectives of the majority of its practitioners. I cannot think of many sociologists who have contributed substantially to the solution of practical social problems or used their specialized knowledge to spearhead an effective social movement. But the best among them, such as Max Weber, Raymond Aron and, in our own country, M.N. Srinivas, have enriched our critical understanding of our own social circumstances.

In a developing country such as ours, there is moral pressure on the social scientist to make some tangible contribution to social reconstruction. The pressure to aid and assist a beleaguered government by finding ways for removing economic and social backwardness was particularly strong in the early years of independence when I was beginning my career as a sociologist. The economists were in the forefront of the effort to find solutions to pressing practical problems, but many sociologists and social anthropologists felt that they too should contribute something.

I have never been attracted by the idea of sociology as a policy science. It can contribute something to policy analysis but very little to policy prescription. Sociologists who place their services at the disposal of the government often come to grief; their advice is either ignored or put to uses contrary to the ones intended. On this point, what Robert Merton (1968: 261–78) had said many years ago about the role of the intellectual in public bureaucracies still holds true to a large extent.

Today, at least in India, young sociologists are no longer excited by the idea of advising the government in the service of society; they are much more enthused by the idea of transforming society through active engagement in social movements. But I doubt that sociology as an intellectual discipline has much more to contribute to social activism than it does to social engineering. In my experience, social activists quickly lose patience with disciplined enquiry and analysis, preferring instead the moral high ground from which they can speak with ease about empowerment and social justice. Social activism can itself follow different paths, for one can be an activist not only in the cause of class struggle or gender justice or environmental protection but also in the cause of *hindutva* and national glory.

Those who opt out of social engineering and social activism do not all have to live in an ivory tower. Indeed, the contemporary Indian university, where this work was largely conceived and written, has an atmosphere that is very different from that of an ivory tower. The sociologist engaged in furthering the advancement of critical understanding is not condemned to playing the role of disinterested bystander. By analysing the forms and functions of social institutions he can help people to gain a deeper insight into the true nature of the constraints under which they live. He can also help them to understand what price they have to pay for every choice they make. If this be the case, then the sociologist does not construct a new society as the engineer constructs a bridge; he only helps to give a focus to the consciousness out of which people create or recreate their own society.

The social activist is by his own free choice a partisan, and partisanship undermines the very conditions of sociological enquiry and analysis. The position adopted here is that society is a field of contending values and interests, and that the sociologist serves his purpose best by not taking sides in the contention. As far as the present author is concerned, it is fairmindedness, and not partisanship, that is the defining virtue of the sociologist.

* * *

The first chapter deals with sociology and common sense. It was written to honour Nirmal Kumar Bose who was endowed with robust common sense as well as a passionate belief in the value of scientific enquiry. It tries to place sociology as a particular branch of knowledge in the widest context of general ideas and beliefs. The point is not so much that sociology should set itself against common sense as that it should try to reach beyond it. Only a handful of individual sociologists have succeeded in changing the common sense of their time; but that, rather than success in a political cause, should be the aim of sociology as a discipline.

The two essays that follow deal with sociology and social anthropology. The first of the two is more general, using a broad definition of sociology so as to include social anthropology. It discusses the scope, aims and achievements of the discipline with special reference to the work done in India, though not by Indian scholars alone, in the last fifty years. The second one provides a more personal account in which the vexed and changing relationship between sociology and anthropology is brought to light.

The next two essays discuss the comparative method in somewhat different ways. They both reflect my long-standing association with Dutch sociology which began in 1984 when I held the Tinbergen chair at the Erasmus University in Rotterdam. The first essay on the comparative method was delivered as the Wertheim lecture in Amsterdam in July 1990 with Professor W.F. Wertheim himself in the audience. The second essay was presented five years later at a seminar in Bangalore, organized by Dutch and Indian scholars under the auspices of the Indo-Dutch Programme for Alternatives in Development. Being on the same subject, there is naturally some overlap between the two essays although I have tried to reduce it as far as possible.

Since I believe that the comparative method is the backbone of sociology, my discussion of it figures in every one of the essays in the collection. I have tried to bring out the significance of the comparative method for sociology by contrasting the latter with area studies in 'Sociology and Area Studies', which was an address delivered to a group of Japanese scholars at Osaka. It seems to me that Japanese scholars are following the path laid down in the United States by maintaining the distinction between sociology and anthropology.

The following three chapters, devoted to religion, politics and economics, constitute a set. Each brings out in relation to a particular set of substantive issues what I consider to be the distinctive features of sociology as an intellectual discipline. They all stress the salience of the comparative method; they all point to the importance of revealing the interconnections among different social factors; and they all stress the need to keep value judgements separate from judgements of facts. The essays on economics and on politics, like the two earlier ones having to do with anthropology, discuss the question of boundaries between neighbourly disciplines.

The last three chapters discuss continuity and change in systems of knowledge with special reference to sociology as a branch of scholarship. Tradition occupies an ambiguous, not to say a vexatious, place in sociology. Sociologists study tradition, but they themselves work within specific traditions of knowledge. The position taken in these essays, as in the work as a whole, is that, while tradition is indispensable to social life, including the organized pursuit of knowledge, we cannot, as sociologists, speak of it in the singular but only in the plural. There are many different traditions, some of great antiquity and others of more recent origin, some restricted to small areas and others cutting across national frontiers. The traditions of science and scholarship are not the same as those of religion or politics; and these various traditions are sometimes, though not always or invariably, in conflict with each other.

Science and scholarship have to do not only with the transmission of existing knowledge but also with the creation of new knowledge. They are sustained not only by tradition but also by innovation. When viewed in a broader sociological perspective, tradition and innovation do not appear as antithetical principles. At the same time, it is difficult to determine, on the plane of individual activity, the conditions for the creation of new knowledge. As Max Weber had put it, 'Ideas occur to us when they please, not when it pleases us' (1946: 136). What the institutions of science and scholarship do is to keep the individual in readiness should a new idea choose to come his way. In my experience, scholars who are obsessed with the pursuit of novelty rarely contribute anything of value to scholarship.

The essays briefly summarized above cover a broad range of topics and issues in sociology, although they are by no means exhaustive. They have been collected together in the hope that they will give the reader some sense of the theory and practice of sociology in its Indian setting. I have included two Appendices dealing with supplementary topics. Appendix I presents an interview conducted by the Swedish anthropologist Stefan Molund in Stockholm in May 1990; it is included here in order to give the reader some idea of how our work appears to a distant but sympathetic observer. Appendix II belongs to a slightly earlier period. It was a keynote address delivered at the third decennial conference of the Association of Social Anthropologists at Cambridge in July 1983. It is reproduced here in order to record my long-standing and continuing engagement with Marxism.

References

Ingold, Tim (ed). 1990. *The Concept of Society is Theoretically Obsolete.* Manchester: Department of Social Anthropology, University of Manchester.

Marx, Karl. n.d. *The Eighteenth Brumaire of Louis Bonaparte.* Moscow: Foreign Languages Publishing House.

Merton, Robert K. 1968. *Social Theory and Social Structure.* Glencoe: The Free Press.

Shils, Edward. 1985. 'Sociology'. In Adam and Jessica Kuper (eds). *The Social Science Encyclopedia.* London: Routledge and Kegan Paul, pp. 799–811.

————. 1997. *The Virtue of Civility.* Indianapolis: Liberty Fund.

Weber, Max. 1946. 'Science as a Vocation'. In H.H. Gerth and C.W. Mills (eds). *From Max Weber: Essays in Sociology.* New York: Oxford University Press, pp. 129–56.

Chapter 1

Sociology and Common Sense*

S ociology in contemporary India is a loosely-defined field of intellectual activity. There are pervasive disagreements about its aims, scope, approach, methods, concepts and subject matter. There are professors of sociology who not only disapprove of the subject as it exists but are sceptical about the very possibility of its existence; and there are laypersons with only a passing acquaintance with its vocabulary who speak confidently about its various branches. Part of the ambiguity and uncertainty characteristic of sociology arises from the fact that it touches the everyday experience of the ordinary person at so many points; and it often appears so close to common sense that there is an inevitable tendency to use the one in place of the other.

On this occasion, I shall confine myself largely to academic sociology or the discipline that is pursued under that name in the universities and institutes of research. This is not to suggest that the subject can have no place outside academic institutions. Auguste Comte and Herbert Spencer, two of the most influential sociologists of the nineteenth century, had little to do with universities, and Max Weber who came after them did much of his work outside the university. At the same time, sociology has been a recognized academic discipline in India for more than seventy

*This is the text of the N.K. Bose Memorial Lecture delivered in Calcutta on 20 June 1996 under the auspices of the Anthropological Survey of India on the occasion of its Golden Jubilee. I am grateful to the Director of the Survey, Dr R.K. Bhattacharya for inviting me to deliver the lecture.

years, and there has been a virtual explosion of the subject in universities and research institutes since independence. It may be useful to look at the work being done in these centres of study and research before enquiring into the relations of the subject to the wider intellectual currents in society.

I wish to argue that for all its own unresolved, and perhaps unresolvable, differences, sociology is distinct from common sense. It has a body of concepts, methods and data, no matter how loosely co-ordinated, for which common sense of even the most acute and well-informed kind cannot be a substitute. For one thing, sociological knowledge aims to be general, if not universal, whereas common sense is particular and localized. Educated, middle-class Bengalis, like other people, educated or uneducated, anywhere are apt to believe that their common sense is common sense as such or the common sense of mankind. One of the lasting contributions of sociology has been to show that common sense is in fact highly variable, subject to the constraints of time and place as well as other, more specifically social constraints.

To say that sociology is distinct from common sense is not to suggest that it should seek deliberately to be arcane or esoteric. Because it is so difficult to disengage oneself from common sense in the analysis of the human condition, and particularly in the study of one's own society, professional sociologists are frequently tempted to take recourse to needless conceptual and verbal sleight of hand. Here I would like to recall N.K. Bose's observation about scientists who, he would say, were of two kinds, those who made complex things simple, and those who made simple things complex, his preference—and mine as well—being for the former. We must surely deplore the mystification of the simple through the display of technical virtuosity but we must also recognize that common sense is not always, or by its own unaided effort, successful in making complex things simple.

Thus, sociology has to steer an uneasy course between two unfruitful alternatives: submergence in the common sense of the scholar's own environment, and absorption in a narrow and self-satisfied technical virtuosity unconnected with the substance of social enquiry. Let me repeat that nothing will be gained by abandoning either common sense or the cultivation of technical skills. Just as common sense is full of snares and pitfalls for the unwary sociologist, so too technical virtuosity becomes a distraction when pursued as an end in itself. In what follows, I shall have very little to say about technical virtuosity, my main concern for the present being with the interpenetration of sociological knowledge and common sense.

* * *

I would like to illustrate the nature of the problem by referring, very briefly, to my experience as a teacher of sociology at the post-graduate level over the last few decades. The question I wish to put before you is why sociology is such a difficult subject to teach. This may appear to be an odd question since, compared to the hard sciences or even economics, sociology is regarded by the majority of students as a soft subject, chosen principally by those for whom other, more attractive or more difficult, options are not open. To be sure, the routine teaching of sociology at both undergraduate and post-graduate levels goes on throughout the country without much apparent exertion from either teachers or students. What I have in mind, on the other hand, is teaching as a serious and unremitting effort to open the mind to new facts and new arguments, and the unsuspected connections among them.

Again, I have in mind not only teachers who are prepared to make the effort but also students among whom a certain interest in the subject may be presumed to exist. The most serious obstacle to the concentration and deepening of the interest is that the better equipped students soon begin to wonder what there is to learn in sociology except a series of terms and concepts and, in the sociology of India, a variety of observations on village, caste, joint family, class, community, urbanization, industrialization, modernization and so on, with which they are already familiar to a greater or lesser extent. Sociology does not have the kind of formal theory that can be readily communicated by the conscientious teacher to an attentive student. It does not confine itself to a body of facts delimited by space and time, as do geography and history to a large extent. It deals with both arguments and facts, but the connections among them often appear loose, open and ambiguous.

In the absence of a clear and established framework, discussion and argument tend to wander in every direction. This may be a good thing in a research seminar but it makes both teaching and learning extremely difficult in the classroom. In a research seminar, the discussion has to be confined at least within the boundaries of the subject specified. In M.A. or undergraduate teaching, on the other hand, one can expect a change of gear from one course to another, and, even within the same course, from one topic to another. While students might easily comprehend, item by item, what is being taught or explained, it is often very difficult for them to grasp the connections among the items. It sometimes appears that every argument as well as its opposite is true; and facts can be marshalled, without too much trouble, to support contrary theories.

In my experience, students find it hard to cope with a subject in which the teacher is unable to provide the one correct answer to each of the important questions, whether it is about class or kinship or religion or politics. The laws of physics, and upto a point the facts of history, no matter how complex or detailed, can generally be stated in forms that can be judged to be either right or wrong. In sociology, the situation is often different, with a greater room for ambiguity and disagreement. Indian students in particular, find it disorienting when their teacher is unable to come out with the right answer to their questions every time. There are of course many teachers who answer all questions with the same air of authority but they are sooner or later found out by their students. Students who can write fluently use their common sense and a superficial acquaintance with names and opinions to cobble together reasonably good answers. Others who may have struggled with the subject but are handicapped by poverty of expression produce answers that are weak, confused and meandering. The examiner is often unsure whether he is giving credit for a well-written essay or for a good knowledge of the subject. Exactly the same problem arises in evaluating manuscripts for journal articles or books; many a trivial article gets published because it is written in good prose, whereas one with more substantial arguments, but badly presented, gets rejected.

Among students, the use of common sense (and fluency in language) is most in evidence in papers dealing with India. After all, every Indian student knows something about caste, class, joint family and Hinduism, and if he has some mental agility, he can write a plausible essay on any of these topics without being too far wrong. But such a student soon finds himself out of his depth when he has to deal with such topics as kinship in Africa, or religion in Indonesia, or social mobility in France. I have always opposed the patriotic zeal of those scholars who would like to confine the teaching of sociology to material relating largely to India. No student can learn how to construct a proper sociological argument unless he is taught to handle empirical material relating to every type of society, his own society as well as other societies.

The most acute pedagogical problem in university departments of sociology in India is to integrate what is taught under sociological theory with what is taught under the sociology of India. So far as I know, there are courses devoted to both major areas in all post-graduate departments of sociology in the country, and so far as I can judge, they are nowhere integrated in even a moderately satisfactory way. I point only to the gravity of the problem without wishing to propose any easy solution to it. The path chosen by most Indian sociologists as they move towards maturity is to steadily jettison the general equipment of sociological knowledge in order to give their undivided attention to the problems of Indian society. I, on the other hand, believe that by turning away from the accumulated concepts, methods and data of sociology in general, we will in the long run only impoverish and not enrich the sociology of India.

In the last forty years, there has been a slow but steady displacement of interest away from the general concepts, methods and theories of sociology towards an increased concentration of attention on the current problems of society, culture and politics in India. Again, I would like to draw on my personal experience to make a point. Thirty years ago, when I went to lecture to students of sociology in universities outside Delhi, my hosts were quite happy to hear me speak on general topics: theories of evolution, types of lineage system, and relations between status and power. Now they mostly want me to speak on reservations, caste politics, communalism and secularism.

Virtually the only active intellectual contact professional sociologists have with new developments in theory and method is through their teaching of students at the post-graduate and, to some extent, the under-graduate levels; those who work in specialized institutes of research largely have to do even without that. Research seminars are generally, if not invariably, on topics dealing with India and there is often a conspicuous absence of a broader comparative or theoretical interest. Then there are the large annual conferences: these are now devoted almost entirely to current affairs, and even the less newsworthy features of Indian society and culture, and their underlying structure, receive scant attention.

Sociology has always and everywhere maintained some concern for current affairs, but that concern does not necessarily drive out other, more academic interests in topics that are remote from the obsessions of newspaper editors and columnists. N.K. Bose maintained a lifelong interest in the distribution of material traits; G.S. Ghurye wrote on dual organization, on *gotra* and *charana*, on Indian costumes and on ancient cities; Irawati Karve wrote a book on kinship organization in India. Such topics have a marginal place in the many regional and national seminars and conferences organized by sociologists today; they have largely been driven out by what are believed to be more socially relevant subjects.

There is no doubt the preoccupation among Indian sociologists, regularly expressed at seminars and conferences, with the appropriateness of the existing body of sociological knowledge to the understanding of Indian society and culture. These discussions are not so much about methods and techniques of investigation as about the presuppositions of sociological knowledge and about the nature of understanding and explanation. They tend to be presented in highly abstract and speculative terms, and rarely lead to any concrete or workable propositions. Alternative approaches to the study of Indian society can hardly produce results unless they are linked to the disciplined practice of a craft; no new approach has emerged in science or scholarship from the mere desire to have a new approach.

* * *

Today, at the close of the twentieth century, it is impossible to practise sociology as a serious academic discipline without drawing on the vast reservoir of sociological concepts, methods and theories created by scholars over the last hundred years. This has been mainly, though not solely, the work of western scholars, and like any accumulated body of knowledge, it contains much that is mistaken, distorted and obsolete. Therefore, in the pursuit of his work, the practising sociologist, whether in the west or in India, has to maintain an alert and critical attitude to it. But that is far from saying that he can set it all aside in the hope that a completely new framework can be created *ex nihilo* by some as yet unrecognized genius nourished by the Indian air. Surely, there is room for an Indian perspective, or, better, several Indian perspectives, but to be viable, they have to address themselves to society and culture as such, and not just to Indian society and culture.

The builders of modern sociology, Émile Durkheim, Max Weber, and others took the whole of human society in its diverse and changing forms as their object of study, even when their primary attention was devoted to their own society. To be sure, their observations on other societies were limited, one-sided and often misleading. But they believed, one and all, that the disciplined application of the sociological method would contribute much to the understanding of their own society; and that this understanding could be deepened and broadened by systematic comparisons between their societies and other societies. They were all convinced that common sense was not enough to reach the understanding they sought, and that they had to fashion new tools of enquiry and analysis to attain their objective.

The sociologist who did most to lay bare the illusion of understanding created by common sense was Émile Durkheim. He argued tirelessly that the systematic investigation of a subject was not possible unless the investigator freed himself from his preconceptions of it. These preconceptions, shaped generally by a limited experience, were not only often wrong but also impediments to the examination of the available and relevant facts.

Early in his career, Durkheim gave a brilliant demonstration of the superiority of his approach over that of common sense through his study of suicide.[1] His argument was that suicide was a social fact whose forms and patterns could not be explained by the known facts of human psychology. Now that we have Durkheim's study and the many others to which it gave rise behind us, this perhaps does not seem a great revelation any longer. But when it first appeared, it did seem startling to discover that social causes were behind what common sense might lead one to believe was the supremely private or individual act. As is well known, Durkheim pursued systematically the distinction between the *incidence* and the *rate* of suicide, and brought together a wealth of data to show that suicide rates varied systematically between societies, and between religious, occupational and other groups within the same society. Further, while suicide rates were on the whole highly stable, they were also subject to fluctuations due to social and economic causes which he sought to identify. One of Durkheim's remarkable findings was that suicide rates go up significantly not only after an economic crash but also after an economic boom.

Not all of Durkheim's observations on suicide have stood the test of time,[2] but that is not the point. The point is that when he had an important idea that appeared to go against common sense, he decided, as a sociologist, to test that idea by systematically assembling a large body of data, and applying to the data, concepts and methods that may also be applied to other domains of life in other parts of the world.

One of Max Weber's most fundamental ideas by which sociology has been enriched everywhere is that the consequences of human action are rarely the same as the intentions of the actors, and that sometimes the two are diametrically opposite. One can say again that it is no great discovery that our actions often miscarry and end in ways that we least expect. But in science and scholarship what counts is not just the original insight but the significance of the domain to which it is applied, and the methods and data by which the insight is tested. Weber's application of the insight in exploring the relationship between religious values and economic action has produced a rich harvest of detailed and systematic studies by generations of sociologists the world over.[3]

Here I would like to make a brief observation on Weber's approach to religion, partly because of its intrinsic importance and partly because it has been frequently misrepresented. The prevailing view among social theorists until Weber's time was that, for good or evil, religion was a great source of social stability. This was Marx's view, and because he believed change to be both necessary and desirable, he assigned a negative value to religion. Durkheim, on the other hand, assigned a positive value to religion because he believed that stability was essential for the maintenance of collective life. Weber's originality lay in his investigating, systematically and with a sharp eye for detail, the profound consequences of the breakthrough in religion for the organization of economic life. In his view, it was neither the commitment to ideal values nor the demands of material existence, but the tension between the two that was the true source of change in society.

* * *

What I have tried to stress so far is that sociology is a disciplined and specialized activity in which the role of originality should not be exaggerated. It is a craft that needs patience and care, and a long apprenticeship to acquire. Its concepts and methods are not things that any intelligent person can construct on his own in order to satisfy a passing intellectual urge. Having drawn attention to the empirical grounding of the discipline in the careful observation and description of facts, I would now like to make a few remarks on two of the fundamental preoccupations of sociology: its rigorous search for interconnections among the different domains of society and its systematic use of comparisons.

Sociology is not about economic, political or domestic life; it is not about class, caste or community; it is not about the ideal of equality or the reality of inequality. It is about the interconnections among all these and other aspects of social life. This constitutes what some have been pleased to call the 'functionalist bias' of sociology. While freely admitting to that bias, I must point out that it does not in any way rest on the presupposition that the interrelations in society are harmonious rather than inharmonious, or stable rather than unstable. Sociology in the last few decades has been invaded by a kind of mindless Marxism for whose proponents the word 'functionalist' has acted like the red rag to a bull. Detailed analyses by sociologists have on the other hand led to the very fruitful distinction between 'social integration' and 'system integration'.[4]

The search for interrelations is laborious and time consuming, and it has its own procedures: survey research, statistical analysis, participant-observation and case studies. It does not always, or even generally, lead to spectacular results, but meaningful and unsuspected connections can be reached only by sifting through masses of connections that are trivial and easily accessible to common sense. It is in this way that the great advances in sociological knowledge have been made, generally incrementally and only rarely by a dramatic breakthrough.

The detailed and systematic examination of interrelations has shown that sometimes economic factors were important where they were not suspected to be and, at other times, the ties of kinship and marriage were seen to have unforeseen consequences on various areas of social life. However, the belief that one single factor or set of factors, whether economic or religious, holds the key to all the interconnections in society has been a hindrance rather than a help in sociological enquiry. Sociology has never been able to make its peace with either the religious interpretation of the world or the materialist interpretation of history.

Patient and systematic studies by sociologists have brought to light many aspects of Indian society where things are not what they seem. I can refer here to only a few examples, and that too very briefly. Shortly after independence, a whole range of village monographs began to be published by trained anthropologists, and these have altered our perception of rural India and Indian society in general. M.N. Srinivas formulated the important distinction between the 'book-view' and the 'field-view' of Indian society,[5] emerging as the principal protagonist of the latter and repeatedly drawing attention to the errors of the former.

Srinivas's most seminal contribution was his exposure of the misperception of caste among educated Indians. He attacked the conception of caste as a rigid and inflexible system based on the division of Hindu society into the four *varnas*. He maintained: 'The *varna*-model has produced a wrong and distorted image of caste.'[6] He was able to show that far from being absolutely rigid and inflexible, the caste system accommodated distinct forms of social mobility. Further, by drawing attention away from *varna* to *jati*, he was able to see more clearly than the political commentators of the day that the role of caste was increasing rather than declining in Indian politics.

My own detailed study conducted in Tanjore district more than thirty years ago addressed itself to the view then widely prevalent that the Indian village was a 'little republic'.[7] I had no difficulty in showing that the village in which I lived and worked for nearly a year was riddled with inequality and conflict; and my reading of village monographs by other social anthropologists, both Indian and foreign, and my general training as a sociologist convinced me that what I had observed and recorded was general rather than exceptional.

Similarly, the work of my colleague, A.M. Shah has exposed, through the systematic analysis of a wealth of empirical material, some common misperceptions about changes in the Indian family system.[8] This misperception arises partly from a confused conception of the joint family, and partly from insufficient attention to the available evidence. Shah's work shows that the proportion of 'joint-family households' was never larger than that of 'nuclear-family households'; that in most sectors of contemporary Indian society, urban as well as rural, there are still many joint-family households; and that the average size of a household in the Indian population has remained roughly the same in the last hundred years.

Despite the rich harvest of studies on practically every aspect of Indian society and culture, there is a striking shortage of studies by Indian sociologists of other societies and cultures. Not only that, in their empirical research, most Indian sociologists confine their attention to their regions of origin: Bengalis to West Bengal, Gujaratis to Gujarat, and Tamilians to Tamil Nadu. It is unfortunate that Indian sociologists have taken so little advantage of the comparative method, because it is in the use of that method mainly that sociology scores over common sense.

Since I attach a great deal of importance to the comparative method and have devoted much time and effort writing about it,[9] I cannot pass it by without making a few brief observations on it. It is useful to begin with Durkheim's statement on the subject: 'Comparative sociology is not a special branch of sociology; it is sociology itself.'[10] The sociologist acquires the habit of comparison so that no matter which process or institution he is examining, he brings to it insights from the study of similar processes and institutions in other societies and cultures. Nor is it a matter of mere habit; rules of procedure have been devised, tested and refined as an essential part of comparative study. There is nothing in the comparative method as such that requires every investigator to cover the entire range of societies, near and distant. As Durkheim has put it, comparisons 'can include facts borrowed either from a single and unique society, from several societies of the same species, or from several distinct social species'.[11]

India, with its large and varied population, offers rich possibilities for comparisons within its own confines. I will conclude this section by referring to two examples of comparisons from my own work, one very restricted and the other very wide in scope. The first was a taluk by taluk comparison in Tanjore district of the relations between the cleavages arising from the ownership, control and use of land, and those arising from caste;[12] it deepened my own understanding of the peculiar combination of factors that leads to class formation in agriculture. The second is a long-standing comparative study of positive discrimination in India and affirmative action in the United States; it has enriched my understanding of the distinction between rights and policies, and of the relationship between distributive justice and institutional well-being.[13]

* * *

Common sense is not only localized—being bound by time, place, class, community, gender and so on—it is also unreflective since it does not question its own origins and presuppositions, or at least does not do so deliberately and methodically. It goes without saying that no sociologist can fully insulate his scholarly work from the presuppositions of his common sense. Our sociology is influenced to a greater or lesser extent by the common sense which is a part of our own social environment, but to what extent is that common sense in its turn influenced by sociology?

Common sense is based on a limited range of experience of particular people in particular places and times. Where it relates to such matters as family, marriage, kinship, work and worship, people are inclined to believe that their way of doing things is the right way or the reasonable way. Other ways of acting in these regards strike them as being not only wrong but also contrary to common sense. This is because they only observe or experience other ways of acting and thinking in bits and pieces, and not in their entire context. Seeing alien and unfamiliar practices in their proper context often makes those practices appear quite sensible; familiarity with a wide range of practices occasionally makes one's own ingrained ways of acting and thinking appear peculiar if not quixotic. An old Chinese poem says:

When I carefully consider the curious habits of dogs,
I am compelled to conclude that man is the superior animal.
When I consider the curious habits of man,
I confess, my friend, I am puzzled.

Comparative sociology is a great help in acquiring and maintaining a sense of proportion.

I would like to avoid inviting the charge of making invidious distinctions among disciplines. At the same time, it is essential to draw attention to the peculiar preoccupation of sociology with the similarities as well as the differences among societies, with comparison as well as contrast. To be sure, historians have recorded diverse beliefs and practices among people at different places and different times over a longer period than have sociologists. But their characteristic tendency has been to study the diversity of beliefs, practices and institutions severally rather than jointly. It is the rare historian who does comparative history, whereas one cannot really escape from comparison and contrast while studying sociology.

Sociology does not simply deal with facts from the entire range of human societies, it seeks to place those facts on the same plane of observation and analysis. The educated layman can hardly be expected to master all the facts with which the sociologist deals. He follows at best the method of apt illustration and no consistent rule of procedure for the selection and arrangement of facts. On the other hand, sociological practice develops a characteristic style of argument that does tend to filter through ever-widening circles in the course of time. Over the long run, the sociological mode of reasoning has had some effect on thinking about education, politics, class and inequality.

Where sociological reasoning acts upon common sense, it tends to moderate both the utopian and the fatalistic elements in it. Common sense easily constructs imaginary social arrangements in which there is no inequality, no oppression, no strife and no constraint on individual choice: a world in which society makes it possible 'for me to do one thing today and another tomorrow, to hunt in the morning, fish in the afternoon, rear cattle in the evening, criticise after dinner, just as I have a mind, without ever becoming hunter, fisherman, shepherd or critic'.[14] Sociology is anti-utopian in its central preoccupation with the disjunction between ideal and reality, between what human beings consider right, proper and desirable and their actual conditions of existence, not in this or that particular society but in human societies as such.

Sociology is also anti-fatalistic in its orientation. It does not accept the particular constraints taken for granted by common sense as eternal or immutable. It provides a clearer awareness than common sense of the range of alternative arrangements that have been or may be devised for the attainment of broadly the same ends. No social arrangement, no matter how beneficial, is without some cost. Social costs and benefits are far more difficult to weigh and measure than the purely economic ones. A finely-tuned judgement is essential for this, and that can be formed only through the disciplined and methodical examination of the varieties of social arrangements created, adopted and replaced by successive generations.

This leads to the question of value-neutrality or, better, the distinction between value judgements and judgements of reality in sociology as against common sense. There is now a considerable body of sociological literature, some of it abstract and technical, on this question, although this is not to say that all disagreements on it have been or even can be settled on purely technical grounds. By and large, there is agreement among sociologists that questions of fact are distinct from judgements of value, and that the two ought to be differentiated as clearly as possible by all the technical means available.[15] The disagreement is about the extent to which the distinction can be consistently maintained in practice, and the best means to be adopted in achieving or approaching that end.

There is an influential tradition in sociological enquiry that views the methods and procedures of the discipline as being, at least in principle, the same as those of the natural sciences. Not only animals, vegetables and minerals, but also men and women and their social arrangements can be made subjects of science.[16] In this tradition, which has generated enormous amounts of useful information and some fruitful analysis, all descriptions and all evaluations are suspect unless they are made in accordance with certain procedures that consciously eliminate, or at least minimize, the investigator's bias; and common sense, in this view, is always a source of potential bias and error.

Not all sociologists view their discipline as a kind of natural science; today perhaps the majority of them view it as a moral science. One of the problems in keeping values strictly separate from facts in the moral or human sciences is that values themselves are an important part, some would say the most important part, of their subject matter. In other words, the sociologist has to treat values as facts, as a part of his data, whether he is studying his own society or some other society, or both. But even here, he has to distinguish as clearly as possible the different kinds of facts with which he has to deal; for instance, the demographic composition of a community as against the religious ideas of its members.

It takes a special kind of discipline—at once intellectual and moral—to insulate the values being investigated by the sociologist from his own personal and social values. In a sense, what the sociologist investigates and the means by which he investigates it are of one piece, more so where the study of one's own society is concerned. This makes the separation between the two particularly urgent on the intellectual plane and particularly difficult on the moral plane. As Max Weber had observed on this question: 'Nor need I discuss further whether the distinction between empirical statements of fact and value-judgements is "difficult" to make. It is.'[17] It is here, and particularly in India, that the sociologist is most frequently tempted to let go of his slippery hold over the resources of his discipline and to revert to plain common sense.

There is now an accumulated body of experiences as well as reasoned discussions relating to the choices involved in the study of one's own society as well as the study of other cultures. The experience shows the significance in all cases of the standpoint of the investigator: in the human sciences, there is no Archimedean point from which the investigator can examine his subject matter as a completely disengaged observer. The same subject reveals different aspects when investigated from different standpoints; although different, the results of these investigations need not be contradictory. Indeed, the advancement of sociological knowledge becomes possible only when investigations made from different standpoints keep themselves open to mutual correction. This is a slow, laborious process that does not, by its very nature, have any final outcome.

In conclusion, it is not true that the sociologist does not or should not express moral preferences. But his moral preferences are or ought to be formed on a somewhat different basis from what is given to each person by his common sense. It is doubtful that sociology can ever attain a state from which it can dictate the moral choices of the individual. Those choices are, in the end, matters of individual judgement and individual responsibility. Sociology can only help a little in giving the individual a better sense of the alternatives available, and of the likely costs and benefits of each of the available alternatives.

Notes and References

1. Durkheim, Émile. 1951. *Suicide: A Study in Sociology.* Glencoe: The Free Press.

2. Giddens, Anthony. 1977. 'A Theory of Suicide' and 'The Suicide Problem

in French Sociology'. In his *Studies in Social and Political Theory*. London: Hutchinson, pp. 297–332.

3. Weber, Max. 1976. *The Protestant Ethic and the Spirit of Capitalism*. London: Allen and Unwin.

See also Gordon Marshall. 1982. *In Search of the Spirit of Capitalism: An Essay on Max Weber's Protestant Ethic Thesis*. London: Hutchinson.

4. Lockwood, David. 1992. 'Social Integration and System Integration'. In his *Solidarity and Schism*, Oxford: Clarendon Press, Appendix, pp. 399–412.

5. Srinivas, M.N. (ed). 1960. *India's Villages*. Bombay: Asia Publishing House, pp. 1–14.

6. Srinivas, M.N. 1962. *Caste in Modern India and Other Essays*. Bombay: Asia Publishing House, p. 66.

7. Béteille, André. 1965. *Caste, Class and Power: Changing Patterns of Stratification in a Tanjore Village*. Berkeley: University of California Press. Delhi: Oxford University Press, new enlarged edition 1996.

8. Shah, A.M. 1996. 'Is the Joint Household Disintegrating?' *Economic and Political Weekly*. Vol. xxxi, No. 9, pp. 537–42. See also his *The Household Dimension of the Family in India*. Delhi: Orient Longman, 1973.

9. Béteille, André. 1990. *Some Observations on the Comparative Method*. Amsterdam: CASA see chapter 4, this volume; see also my *Society and Politics in India: Essays in a Comparative Perspective*. London: Athlone Press, 1991.

10. Durkheim, Émile. 1938. *The Rules of Sociological Method*. Glencoe: The Free Press, p. 139.

11. Ibid., p. 136.

12. Béteille, André. 1972. 'Agrarian Relations in Tanjore District, South India'. *Sociological Bulletin*, Vol. 21. No. 2, pp. 122–51.

13. Béteille, André. 1987. 'Equality as a Right and as a Policy', *LSE Quarterly*. Vol. 1. No. 1, pp. 75–98. 'Distributive Justice and Institutional Well-being', *Economic and Political Weekly*. Vol. xxvi. Nos. 11 & 12, pp. 591–600. 1991.

14. Marx, Karl and Friedrich Engels. 1968. *The German Ideology*. Moscow: Progress Publishers, p. 45.

15. Durkheim, Émile. 1974. 'Value Judgements and Judgements of Reality'. *Sociology and Philosophy*. Glencoe: The Free Press, pp. 80–97.

Max Weber. 1949. *The Methodology of the Social Sciences*. Glencoe: The Free Press.

16. Durkheim, Émile. *The Rules of Sociological Method*. op. cit.

17. Weber, Max. *The Methodology of the Social Sciences*. op. cit. p. 9.

Chapter
2

Sociology and Social Anthropology

S ociology is a loosely-defined field of study and research in India as in other parts of the world. There are many different approaches to it, and even different conceptions of its scope. If we add social anthropology to it or include it in an extended definition of the subject, the scope is broadened even further. In India, there has been a closer relationship between the two than in many other countries, and this may prove to be a source of their strength. But even here, there is no universal agreement about the relationship. Some regard the two as practically synonymous; others maintain that they stand in a special relationship to each other; and yet others believe that anthropology is no more closely related to sociology than are other cognate disciplines such as history, political science and economics.

This article presumes a close relationship between sociology and social anthropology; such a relationship has existed in the past and is likely to continue into the future. It takes into account the work of social (and also cultural) anthropologists in a way in which it does not take account of the work of historians, economists and political scientists. While emphasizing the study of Indian society and culture by Indian scholars, it also pays attention to the important contributions of scholars from other countries.

To say that the relationship between sociology and anthropology is a close one is not to suggest that it is free from tension. My own view of it has changed somewhat, partly as a result of changes in the orientations of the disciplines (Béteille 1975, 1993). Under the circumstances, it is difficult to avoid ambiguity of expression in an article of such a wide scope. In what follows, I have tried to cover sociology and social anthropology together, hoping that the context will make it clear when I use the term 'sociology' to include both and when I use it to cover the one as against the other. Needless to say, the ambiguity of expression is heightened by the fact that 'anthropology' has several faces of which 'social anthropology' is only one.

Since I have adopted the more inclusive conception of the subject, I would like to stress at the outset the variety of issues and problems that have received attention within it. In one obvious sense, sociology is what sociologists do, although it is not easy to describe succinctly and accurately the results of what they do. More than in most other disciplines, sociologists have to respond to a fluid and changing reality. The sociologist (or social anthropologist) may find that not only have his concepts and methods become out of date, but that the very subject of his investigation has changed its shape within the span of his own professional career.

In a discipline whose subject matter is itself in a continuous state of flux, it is an advantage to maintain open frontiers. Sociology is not a very old discipline in India, and those who occupied prominent positions in it, in the years immediately before and after independence, came to it from a variety of other, older disciplines such as Sanskrit, economics and political science. They brought with them a variety of different concerns and approaches, and this variety is still reflected in the conceptions of the discipline held by its current practitioners.

While adopting an open and flexible approach to a relatively new and growing subject, it is essential to maintain some sense of the distinctive features of the discipline if a coherent and meaningful account of it is to be attempted. In the broadest sense, sociology and social anthropology deal with social relations, social processes, social structures, social institutions and social change in all societies comparatively in order to deepen the understanding of each society. Some would say that sociology is at best a subject and not quite—or not yet—a discipline. Nevertheless, it has in course of time accumulated a body of concepts, methods and data that, no matter how loosely integrated, gives it a distinctive shape and character.

The main work of interpretation and explanation in sociology is to place human actions and events in the context of the social processes, structures and institutions within which they occur. Its concern is as much with actions and events as with their social context. Understanding this context requires the formulation of concepts and methods that have to be systematically applied. These concepts and methods are of little value in themselves; their value lies in their use in the collection, arrangement and interpretation of empirical material. We have today, as a result of sociological enquiry and investigation, a much larger body of reliable data than we had fifty years ago on virtually every aspect of Indian society and culture: village, caste, kinship, religion, economics, politics and stratification. This abundance of empirical material creates its own embarrassment: it has to be continually sifted through the application of concepts and methods to yield meaningful sociological accounts.

Sociological reasoning is informed by two distinctive tendencies: the search for interconnections among elements in a given social context, and the comparison and contrast of different social contexts. Sociology is at the same time general and particular in its concerns. Its theoretical aim is general, for it seeks to understand how societies are constituted, how they function and how they change; at the same time, it must address itself to the facts of each particular society or section of it. A sociological account, no matter how consistent logically, cannot be adequate unless it is informed by a detailed knowledge of the available and relevant facts.

To describe the data of sociology as particular, and its concepts and methods as general is of course misleading, because in any scientific work, the latter have to match the former. In every branch of scholarship, matching concepts and methods with the data is a difficult art in which complete or sustained success is rarely achieved. Anxiety over their mismatch is a perennial feature of Indian sociology, and it gives rise to disagreements that are not always made explicit.

The anxiety referred to above is deepened by the awareness of a disjunction that is in some respects specific to the Indian situation. In the last hundred years or so, a large reservoir of theories, concepts, terms, methods and procedures has been built on which sociologists draw for their work in every part of the world. The tools of sociological enquiry and investigation were initially created by sociologists in England, France and Germany, and many of the basic ones among them were already in place when the subject began its career in the third and fourth decades of the twentieth century in India. In this regard, India—like other countries in Asia and Africa—had the advantage of a latecomer, as well as its disadvantage.

The advantage lay in the fact that when Indian sociologists began their work in the twenties and thirties, they did not have to create anew all the tools of their trade, but found a readymade stock at their disposal that could be put to use in their work. But this meant two things. One, it stifled, at least to some extent, the creativity and innovation of Indian sociologists on the theoretical and methodological planes, encouraging the lazy habit of applying whatever was readily available to every kind of problem: why, some of them must have asked, try to reinvent the bicycle? Two, it established a gap on the plane of concepts, methods and theories between western sociologists and their Indian counterparts. This gap still remains very wide, and some would say that Indian sociologists have failed to be innovative theoretically and methodologically because of their passive dependence on the work of western scholars.

More serious than the charge of passivity is the argument that concepts and methods in the human sciences are, for all their claims to universal validity, always coloured, to a greater or lesser extent, by the cultural matrix of their origin and provenance. An uncritical application of those concepts and methods to other and different contexts entails the risk of distorting not only analysis and interpretation, but also the collection and arrangement of empirical material. It is argued that such categories as family, class and nation do not mean the same things in all places, and when they are turned directly into sociological concepts, they do not fit the reality equally well everywhere.

Beginning with the work of Evans-Pritchard (1962), social anthropologists have become increasingly sensitive to the problem of translating the categories developed in one cultural context for use in a different context. In some ways, the problem of translation has always bedevilled sociologists since they have been unable to devise technical terms that are clearly distinct from the words used in everyday language. It is well known that there is no exact English equivalent for the French term 'sacré' used extensively in the sociology of Durkheim, or the German term 'Politik' used similarly in that of Weber. For all that, Anglophone sociologists have more or less successfully adapted the concepts to the requirements of their work.

The problem assumes a different magnitude, and some would say that it becomes qualitatively different, when we move from the western to the Indian context. Here the problem of translation is of a different order, and not merely in the literal sense of the word 'translation'. This may be illustrated by referring to the recent discussion of the concepts of 'secular', 'secularization' and 'secularism'. Some have argued that these terms as they are generally used in sociology, are the products of the Enlightenment in Europe, and as such they are limited not only in their origin but also in their reach (Madan 1987). It is therefore maintained that even though there might be some indication of 'secularization' in India, the very method of studying the relationship between religion, society and politics in India is flawed by the application of a perspective that is limited and distorting.

Of course, even those who are troubled most by the distortion caused by the application of western concepts and terms do not themselves desist wholly from drawing upon the common stock of sociological tools for their own work. The question is not simply whether it would be desirable but whether it would be at all possible to do otherwise. Much ground has already been covered by sociologists in India in the last seventy to eighty years; three or four generations of them have built up a cumulative body of information and knowledge; and some of them at least have shown considerable skill in drawing from the common reservoir of concepts and methods and adapting them to their own requirements, and even devising new tools of enquiry and analysis. It would be too much to expect them now to turn their backs on this entire body of work in the hope of creating a whole new approach and discipline. In any case, the main aim of this article is not to propose such an alternative even in outline but to provide a critical account of the existing body of knowledge in sociology and social anthropology as they are understood today.

It is to the credit of sociologists and anthropologists working in India that they have not allowed their genuine concern for alternatives to existing approaches to seriously interfere with the continuous pursuit of their craft. Three quarters of a century after its inception, sociology in India is now more than merely an individual intellectual pursuit. It is a discipline with a recognized place in universities and institutes of research; it has its own professional associations, national and regional, and its own scholarly journals. The institutionalization of sociology, particularly since independence, has contributed substantially to the growth and consolidation of the discipline.

Sociology and social anthropology are now taught in many of the post-graduate departments in Indian universities through the length and breadth of the country; they are also taught in numerous undergraduate colleges. These subjects were taught in only a few universities in the pre-independence period when the size of post-graduate departments was generally small. Given the size and diversity of the country, the quality of teaching and research in the universities today is highly uneven. This is aggravated by the rapid and sometimes ill-judged expansion of universities and colleges.

Here a certain aspect of the differentiation between the two disciplines may be noted. The first department of anthropology was started in the University of Calcutta in 1922, and initially universities in the eastern region developed departments of anthropology rather than sociology. The first department of sociology was started at about the same time in the University of Bombay; and universities in the western region began in their turn with departments of sociology rather than anthropology. This changed after independence, but a noteworthy feature of developments thereafter is that attempts to establish departments jointly of sociology and social anthropology have been largely unsuccessful.

Apart from the universities, sociological research is actively conducted in several of the institutes of research set up mainly after independence and now supported by the Indian Council of Social Science Research (ICSSR), such as those in Delhi, Bangalore and Surat. The Council has been an active promoter of sociological research, although here again the quality of the research has been highly uneven. Shortly after it was set up, the ICSSR commissioned surveys of the research being done in the country in sociology and social anthropology, as of other social science disciplines. Even a casual glance at the three volumes that were the outcome of this survey will suffice to give an idea of the range and depth of the research in these fields already in progress by the seventies (Srinivas, Rao and Shah 1972).

The growth of centres of study and research has been accompanied by a steady increase in the number and variety of publications by professional sociologists and social anthropologists. Apart from the steady and widening stream of scholarly books, there are professional journals. Reflecting to some extent their differences in origin, background and professional organization, there are different scholarly journals associated with sociology and social anthropology, although individual scholars publish their articles in some or all of these, according to their intellectual interests. The oldest surviving professional journal is *Man in India*, started in 1922 and catering to prehistoric archaeologists, physical anthropologists and cultural anthropologists as well as sociologists. *Sociological Bulletin* began its career just after independence, in 1951; it owes its special significance to the fact that it is the journal of the Indian Sociological Society, also established in 1951. The other important journal, which has offered its pages to both sociologists and anthropologists, is *Contributions to Indian Sociology* which began publishing in 1957. In addition, there are periodicals, not devoted solely to sociology or social anthropology, in which scholars in these disciplines publish regularly, the most notable being *Economic and Political Weekly*.

The publication of *Sociological Bulletin* is one of the two principal activities of the Indian Sociological Society. Its other principal activity is the sociological conference, now held annually every winter. The Society has well over a thousand life members, including more than a hundred foreign life members. Although not every member attends each conference, it nevertheless has a large attendance. Working papers are presented and discussed in small groups, and there are plenary sessions addressed by both individual speakers and panels of speakers.

The Society chooses a particular theme for special attention at each annual conference. Some of the themes chosen for the annual conference in recent years are: Identity, Equality and Social Transformation (Mangalore, 1993); Cultural Dimensions of Social Change (New Delhi, 1994); Challenge of Change and Indian Sociology (Bhopal, 1995); and Ecology, Society and Culture (Kolhapur, 1996). It may be noted that the choice of themes reflects a broad concern with problems and issues that are not merely sociological in a narrow academic sense but also social in the wider sense—the thrust is to convert social issues into sociological problems. The discussion of the issues inevitably remains inconclusive. Nevertheless, it influences the nature of sociological discourse in the long run. More generally, the annual conference serves to give unity and continuity to the profession by bringing together sociologists of different generations and from different parts of the country.

* * *

Before entering into a fuller consideration of the work being done by sociologists and social anthropologists in India, I will discuss briefly some of the basic issues and problems in whose light this work has to be considered. Here we have to keep in mind the fact that the discipline has grown in India as much through teaching at the post-graduate and undergraduate levels as through research in the restricted sense of the term. With the notable exception of Patrick Geddes who lectured briefly on the subject in Calcutta and Bombay around the end of World War I, the teaching of sociology has been conducted from the very beginning by Indians: L.A.K. Iyer and K.P. Chattopadhyay in Calcutta, G.S. Ghurye and K.M. Kapadia in Bombay, and Radhakamal Mukherjee and D.P. Mukherji in Lucknow. Some of the early teachers, though by no means all, were trained in the west, but they all brought to their teaching and research, perceptions and concerns formed by their experience as members of Indian society.

Teaching is shaped not only by the perceptions and concerns derived from the teacher's social environment but also by the books that are used by him. In the early phase, most of the books used by teachers and students were written by European and American scholars who had very little direct experience of the Indian reality. Soon Indian scholars began to write their own books which they also used in their teaching. The stream of publications by Indian sociologists in the decades since independence has not driven out books produced in the west. Indeed, there are many Indian scholars who now not only publish their books and papers in Europe and America but also write them there in part or in full. The choice of books, in terms of both quality and provenance, remains an important issue in the teaching of sociology in India, and there is considerable variation between universities in what gets chosen. The diversity contributes to the strength and vitality of the subject in India, and also to some of its confusions.

An important concern of students of Indian society and culture is the understanding of the Indian tradition, its unity, integrity, stability, resilience, vulnerability and capacity for change. Sociologists address this problem in a particular way through the examination of the present as well as the past. Understanding the past in the present is an important problem for sociologists everywhere, whether of a conservative or a radical persuasion, but the problem is particularly compelling in India because of the richness and depth of its tradition and its continued strength in contemporary life.

Sociologists and anthropologists, whether Indian or western, have sought to integrate the findings of classical studies with their work on contemporary India much more widely and actively than has been the case with sociological studies of contemporary western societies. Among the outstanding names are G.S. Ghurye, N.K. Bose, Irawati Karve, Louis Dumont and McKim Marriott. Several prominent members of the first and second generations of Indian sociologists—Benoy Sarkar, G.S. Ghurye, K.P. Chattopadhyay, K.M. Kapadia and Irawati Karve—were either trained as Sanskritists or well versed in the classical literature. They tried to use their familiarity with that literature in their investigation of contemporary forms of family, marriage, kinship, clan, caste, sect and religion. In European and, even more, American sociology, tradition is a specialized topic of enquiry (Shils 1981). In the sociology of India, it features as a general concern in the study of many different topics.

The real disagreement among sociologists of India is not over the importance of tradition as a subject of study; it is over the possibility—and also the need—of drawing upon tradition to develop a distinctive method for the study of society and culture. This is not the place for examining the merits of the different arguments. Suffice it to say that some would argue that the mismatch between methods and data in Indian sociology arises precisely because the Indian tradition is ignored in formulating the appropriate approach to the problems under study. Others would say that tradition can be adequately taken into account by applying to its study concepts and methods drawn from the common pool of sociological knowledge.

The Indological approach, which has been advocated by such diverse scholars as Louis Dumont (1966) and A.K. Saran (1962), has to be distinguished from the historical approach which seeks to relate contemporary social institutions and processes to their immediate historical settings, especially in the colonial period. Here there are obvious parallels with the historical sociology of such western scholars as T.H. Marshall (1977) and Charles Tilly (1981), although the themes addressed are naturally different. In India, as elsewhere, not all sociological enquiry is equally informed by a historical perspective. Some enquiries pursue an institution (such as the university), ideology (such as nationalism) or a movement (such as the peasant movement) across a particular stretch of time, and here the work of the historically-informed sociologist differs little from that of the sociologically-informed historian. Other enquiries focus more specifically on present social arrangements, with only passing attention to the historical context of those arrangements.

While the historical approach in one or another form has been used by many sociologists, it has been favoured particularly by Marxist sociologists or those under the influence of Marxism. Some of the most influential historians of India have been Marxists, and it cannot be denied that there is some affinity between the materialist interpretation of history and certain influential sociological approaches (Evans-Pritchard 1965: 76–7). A good example of the use of the historical approach from this point of view is the work of A.R. Desai (1959) on the social background of Indian nationalism, which has received considerable attention from students of sociology, history and politics in India. The historical approach has also been widely used by sociologists engaged in the study of agrarian relations.

Sociology in India has benefited above all from the contributions of descriptive and analytical ethnography as exemplified by the work of a long succession of scholars, beginning with S.C. Roy and L.A.K. Iyer. As compared to Indology and even history, ethnography was something of a new departure for Indian scholars, and it has remained central to sociological studies of India. Ethnographic enquiry began as a very different kind of intellectual pursuit from Indological or even historical scholarship. Its requirement of field investigation was based on the model of the natural sciences rather than that of humanistic scholarship. Whereas Indologists and historians devoted themselves to noble, lofty and elevated subjects, ethnographers seemed to go out of their way to observe and describe the habits and customs of poor, humble and illiterate people; before independence, social anthropologists devoted themselves to a very large extent to the study of tribal communities. Fei Hsiao-tung (1939), the pioneer of Chinese ethnography, has reported how the whole approach of this work appeared unprofitable, unattractive and even perverse to the traditional Chinese intelligentsia immersed in the learning of books. Ethnographic enquiry was, if anything, even more alien to the Brahminical than to the mandarin intellectual tradition.

If sociological enquiry in India is concerned with tradition, it is no less concerned with modernity and modernization. Indeed, the two concerns are closely related, as is evident from the titles of such influential works as *When a Great Tradition Modernizes* by Milton Singer (1972) and *Modernization of Indian Tradition* by Yogendra Singh (1973). These twin concerns with tradition and modernity present important challenges, both empirically and normatively, to sociologists of India, many of whom show a marked ambivalence towards each.

Indian intellectuals were made conscious by their colonial rulers of the fact that theirs was a static, not to say stagnant, society with very little inherent capacity for change; the idea of the Asiatic Mode of Production was, after all, adapted from the writing of James Mill on India. From the beginning of the nineteenth century, under the impact of the colonial encounter, they turned their thoughts to the regeneration and transformation of their society. Some sought to base the regeneration on a modified concept of Indian values while others called for a more radical break with the past. This debate about adapting traditional values to present needs and making a break with the past is an important aspect of the Indian intellectual climate to this day, and it naturally colours the work of contemporary sociologists.

India's independence in 1947 marks a kind of watershed not only politically but also intellectually. As I have noted, there was a marked expansion in the work of sociologists, accompanying the growth of universities and other centres of advanced study and research. Part of this institutional growth was itself a response to the perceived need for coping more adequately with the demands of modernization. It will be fair to say that among Indian social scientists in general, the revival of tradition took a back seat in the first two decades of independence, their sights being set more firmly on the challenges and possibilities of development and modernization. But before long, a kind of disenchantment set in, and just as tradition had been questioned and criticized in the earlier phase, there emerged in course of time a more sceptical and critical attitude towards modernity.

No matter which institution the sociologist studies in contemporary India—village, caste, temple, factory, laboratory or hospital—he cannot help observing and recording the changes taking place in it. To some extent, this is so irrespective of his attachment to tradition or to modernity as a value. All studies of change are of course made within some kind of framework, explicit or implicit, of description and analysis. There has been much debate in India, as elsewhere, between Marxists and non-Marxists over the adequacy in the understanding of change of the 'structural-functional' framework, used extensively by social anthropologists, particularly in their case studies.

The study of social change has often been driven by the urge to give direction to it by analysing its causes and conditions. In the early years of independence, much hope was placed on the transformation of society through conscious and planned effort. The country had fashioned a new Constitution that set its back on the old hierarchical order. Planners, policy-makers and educators applied themselves to the removal of poverty, illiteracy, superstition, inequality, oppression and exploitation, and to the creation of a new social order based on equality, justice, freedom and material prosperity. Naturally enough, Indian social scientists did not wish to fall behind in this exciting venture.

In all this, the lead was taken among social scientists by the economists, for it was widely believed then that social change would be driven in the desired direction by economic development. But economic development itself had to be broadly conceived and, in any case, it could not be understood or managed without taking into account its social causes and consequences. Hence sociologists and social anthropologists were from the beginning associated, though not as major players, with research on development and change. Such research is conducted at many places, in the universities of course, by agencies of the government, and in autonomous research institutes. The latter were often set up with the specific objective of providing the intellectual tools for analysing and recommending change. This is often evident from their very names: Institute of Economic Growth, named at first Institute for the Study of Social and Economic Growth (Delhi); Centre for the Study of Developing Societies (Delhi); Institute for the Study of Social and Economic Change (Bangalore); Centre for Development Studies (Trivandrum); and Madras Institute of Development Studies (Madras), to name only the more prominent ones supported by the Indian Council for Social Science Research.

Before closing this section, I would like to point to two important dilemmas that are an inescapable part of the predicament of the sociologist as an intellectual in contemporary Indian society. The first, to which I have already alluded, relates to the tension between tradition and modernity that is pervasive not only in what the sociologist studies but also in his own intellectual make-up. Sociological enquiry as we know it, whether in the west or in India, makes some kind of break with traditional forms of knowledge. At the same time, it has to address itself in India not only to traditional social arrangements but also to traditional norms and values. Is the orientation characteristic of modern systems of knowledge adequate for a sympathetic understanding of those norms and values?

This leads to the second and deeper issue of the relationship between value judgements and judgements of reality in sociological enquiry. This has always been a vexed issue, and nowhere and at no time have sociologists achieved complete consensus on it. There are those who believe that a separation can and should be maintained between the two; there are others who argue that this separation is unnecessary and undesirable, and that it impoverishes both thought and action; and there are those who say that although the seperation is in principle desirable, it is extremely difficult to maintain in practice. This article is written from the viewpoint of the third position (Béteille 1992), although the majority of Indian sociologists would probably like to maintain a closer relationship between facts and values than the present author.

* * *

While debates over approach and method continue to be very important, the real progress of sociology and social anthropology has been through the steady flow of substantive studies in a variety of different fields. I will dwell mainly on the work done since independence, that is, during the last fifty years, although that work would amount to little without the groundwork prepared in the earlier phase. Even then, the field is vast, and I will deal specially with those areas that have received continuing attention during this period in both research and teaching. I will take account of work done by both Indian and foreign scholars as I believe that their collaboration is a major source of the vitality of the discipline. In entering into empirical social enquiry, Indian sociologists and social anthropologists were moving against the grain of the Indian intellectual tradition whose strength lay in formal disciplines such as mathematics, grammar, logic and metaphysics rather than empirical disciplines such as history and geography.

A major development that began immediately after independence was the entry by professional sociologists and social anthropologists into village studies. In their earlier empirical work, Indian anthropologists, like anthropologists everywhere, had concentrated on 'tribal' or 'primitive' communities. Village studies today are a continuing source for the deeper and wider understanding of society, economy and polity in contemporary India. They are significant at more than one level. They are important not only for their substantive findings but also for the grounding they provide to scholars in the craft of their discipline. It is in and through the village that the Indian social scientist began to grasp the significance of what Srinivas has called the 'field-view' as against the 'book-view' of Indian society. The enthusiasm for village studies in the sixties and seventies created something like a community of scholars, Indian as well as foreign, who interacted, or at least communicated, actively with each other over their work. At least among Indian scholars, the distinction between sociology and social anthropology, which remained an obdurate feature of western social science, was largely set aside in the pursuit of this common venture.

From the fifties into the seventies, sociology and social anthropology in India were virtually dominated by village studies, having largely displaced the study of tribes among whom anthropologists in the pre-independence period mostly did their fieldwork. Village studies are still extensively conducted in every region in the country, and they raise a number of important questions about the nature of Indian society. Is the Indian village a 'little republic' as was widely believed the fifties? Was it ever a little republic? One study after another showed that the Indian village is not and probably never was an isolated and self-sufficient community of equals. Through their detailed analyses of inequality and of the conflict of interests in the village, sociologists began to question the very idea of community as applied to the village as a whole.

Part of the impetus for village studies came from the ideas of Gandhi, Tagore and many others who saw India as a land of villages. Many anthropologists took the position that the village was a kind of microcosm in which the macrocosm of the wider world was reflected in miniature. Few of them confined their attention exclusively to the village, but examined the networks based on the ties of marriage, kinship, economics, politics and religion that stretch outward from the village. Not only are new villages being taken up for investigation but also some of the old ones are being restudied (Breman, Saith and Kloos 1997).

In the wake of independence, the Indian village occupied the minds of many, and not merely of professional social scientists. There were those interested in village studies and those interested in village reconstruction, and there was convergence of interest and collaboration between them. Jayaprakash Narayan presented a document entitled *A Plea for the Reconstitution of Indian Polity* in which the village was given pride of place. The Community Development Programme generated a variety of investigations to which sociologists made contributions; notable among these was *India's Changing Villages* by S.C. Dube (1960). After the social anthropologists had opened up the village as a field of study, scholars from other disciplines followed. It will not be unreasonable to claim that village studies, more than any other kind of enquiry, brought the work of social anthropologists to the attention of scholars in such diverse fields as political science, economics, demography, history and geography in the first two decades after independence.

Closely associated with village studies were studies of caste. Discussions of caste had of course figured in the writings of Indologists and historians long before the era of village studies. But the fifties and sixties witnessed the beginning and consolidation of a somewhat different approach to the study of caste. The new approach lay in the move away from the 'book-view' to the 'field-view' of the subject. Here, the brief essay by Srinivas (1962), '*Varna* and Caste', was a turning point. The essay was a trenchant attack on the book-view of caste based on the *varna* model which, according to Srinivas, gave a distorted and misleading picture of the Indian social reality. Srinivas argued that the real operative units of the system were not *varnas* but *jatis*, and that these had to be understood in their local and regional contexts, and not in terms of some general and purely formal scheme.

Srinivas's work opened the way for an examination of the dynamics of caste in contemporary India. Caste could no longer be viewed as a harmonious system in which each part maintained itself in its appointed place in an unchanging order. There were fierce conflicts of interest between castes at the village level, the district level and the regional level. By drawing attention to the enhanced role of caste in democratic politics, Srinivas brought the work of sociologists and social anthropologists to the attention of the wider public. If it is a commonplace among journalists today to speak of Indian politics in terms of caste, they owe something to the work begun by sociologists and social anthropologists in the sixties.

Close examination of the operation of the system on the ground also showed that the hierarchy of caste was not as rigid and inflexible as it had been assumed to be. The analysis of caste mobility through the process described by Srinivas as 'Sanskritization' altered the perception of Indian society not only among sociologists and political scientists who study the present but also among historians who study the past.

In India, the best empirical material has come out of qualitative research based on intensive fieldwork, although survey research and quantitative analyses have also made some contribution. These researches examine in detail structure and change in a variety of specific institutional domains: kinship, religion, economics and politics. We have, as a result, a much fuller knowledge not only of Indian society and culture in general but also of the variety of institutions that are their constituent parts.

We may begin with family, marriage and kinship. Detailed empirical research has altered, and to some extent corrected, some common misperceptions about the contemporary as well as the traditional forms of these important aspects of Indian society. A.M. Shah (1973, 1998) has shown that the Hindu family was often small in size and simple in morphological form even where it was joint in its legal form; and I.P. Desai (1964) demonstrated that the 'sentiment of jointness' retains much of its strength even after families have been legally partitioned. Shah has demonstrated through a careful analysis of demographic material that the size of the Indian household was on average always relatively small, and that there is little hard evidence to support the view that there has been a significant change in the balance of nuclear and joint households from the beginning to the end of the twentieth century. Ramkrishna Mukherjee (1983) has used survey research to analyse the composition of different types of families in contemporary India.

The ties of kinship and marriage extend beyond family and household, and they have been examined through case studies by a number of anthropologists, notably A.C. Mayer (1960) and T.N. Madan (1965). Madan's work examines the ties of the individual not only with his patrilineage but, through bilateral filiation, with a variety of other relatives, near and distant. Not only is the family embedded in the wider kinship structure, but that structure itself is embedded in caste. Mrs Karve (1968) presented the challenging argument that, given sufficient patience and care, it could be shown that each *jati* was a single genealogical system. Adrian Mayer demonstrated the linkages between caste, subcaste, kindred of recognition and kindred of co-operation through his field investigations in the Malwa region of Madhya Pradesh.

The work of Srinivas (1952) on the Coorgs was a watershed in the sociological study of religion. It examined in detail the operation of religious belief and practice in the setting of a small and relatively compact community. Following Radcliffe-Brown, Srinivas adopted a structural-functional framework and showed how ritual and belief contribute to the unity and identity of groups at different levels: the household, the village and the region. But unlike most anthropologists of his time, Srinivas also examined the relationship between local religious belief and practice and the wider universe of a world religion. This study opened the way for examining the interplay between local and wider religious systems. The wider study of Hinduism has again led back to the examination of religious texts, now in a perspective enriched by empirical investigations in the field.

The wider study of Hinduism has drawn attention to two important aspects of the relations between religion, society and politics in contemporary India. These are secularism and communalism, each of which may be viewed in terms of both ideology and practice. Communalism is not an easy subject to study by means of the conventional methods of sociological enquiry, whether through survey research or participant-observation. For a long time, it was studied more widely by historians than by sociologists, but the latter have now begun to enter the field where they find much scope for collaboration with the former. Sociologists have, on the other hand, been more at ease with secularism, or at least secularization, in the study of which they can have recourse to a much wider body of comparative material in their own discipline.

In the village studies they undertook, some social anthropologists turned their attention to local-level politics, and an empirically-grounded political sociology made its beginnings in India in the sixties. This acquired added impetus from the enthusiasm for the institutions of Panchayati Raj in the country. Political scientists who had till then concerned themselves mainly with national and state politics, also turned their attention to local-level politics, and the convergence of their interests with those of social anthropologists led to some very fruitful collaboration. An outcome of that collaboration was the book *Caste in Indian Politics* edited by Rajni Kothari (1971). Sociologists, social anthropologist and political scientists have also worked in association in the study of elections.

Sociologists and social anthropologists have studied economic structures and processes, particularly in the rural areas. The traditional village economy of land and grain with its associated crafts and services has been undergoing many changes. *Jajmani* relations are breaking down, and the old relations between patrons and clients are being altered by the cash nexus and demands of the market (Breman 1974). Economists and anthropologists now discuss and debate with each other the choice of methods best suited to the investigation of these and other problems (Bardhan 1989).

A central problem in Indian society as well as the sociology of India is that of inequality. One of the early village studies (Béteille 1965) addressed itself to class and stratification in an effort to bring together some of the central conceptual and theoretical concerns of classical sociology with the method of intensive fieldwork distinctive of social anthropology. This study examined the changing relations between caste, class and power in a single village, though it also drew attention to the action of external forces in initiating or hastening the change. Similar studies have been and are being made in many parts of the country and outside (Gough 1981; Wild 1974).

The more general problem of inequality has been examined in a variety of sociological perspectives of which two are of particular significance. The first of these is best exemplified in the work of Louis Dumont (1966) which has had far-reaching influence among sociologists of India. In this work, the defining feature of Indian society is seen as hierarchy, itself an aspect of holism; and hierarchy is sharply distinguished from both stratification and class. Hierarchy is conceived by Dumont and his followers in terms of values, and in this conception, status is given primacy over power. Caste is the most striking institutional form taken by hierarchy, although in a more general way, both religion and kinship are also permeated by it. This distinctive approach to Indian society and culture found its fullest expression in the influential journal *Contributions to Indian Sociology*, particularly in its earlier phase.

A very different, though no less influential, approach to inequality derives its inspiration from Marxian theory, and its exponents have published extensively in *Economic and Political Weekly*. Here the emphasis is on class and material interest rather than caste or hierarchical status. In the study of contemporary India, sociologists continue to disagree on the importance to be assigned to caste and to class. The study of class brings together the work of sociologists, economists, political scientists and historians. The subject can and has been studied at different levels, and sociologists and anthropologists have probably made their best contributions to it by studying it in the context of agrarian relations at the local level. Not all sociologists who study class adopt the Marxian framework, and of course class and caste are often studied together. A number of sociologists have also addressed themselves to the problems of stratification and mobility in relation to the modern occupational structure (D'Souza 1977).

Caste and class are brought together in the study of not only stratification but also politics. I have already alluded to studies by sociologists of caste politics at various levels; these studies tend to be descriptive and analytical and do not generally have any clear or distinctive normative orientation. For Marxists, on the other hand, the politics of class is a matter not only of theory but also of practice. Partly as a result of the evidence brought to light by sociologists in the last two or three decades, Marxists are now inclined to give more attention to caste in their political analysis than before.

The role sociologists assign to caste in politics depends to some extent on their assessment of the significance of collective as against individual identities in Indian society. This is a subject of continuing interest which was sharply posed by Dumont's contrast between India and the west, in which India is characterized, on the plane of values, by holism and hierarchy, and the west by individualism and equality (Dumont 1966, 1977). Dumont's categorical assertion that the individual has no place in Indian society has of course been questioned (Béteille 1987; Dumont 1987). At the same time, sociological investigation and political experience both show the continuing importance of collective identities of every kind.

When we examine Indian politics sociologically, we find that caste does not operate alone but together with a whole family of collective identities based on language, religion, sect, tribe and so on. The terms 'ethnic group', 'ethnic identity' and 'ethnicity' have been used for referring to their operation, and it is interesting that the word *jati* or *jat* is now widely used in more than one Indian language to refer to the identities not only of caste in the narrow sense but also of language, religion, sect and tribe. Their constitution and operation are now being increasingly studied by both sociologists and political scientists (Gupta 1996).

I have described selectively rather than exhaustively some of the areas through whose investigation sociological study and research have grown continuously in the last fifty years. Village, caste, kinship, religion, politics, economics and stratification may be described as established or core areas because of the length of time over which they have received attention and the number of scholars who attend to them in their teaching as well as research. While work continues to be produced in each of these areas, a number of new areas have come into prominence in the last couple of decades, and some of the most interesting and original work is now being done there.

Among the new developments, pride of place must be assigned to gender studies of which there has been a veritable explosion worldwide, and in India since the eighties. A good idea of the work being done by sociologists in this field may be formed by seeing the interdisciplinary *Indian Journal of Gender Studies*, the founding editor of which is a sociologist. It would be fair to say that until only a couple of decades ago, men and women were given unequal attention in all fields of sociological enquiry with the possible exception of family, marriage and kinship. This has now changed substantially, and women receive far more attention, although still rather less than their due share of it, in every field of sociological enquiry, including economic sociology, political sociology and social stratification. More important than that, the concern with gender has brought a new perspective into sociology that has enriched not only its data but also its concepts, methods and theories.

The impetus to the development of women's studies has come from a variety of sources. Firstly, it is a worldwide phenomenon, and the cross-fertilization of ideas across countries and across continents has been remarkably quick and effective. But in India, institutional support has also played a part. A turning point in this development was the publication of the influential report, *Towards Equality*, of the Committee on the Status of Women in India (Government of India 1974). Today, women's studies receive active support from both the Indian Council of Social Science Research and the University Grants Commission. The former supports the Centre for Women's Development Studies, and the latter provides special assistance for programmes of women's studies in several universities.

A second relatively new interest that has already made its mark and is likely to extend its influence among sociologists is the study of the environment (Guha 1994). This is an area in which research and policy are closely combined. Sociological research on the environment does not arise from academic interest alone, but is also driven by the active concerns of governments and non-governmental organizations.

Health and medicine are also attracting increasing attention from students of human society and culture. There are innumerable issues, and even to list them would be impossible here. We now understand more clearly, partly through the work of anthropologists, that the very conceptions of health and disease are themselves cultural constructions, at least to a large extent. There are large variations across cultures and within them in real and perceived illnesses, and sociologists and anthropologists play a crucial part in mapping these variations. They also play a part in analysing alternative systems of knowledge and practice in the diagnosis and treatment of disease.

There are alternative systems not only of medicine but also of science itself. It is a truism that scientific research is conducted in different ways in different social settings. There are differences in the resources available, in institutional facilities, and in the material and symbolic rewards of scientific work (Visvanathan 1985). Beyond these is the question of the hegemony and authority exercised by science and scientists in the metropolitan centres over their counterparts in the less developed countries; part of the impulse for the sociology of science in India, as for other branches of sociology, comes from the urge for national self-reliance (Uberoi 1978).

We must note that sociology and social anthropology have been criticized everywhere by radicals of various persuasions for their conservatism, for the bias inherent in their theoretical orientation towards order and stability as against conflict and change. It is undeniable that sociology has had very little success in developing an adequate theory whereby change and conflict can be explained. Not only that, its conventional methods, whether based on intensive fieldwork on a single site or on survey research on dispersed populations, cannot be easily adapted to every type of enquiry. Inevitably, certain issues and problems, not easily amenable to description and analysis by conventional methods, receive little or no attention from academic sociologists, and this becomes a source of disquiet among the consumers of sociology.

Those who observe and experience life in contemporary India are struck by the pervasive violence, both private and public, by which it is marked.

Sociologists of the family and political sociologists are beginning to take note of it in their respective studies. But the subject of violence needs to be addressed on its own terms, for it provides challenges and opportunities for sociological enquiry across its entire range. Some interesting work has already emerged as a result of this particular concern (Das 1990).

* * *

Today, the sheer volume and diversity of the sociological output would justify the observation that the subject has come of age in India. Has the work of sociology in India acquired a distinctive identity? If such an identity exists underneath the sheer variety of the work being done, it is unlikely that it can be represented by any simple formula.

It should be obvious from what has been described in the preceding section that sociology in India cannot be understood as a simple application of theories and methods developed elsewhere. Nor can its development within the country be explained in intellectual terms alone, as the unfolding of a few elementary principles applied successively to the various segments of an external reality. On the plane of ideas, there is the general stock of sociological knowledge on which, as I have repeatedly indicated, sociologists working in India, both Indian and foreign, have drawn freely and continuously. Beyond this there is a rich and active, though often confusing, intellectual life in India which never ceases to provide stimulus to sociological enquiry. Finally, there is the distinctive experience of a complex and changing society that gives something of its own colour to the studies, no matter how general or abstract, that are based on it.

The Indian experience offers significant material for examining the relationship between facts and values in the study of human society. Sociologists and social anthropologists in India have been influenced, one and all, though in varying degrees, by concepts and methods that are largely of external provenance. These concepts and methods have themselves been shaped, to a greater or lesser extent, by values that are too freely assumed to be universal; to the extent that these assumptions are subjected to critical scrutiny in the course of enquiry and investigation, the scope of sociology itself becomes enlarged. For new concepts and methods do not emerge unless the existing ones are tested through actual enquiry, if found wanting, they are either discarded, modified, or replaced.

New insights do not emerge in an empirical science solely from the internal critique of the intellectual apparatus of the discipline. Their emergence depends also on the extent to which new experiences are purposefully and methodically addressed. Every Indian sociologist has a larger life outside the classroom and the study, which forces him not only to observe and experience reality but also to make judgements on it. The judgements that are formed by everyday experience and that give shape to it seep into the formulation of his sociological problems. This is true everywhere, and it would be remarkable if the dependence on 'alien' concepts and methods were to insulate the Indian sociologist completely from the concerns and judgements created by everyday experience.

Sociology has developed in different ways in different climes, and it is not uncommon for the discipline to acquire something of the colour of the environment in which it grows. As far back as in the 1930s, Karl Mannheim (1953) wrote two essays in which he contrasted the orientations of German and American sociology: one of his arguments was that the Americans sought to be more 'scientific' and value neutral in their sociology than did the Germans.

Sociology has often had a close association with social policy. At the same time, its autonomy as an intellectual discipline may be compromised if it is too narrowly defined as a 'policy science'. Raymond Aron is reported to have observed, somewhat disparagingly, that the trouble with British sociology in the post-War years was that it was too closely concerned with trying to make intellectual sense of the political problems of the Labour Party (Halsey 1987).

Sociology will be greatly impoverished if it chooses as its sole or even its main concern the task of making intellectual sense of the political problems of any party or, indeed, any institution of society, including the state and the church. Indeed, sociology cannot achieve its proper purpose without maintaining some distance from the church and the state, and from day-to-day political concerns in general. Commitment to one's own values in the pursuit of sociological research has to be clearly distinguished from partisanship in the cause of the established institutions of society (Béteille 1981). The former fertilizes it, the latter sterilizes it.

In India, the state has not dictated or directly interfered with socio-logical research, though the Indian Council of Social Science Research, funded by the government, has made weak and, on the whole, ineffectual attempts to establish the priorities of research. State funding has led to research that has been critical more often than approving of the work of governments. Sociologists employed by agencies of the government have made little impact on either teaching or research in their discipline, although an exception may be made of the Anthropological Survey of India.

In India, political parties and sociologists have made very little direct use of each other, and, on the whole, this has been to the advantage of both. The influence of religious organizations has been equally weak, and sociologists have rarely received financial support from corporate capital or felt inhibited from attacking its interests. For all its many sins, it has to be admitted that Indian society has allowed sociologists to do their work in freedom without any organized interference.

Despite maintaining distance from state and party, or perhaps because of it, sociology in India has been marked by a strong moral and even political impulse. Here there is a striking difference between Indian and non-Indian students of Indian society and culture. The former are engaged to a far greater extent, politically and morally, not only in their selection of problems but also in their style of argument than western scholars, whether the latter are anthropologists writing about India or sociologists writing about their own society. At the same time, what is noteworthy about this engagement is more often its vehemence than its focus.

In reviewing the work of Indian sociologists, one is struck by a much greater sense of urgency to make their work socially relevant than in the work of European or American sociologists; some prefer to speak of cultural authenticity in place of social relevance (Seminar 1972). This is combined with the persistent criticism from within and outside the discipline that it is enslaved by imported methods, concepts and theories, and is as such remote from the Indian reality. All of this is valid to some extent, for it is true that sociologists in India lean a little too heavily on methods and concepts that were developed in other contexts. It is also true that they are concerned almost single-mindedly with making intellectual sense of the Indian experience; Indian sociologists have paid very little attention in their research, though not in their teaching, to other societies and cultures. But posing the problem in extreme terms does little to bridge the gap between what ought to be addressed and how it ought to be addressed.

It is necessary to understand and appreciate the impulse to make sociology and social anthropology socially relevant. This impulse can serve to stimulate the most fruitful intellectual work; it can also lead to slipshod, superficial and unfocused research of no lasting value. To adapt a phrase from Max Weber, research is a slow boring of hardboards, whereas urgent problems call for immediate solutions. Indian sociologists are often impelled to undertake research that is ill-conceived and unproductive, not so much under directives of government or party as from the pressure of public opinion.

The questions that come up for discussion in seminars, conferences and congresses of sociologists and anthropologists are more likely to be poverty, inequality and untouchability than rates of mobility, forms of ritual or types of marriage. The former are perceived as socially relevant and the latter as merely academic, and the contrast expresses not merely a distinction but also a judgement. Not everybody believes that a choice has to be made between the two, but where such a choice must be made, the bias is in favour of the socially relevant.

Turning a social problem into a sociological one calls for a delicate combination of skills that cannot be simply conjured into existence by well-meaning sociologists, still less by committees of well-meaning sociologists. And yet, the expansion of the profession and its continuing concern for urgent problems has spawned a large number of such committees to deliberate upon the priorities of research. In the deliberations and recommendations of these committees, the line is easily crossed between sociology and current affairs.

Where sociology merges with current affairs, the craft of sociology suffers. With the phenomenal increase in the size of the profession in the last two or three decades, the problem of maintaining quality in research has become worrisome. After all, sociological research must be not only relevant and meaningful, it must also be technically adequate. In India today, the dilution of technical skills appears to be a larger threat to the identity and character of sociology than its disengagement from socially relevant and meaningful problems. The Indian Council of Social Science Research sponsors programmes of training for research workers, but these have so far been rather narrowly focused on research methodology. The Council is now actively considering proposals to reorganize its training programme to give it a broader base.

Technical skills not only take time and effort to acquire, they cannot be easily applied to a problem simply because it demands urgent social attention. The tendency is then to apply common sense to the solution of sociological problems. Many people, including some sociologists, believe that sociology is in any case a form of common sense, embellished more or less by the use of technical vocabulary. But sociology cannot grow as a serious intellectual pursuit unless it disengages itself, at least to some extent, from common sense (Béteille 1996). This does not mean that it should turn its back on common sense and seek refuge in technical virtuosity. It must, on the other hand, place the categories of common sense themselves under critical scrutiny; only then will it be able to contribute to the renewal of common sense, which is perhaps the most significant among its uses.

Is there a sociological mode of reasoning, and has it made any impact on the thinking of persons outside the discipline and the profession? These are both difficult questions to answer, the second perhaps even more difficult than the first. But even if no ready answers are available, the questions themselves cannot be set aside as trivial or sterile.

If there is a sociological mode of reasoning, it consists in a patient, methodical and unremitting effort to relate the actions and ideas of men and women in mutual interaction to the structures and institutions of a complex, amorphous and changing social reality. The task appears more promising but it also becomes more challenging when those engaged in it are located within the society whose many faces they are seeking to understand, interpret and explain. It can neither be accomplished by any individual scholar nor by any single generation of scholars. Indian sociologists have benefited greatly from the work of scholars in other countries, but they must also be mindful of the work of their predecessors, both within and outside the country, for it is only by building on what has been already accomplished that a discipline and a profession moves forward. A major problem in India has been that every new generation of sociologists, while eager to benefit from the work of the best and the most advanced scholars outside the country, seems to write as if it is the first generation of sociologists within the country.

References

Bardhan, Pranab (ed). 1989. *Conversations Between Economists and Anthropologists*. Delhi: Oxford University Press.

Béteille, André. 1965. *Caste, Class and Power*. Berkeley: University of California Press.

———. 1975. *Six Essays in Comparative Sociology*. Delhi: Oxford University Press.

———. 1981. *Ideologies and Intellectuals*. Delhi: Oxford University Press.

———. 1987. 'Reply to Dumont'. *Current Anthropology*. 28 (5), pp. 672–77.

———. 1992. 'Religion as a Subject for Sociology'. *Economic and Political Weekly*. Vol. xxvii (35), pp. 1865–70, see chapter 7, this volume.

———. 1993. 'Sociology and Anthropology'. *Contributions to Indian Sociology*. (n.s.) 27 (2), pp. 291–304, see chapter 3, this volume.

————. 1996. 'Sociology and Common Sense'. *Economic and Political Weekly.* Vol. xxxi (35–37), pp. 2361–5, see chapter 1, this volume.

Breman, Jan. 1974. *Patronage and Exploitation.* Berkeley: University of California Press.

Breman, Jan, Peter Kloos and Ashwani Saith (eds). 1997. *The Village in Asia Revisited.* Delhi: Oxford University Press.

Das, Veena (ed). 1990. *Mirrors of Violence.* Delhi: Oxford University Press.

Desai, A.R. 1959. *Social Background of Indian Nationalism.* Bombay: Popular Book Depot.

Desai, I.P. 1964. *Some Aspects of Family in Mahuva.* Bombay: Asia Publishing House.

D'Souza, V.S. 1977. *Inequality and Integration in an Industrial Community.* Simla: Indian Institute of Advanced Study.

Dube, S.C. 1960. *India's Changing Villages.* London: Routledge and Kegan Paul.

Dumont, Louis. 1966. *Homo Hierarchicus.* Paris: Gallimard.

————. 1977. *From Mandeville to Marx.* Chicago: University of Chicago Press.

————. 1987. 'On Individualism and Equality'. *Current Anthropology.* 28 (5), pp. 669–72.

Evans-Pritchard, E.E. 1962. *Essays in Social Anthropology.* London: Faber and Faber.

————. 1965. *Theories of Primitive Religion.* Oxford: Clarendon Press.

Fei Hsiao-Turg. 1939. *Peasant Life in China.* London: Routledge and Kegan Paul.

Gough, Kathleen 1981. *Rural Society in Southeast India.* Cambridge: Cambridge University.

Government of India. 1974. *Towards Equality: Report of the Committee on the Status of Women in India.* New Delhi: Government of India.

Guha, Ramachandra (ed). 1994. *Social Ecology.* Delhi: Oxford University Press.

Gupta, Dipankar. 1996. *Context of Ethnicity.* Delhi: Oxford University Press.

Halsey, A.H. 1987. 'Provincials and Professionals: The British Post-War Sociologists'. *LSE Quarterly.* 1 (1), pp. 43–74.

Karve, Irawati. 1968. *Hindu Society: An Interpretation.* Poona: Deshmukh Prakashan.

Kothari, Rajni (ed). 1971. *Caste in Indian Politics.* New Delhi: Orient Longman.

Madan, T.N. 1965. *Family and Kinship.* Bombay: Asia Publishing House.

————. 1987. 'Secularism in its Place'. *The Journal of Asian Studies.* 46 (4), pp. 747–59.

Mannheim, Karl. 1953. *Essays in Sociology and Social Psychology*. London: Routledge and Kegan Paul.

Marshall, T.H. 1977. *Class, Citizenship and Social Development*. Chicago: University of Chicago Press.

Mayer, A.C. 1960. *Caste and Kinship in Central India*. London: Routledge and Kegan Paul.

Mukherjee, Ramkrishna. 1983. *Classifications in Social Research*. Albany: State University of New York.

Saran, A.K. 1962. 'Review of *Contributions to Indian Sociology*, No. IV'. *Eastern Anthropologist*. Vol. xv (1), pp. 53–68.

Seminar. 1972. 'The Social Sciences'. *Seminar*. No. 157.

Shah, A.M. 1973. *The Household Dimension of the Family in India*. Delhi: Orient Longman.

———. 1998. *Family in India*. New Delhi: Orient Longman.

Shils, Edward. 1981. *Tradition*. Chicago: University of Chicago Press.

Singer, Milton. 1972. *When a Great Tradition Modernises*. Delhi: Vikas.

Singh, Yogendra. 1973. *Modernisation of Indian Tradition*. Delhi: Thomson Press.

Srinivas, M.N. 1952. *Religion and Society among the Coorgs of South India*. Oxford: Clarendon Press.

———. 1962. *Caste in Modern India and Other Essays*. Bombay: Asia Publishing House.

Srinivas, M.N., M.S.A. Rao and A.M. Shah (eds). 1972. *Survey of Research in Sociology and Social Anthropology*. Bombay: Popular Prakashan, 3 vols.

Tilly, Charles. 1981. *As Sociology Meets History*. New York: Academic Press.

Uberoi, J.P.S. 1978. *Science and Culture*. Delhi: Oxford University Press.

Visvanathan, Shiv. 1985. *Organizing for Science*. Delhi: Oxford University Press.

Wild, R.A. 1974. *Bradstow*. Sydney: Angus and Robertson.

Sociology and Anthropology: Their Relationship in One Person's Career

I am asked from time to time whether I am an anthropologist or a sociologist. The question is not always asked out of curiosity, for there is sometimes the hint that I might be making larger professional claims for myself than are justified. With more than thirty years of teaching and research behind me, I am now able to take the question with some detachment; but it was not always so, particularly at the beginning of my professional career.

The relationship between anthropology and sociology has interested me for a very long time, and when I was asked in 1972–3 to give the first UGC (University Grants Commission) national lectures in sociology, I chose that as the subject of my introductory lecture (Béteille 1974a: 1–20). At the University of Punjab in Chandigarh, after my second lecture, Victor D'Souza, the kindest of hosts, walked up to me and, pumping my hand with feeling, said: 'That was scintillating; but . . . it was anthropology, not sociology'. Similar remarks were repeated many times over at other places where I lectured. At that time, they only reinforced my zeal for reasserting the unity of sociology and social anthropology.

When I began to teach in the newly-created department of sociology at Delhi in 1959, I did not have any degree in sociology, but had degrees only in anthropology. I was interrogated on this in my interview by the Vice Chancellor, Dr. V.K.R.V. Rao. I doubt that I would have stood up to Dr Rao's interrogation as well as I did without the sympathetic presence on the selection committee of Professor Srinivas who was, of course, a great partisan for social anthropology. I was let off rather lightly by Dr. Rao who had little personal interest in the kind of boundary dispute in which I soon became involved.

It did not take me long to realize that the disputes over social anthropology and sociology were not just about ideas but also about jobs. The first twenty years after independence witnessed a great expansion in the Indian university system. New universities were created, and old ones enlarged. As relative latecomers, sociology and anthropology had sometimes to contend for the same places. As it happened, persons with degrees in sociology were rarely considered for positions in departments of anthropology, but some with degrees in anthropology, like myself, managed to slip into sociology departments. The invasion of departments of sociology by anthropologists naturally created a certain resentment among those who felt that they had the first claim on those departments.

For all his partiality towards the anthropological approach, Srinivas, one would think, had excellent professional credentials when he took charge as the first head of the department of sociology in the University of Delhi, for he had both an MA and a PhD degree in sociology from the University of Bombay, in addition to his Oxford DPhil in social anthropology. But even that might be questioned by a champion of disciplinary purity. One such person was the late Professor Kewal Motwani (1961: 11–12) who was tireless in his effort to expose the misdeeds of academic appointments committees. He was not at all convinced that persons like M.N. Srinivas were qualified to be professors of sociology. Srinivas did have degrees in sociology, but those degrees would not stand up to proper scrutiny, for he had secured them under the tutelage of G.S. Ghurye who himself lacked the proper credentials since he had worked for his own PhD at Cambridge with W.H.R. Rivers, who was not a sociologist at all but an anthropologist. Professor Motwani himself had secured his PhD in sociology from the State University of Iowa, and he advocated a particular brand of sociology which was to be based on the teachings of Manu.

When I travelled abroad in the 1960s and 1970s, I tried to learn about the relationship between sociology and social anthropology in the universities there, and found that everywhere, or almost everywhere, it was an uneasy relationship. At least in Britain, the problem was in some respects similar to the one I had experienced in India. David Glass, then the Martin White Professor of Sociology at the London School of Economics, would complain that many of the new appointments in sociology in

Britain went to anthropologists, a fact that he attributed in large part to the disproportionate influence of the Oxbridge establishment in British academic appointments; till the mid-1960s, Oxford and Cambridge had anthropology but no sociology. The mistrust of sociology in English academic circles and the indulgent attitude towards anthropology were described with biting humour by George Homans (1962: 113–19) in a BBC broadcast in the 1950s.

What I could not help noticing at that time was that anthropologists and sociologists found it difficult to remain together in the same department, and that a composite department tended to split into two, not only in India but also in Britain and elsewhere. I had the chance to see how this happened in one outstanding department in Britain, at Manchester. There, in 1949, Max Gluckman had set up a new department which was to give expression to a new kind of unity, that of social anthropology and sociology in place of the old one based on the association between social anthropology, physical anthropology and prehistoric archaeology. Nothing could have appeared more reasonable than the new arrangement to Radcliffe-Brown and his followers in Britain and elsewhere. Yet the union at Manchester did not last very long. When I first went there, as a Simon Fellow in 1965–6, Peter Worsley had already been appointed to a second chair, as professor of sociology, and soon after that, Clyde Mitchell took up the third chair as professor of urban sociology. Cracks had begun to appear in the department while I was there, and when I revisited Manchester a few years later, there were two separate departments, one of sociology and the other of social anthropology. Later still, in 1985, I gave a talk at the department of social anthropology in Manchester; it was well attended, and I was later told, I do not know with how much truth, that it had been a long time since so many sociologists had come to attend a talk in the department of social anthropology. I noted the division of a single department into two departments in Canada also during a visit in 1975, and the story is of course a familiar one to observers of the Indian university system.

In 1959, I would have been happy to accept a lectureship in any post-graduate department, whether of sociology or anthropology. After completing my MSc in anthropology from the University of Calcutta, I had worked for a year and a bit in the Sociological Research Unit of the Indian Statistical Institute. My stay there had confirmed my belief that I had no great talent for research, whereas I had a rooted conviction that I would make a good teacher. It was a lucky accident for me that I got a job in Delhi when I did, for at that time I was prepared to change my place in the Indian Statistical Institute for a lectureship in a decent undergraduate college. Perhaps I would have regretted a lifetime spent as a college lecturer, but I think that I would have regretted it less than a life spent in even a senior position in an institute of research.

I was fortunate to find almost at the beginning of my professional career a place where I did not have to choose between teaching and research. I have sometimes wondered why I have always carried such deep misgivings about a career devoted wholly to research but not about one devoted to teaching. Teaching, even at the undergraduate level, enables one to remain in daily contact with great ideas and is, to that extent, a source of satisfaction to someone who cares for the life of the mind, for it is rarely that one has a great idea of one's own. For me, teaching MA students has meant thinking, talking and arguing almost every day about Weber, Durkheim, Malinowski, Mannheim, Aron, Lévi-Strauss, Evans-Pritchard and numerous others. Since I have carried a relatively light load of teaching, I have been able to read fairly extensively, if somewhat aimlessly, the works of some of the great historians, political theorists, economists, jurists and philosophers, and, occasionally, also to discuss them with my students. I have been able to do all this without any sense of guilt about wasting my time or anybody else's.

Research requires a sharper focus, and, if it is to yield results of any value, a much higher concentration of intellectual energy. The life of a full-time researcher in an institute of social science research, it has seemed to me, must be either terribly exhausting or terribly dreary. I have never been strongly attracted by the little I have seen of it at first hand: designing questionnaires, gathering data, tabulating and analysing it, and, then what to me is the dreariest part of it all, writing an endless succession of reports, destined for the most part to languish in filing cabinets. One can of course think of doing research in a more creative way; but then one needs enormous confidence, certainly more than I have in myself, to feel that one can do creative or original work year after year throughout one's life.

As I have said, I did not have to make the choice between teaching and research. Nor did I make any choice, in accepting my first university position, between social anthropology and sociology. I think that at that time I had a weak preference for sociology, but I would certainly not have rejected a position in a department of anthropology had one been on offer. I had studied anthropology for four years continuously, and at the end of that period, it had lost some of its freshness for me. The prospect of teaching a subject that was a little different from the one I had studied appeared quite alluring.

As an undergraduate, I had been attracted to anthropology by its exotic concerns and, its remoteness from everyday life. I had given up physics to do anthropology, but what took me to it initially was not social anthropology at all but palaeontology or the study of fossil men. During the four years that I spent in the department of anthropology, I read fairly widely in physical anthropology and prehistoric archaeology as well as social anthropology. My first published paper, written with two of my teachers, D. Sen and G.S. Ray, while I was still a student, was on Palaeolithic archaeology (Sen et al. 1956). I toyed with the idea of becoming an archaeologist, but N.K. Bose, whom I had come to know by then, told me firmly and decisively that I should stay with social anthropology since I had less aptitude for fieldwork than for writing.

Although I read extensively in social and cultural anthropology, what really attracted me was the descriptive or ethnographic rather than the theoretical side of the literature. I was fascinated by the endless variety of customs and the coexistence of so many different forms of life among human beings who were yet fundamentally alike. By contrast, I found the theories constructed by anthropologists weak and unconvincing. Evolutionism and diffusionism had had their day, and I did not find functionalism, as a theory, to be any better. The writings of Marx and Weber had no place in the anthropology we were taught. I knew Durkheim at that time mainly as the author of *The Elementary Forms of the Religious Life*, but then I had been completely convinced by Goldenweiser's review (1915) in *American Anthropologist* that his facts were all wrong. So I did not accept his theory that in totemism the real object of worship was the clan.

After four years of 'primitive ethnography', I had had a surfeit of exotic customs: levirate and sororate; prohibited degrees in marriage, and marriage with the mother's mother's brother's daughter's daughter; the cousin who is called 'uncle' and the cousin who is called 'niece'; homoeopathic magic and contagious magic; couvade and the avunculate; *churinga, nurtunja* and *waninga*; and so on. I had begun to feel some sympathy for the popular view that anthropology was 'the study of oddments by eccentrics'. It cannot be denied that, through all its transmutations, the subject has retained a somewhat exaggerated concern for the uncommon and the exotic. By the end of the 1950s, I had begun to tire of it.

My immersion in the literature of anthropology as I knew it then meant that I was falling behind on subjects that were of central concern to the brightest among my friends outside of anthropology, such as class, inequality, conflict, capitalism, socialism and democracy. Some of these friends were uncommonly clever and also extremely well-read, and even in the best of circumstances, it would not be easy to keep pace with them. I could of course tell them that there was no such thing as 'primitive communism' or that the belief in a universal stage of matriarchy was mistaken, but that did not carry one very far. I had begun to feel that sociology rather than anthropology, or at least the kind of anthropology that I had learnt, would give me the intellectual equipment to cope with the problems that arose in my immediate environment.

Thus, I was doubly fortunate in securing a lectureship in sociology at the Delhi School of Economics when I did. I had already discovered that the best way of learning was by teaching, and I was glad to be able to explore new fields of ideas and to work through new books and new authors. My close association with Srinivas, who had worked with some of the leading anthropologists in the world—Radcliffe-Brown, Evans-Pritchard, Fortes, Gluckman and others—made me re-examine the anthropology that I had learnt earlier, and prevented me from moving too far away from it too quickly. So, although I entered deeply into the worlds of Max Weber and Raymond Aron, I did not abandon Radcliffe-Brown and Evans-Pritchard.

The unity of sociology and anthropology was an article of faith with Srinivas, and nothing could have suited me better at the beginning of my own academic career. Although I admired Srinivas very greatly, his tastes and preferences in intellectual matters were often different from mine. He had many accomplishments while I was a neophyte. My one advantage over him was my reading knowledge of French, which gave me some familiarity, however limited, with the French intellectual tradition. Srinivas did not mind the French, but he seemed to have a prejudice against the Germans which, I suspect, he had acquired from Radcliffe-Brown. I, on the other hand, was greatly impressed by the German intellectual tradition, at least in social theory, although I did not read any German.

I carried several elements from anthropology into my teaching of sociology, and most of them have remained with me, though not without some transmutation. My interest in the comparative approach became fixed fairly early, and I believe that the kind of teaching I have had to do in Delhi has had an important part in it. The very first course I taught in 1959–60 was in political sociology, and that included segmentary and centralised systems in tribal Africa, the political systems of highland Burma, politics in a small town in England, together with Max Weber's work on power and authority. From the very start, I took to heart Radcliffe-Brown's view that social anthropology was another name for comparative sociology. For me the comparative approach calls for the ability and, above all, the willingness to place all societies, one's own as well as others', on the same plane of observation and enquiry. A sociologist who confines his attention entirely to his own society is only half a sociologist, and one who excludes it from his consideration is hardly a sociologist.

Soon after I came to Delhi, I was persuaded by Srinivas of the fundamental importance of the idea of social structure as developed by his two Oxford teachers, Radcliffe-Brown and Evans-Pritchard. I used that idea extensively in my early teaching and writing, and it made its way into my very first book, *Caste, Class and Power* (1965). But in course of time, I came to realize increasingly the limitations of that idea. I have now come to feel that I might have done better had I given more thought to the idea of social institutions than to that of social structure as I viewed it then. This is because the first concept can accommodate better than the second the meanings that people assign to the social arrangements in and through which they live.

Finally, I have retained an inherent scepticism, derived from the great tradition of anthropological fieldwork, about models that provide elegant theoretical solutions to the problems encountered and experienced in everyday life. I was from the start on Malinowski's side against Radcliffe-Brown in the former's attack on 'kinship algebra' (Béteille 1993b). The importance of fieldwork, the encounter with life as it is actually lived, was constantly brought to my attention by Srinivas and, even before him, by N.K. Bose in Calcutta. I was made all the more aware of its importance since, unlike Bose and Srinivas, I have never been a successful fieldworker.

One does not have to excel in fieldwork in the technical sense in order to be continually preoccupied, as I have been, with the untidiness or, even, the messiness of social life (Béteille 1991: 1–14). It is true that it was intensive fieldwork that transformed anthropology from a 'study of oddments by eccentrics' into the exciting intellectual venture it became with Malinowski and his pupils. Max Gluckman once explained to me that it was this experience, rather than any preoccupation with 'social structure' as against 'culture', that made British anthropologists in the 1930s and 1940s appear different, at least in their own eyes, from their American colleagues. At the same time, one may carry a deep sense of the richness, the complexity and the ambiguity in social and political processes without undertaking anthropological fieldwork, as may be easily seen from the life and work of Max Weber.

It should be obvious from the reference to Weber that I did not rely in my teaching and writing solely on what I had learnt as a student of anthropology; indeed, in the 1950s, the name of Max Weber hardly figured in discussions among anthropologists in India or, for that matter, in Britain. As I settled down to teaching in Delhi, I began to re-examine my intellectual resources while expanding my interest in a number of different directions. Among the many new authors I discovered, the most important was Max Weber, whom I have regarded over the last thirty years as the greatest of all sociologists. This is in a way ironical, for I am greatly attracted by a clear and lucid style, as in the writing of Maitland, for instance, or Keynes, and Weber's prose is anything but clear and lucid.

I also found a new area of intellectual interest in the study of social inequality in its many forms and manifestations. Since this interest has remained with me for more than thirty years, I find it annoying not to be able to recall exactly when, where and how it originated. Inequality hardly figured as a topic in the social anthropology I had read in Calcutta, and, as far as I recall, it was not a major interest with Srinivas, so my interest must have been, at least to some extent, my own creation. Certainly my new interest made it easier for me to justify my place in a department of sociology, for what could be regarded as more central to the discipline than class and stratification?

Although class and stratification are pre-eminently sociological subjects, I incorporated into their study certain basic elements acquired in my training as an anthropologist. My first book examined the changing relationships between caste, class and power through the intensive study of a single village of the kind commonly undertaken by anthropologists in India and elsewhere. I was criticized by certain anthropologists for introducing the concept of class which they regarded as inappropriate in the context of village India, but I did not take their criticism to heart and proceeded in later studies to explore the contours of the agrarian class structure at the district and regional levels on the basis of the insights I had gathered through my village study (Béteille 1974b).

Having cut my teeth on a community study, I became eager to explore wider fields of enquiry. An opportunity soon came my way when I was asked to put together a selection of readings on social stratification for a series that was being launched by Penguin Books. I decided to put to the test the comparative approach I had acquired as a student of anthropology in Calcutta and extended as a teacher of sociology in Delhi. I was determined to give fair representation in my selection to all the major types of society: tribal, agrarian and industrial. The plain fact is that, after the great enthusiasm for the comparative approach shown by the generation of Durkheim and Weber, sociologists in Europe and America had settled down to the study of western or industrial societies, and social anthropologists to the study of tribal or 'primitive' societies. An Indian seeking to understand his own society had to take into account social formations of the greatest variety, from the simplest to the most complex, and I found the division of labour, that had grown in the west between anthropology and sociology, artificial and constricting. I was fully convinced, at least into the mid-1970s, that the unity of sociology and anthropology could only be to the advantage of sociology and never at its cost.

Naturally, my approach to the problem of inequality has grown and developed over the last thirty years, and I will now make a few observations on it in so far as it illustrates a change in my general approach to social enquiry. When I started, my general approach was markedly influenced by *A Natural Science of Society* and *The Rules of Sociological Method* which took for granted the separation of facts and values. It changed over time, at first very slowly, as I came to realize the complex nature of the relationship between judgements of fact and judgements of value in social enquiry. As I look back, I can discern this process in my choice of words for the titles of my books. My first two books carry the word 'stratification' in their subtitles; my later books use 'inequality' instead. The shift in terminology was a signal of my growing awareness that sociology was a moral rather than a natural science (Béteille 1983: 1–27).

One of the constant preoccupations in my early work on the subject was with the coexistence of different dimensions of inequality and their mutual irreducibility. Since I worked in the close proximity of economists, it was important for me to show that inequality was not just a matter of income or wealth, or even class, but that it was also, and independently, a matter of status (or esteem) and of power (Béteille 1977, 1993a). Strange though it may sound, it took me many years to grasp the significance of the simple truth that not only does inequality have several dimensions, but that equality, too, has more than one meaning. A consideration of the many tensions between the ideal of equality and the pervasive presence of inequality has forced me to reconsider many times over the possibility as well as the limitations of a value-free sociology.

I ought to pause here to make a brief observation on my own attitude to a value-free sociology (Béteille 1983: 1–27; 1992). I have always been deeply committed to it while being aware, more acutely now than in the past, that the enterprise is constantly at risk. There may be several positions on this. The one from which I started, which may be characterized as that of Durkheim in *The Rules of Sociological Method*, I find the least satisfactory today. According to it, one must never allow judgements of value to intrude into the observation, description and analysis of facts, and, to ensure that, it is enough to take a few elementary precautions; I was once rebuked in a review by David Pocock for failing to take those precautions.

A second position is the one I associate with the 'Theses on Feuerbach', and the writings of such Marxists as Lukacs, Korsch and Gramsci. It is based on the doctrine of the unity of theory and practice, and stresses commitment, engagement and partisanship in its approach to society and politics. A sociologist who makes inequality the subject of his concern in India cannot escape being asked or, rather, exhorted to declare his own values and to show how they can be realized. To merely study inequality, or to observe, describe and interpret its many and changing forms is, in this view, to share some complicity in a terrible social evil. I have encountered much hostility to my view that the understanding and interpretation of inequality is an important task in itself. What most persons want, or seem to want, from the sociologist is some practical solution to the problem of inequality as they see it. But the most important lesson that I have learnt—and tried to teach—as a sociologist is that things cannot be changed simply because men of goodwill are uneasy in their minds about them.

To try to understand things without adopting a partisan position is not necessarily to be indifferent to them. It is difficult to see how a sociologist can remain consistently indifferent to his own society, or to the world in which he lives. But he must also act with restraint, be attentive to interpretations that go against his own preferences, and not make exaggerated claims on behalf of his discipline. To be sure, one has to exercise judgement as a responsible citizen, but one cannot claim in matters concerning fundamental values any special privilege by virtue of being a sociologist. For it is the case that on such questions as whether equality of opportunity is more fundamental than distributive equality, or whether the two can be harmoniously combined, social theory can say very little that will be universally accepted.

Here I have to note that on these and related questions, my views have been significantly influenced by the economists among whom I have worked, though not always in ways they would approve. I have said that I was lucky in securing at the beginning of my professional career a lectureship in sociology in a strong post-graduate department. The location of that department in the Delhi School of Economics has enabled me to take advantage of the presence of a number of outstanding economists in my immediate environment. To name only a few, I have shared my interest in the agrarian class structure with Professor K.N. Raj, and my interest in inequality with Professor Amartya Sen, and, more recently, Professor S.D. Tendulkar.

In the 1960s and 1970s, economic science occupied a position of undisputed pre-eminence among the humanities and the social sciences throughout the country; and we still have many more outstanding economists than outstanding sociologists. Holding one's own in a discussion with economists has never been easy, but it has had its rewards. What I found least attractive in the economists I knew in the 1960s and 1970s was their self-assurance. They were self-assured when it came to theory, and equally so when it came to policy. This self-assurance apart, some of them, particularly the economic historians, had a sense of the importance of material reality that was a constant challenge to my own understanding of the world. It is this sense of the importance of material things that has sustained the attraction for me of the works of Marx and Weber. But Weber has had the greater attraction simply because his work conveys, at least to me, an equally strong sense of the importance of ideas, beliefs and values.

The changes that have taken place in my ideas over the years have come less from a succession of well-planned or organized research projects than from the everyday demands of teaching, including the supervision of research students. As I look back, these changes appear incremental rather than dramatic, although their cumulative effect has not been inconsiderable, at least in some respects. I would like in the end to dwell a little on some of these changes, with special reference to my changing conception of the nature of sociology and its relations with other disciplines.

The modern university has a division of labour, and its members have to work within it—as teachers, as students, as examiners and as examinees. One need not treat the existing division of labour as sacrosanct and unalterable. Rather, one should adopt a flexible attitude towards it in the knowledge that it has changed in the past and will change in the future; but in a university, with its division into faculties and departments, one cannot wish it out of existence. Within such a system, it is a little difficult to take very seriously the argument that human knowledge is single and indivisible, and therefore it does not matter whether what one is doing is called sociology or psychology or linguistics.

Every teacher has to explain to his students what sociology is about, and to provide a working definition of it. But that is only one side of the story. The conception of sociology that teachers present to their students in the classroom rarely fits well with the conception of it implicit in their discussions at seminars and conferences. The latter is very loose indeed, and, at least in India, it tends to oscillate between a commentary on current affairs and a vague philosophizing about man, society and culture. This makes it all the more necessary for the sociologist in this country to keep his own conception of the subject under constant scrutiny. One obvious way to do this is to compare and contrast it with neighbourly disciplines such as anthropology, history and economics.

As I have tried to explain already, sociology is for me the systematic study of the nature and forms of social life, with the emphasis now more on social institutions than on the structure of groups, classes and categories, although that still remains important in my view. It is, above all, comparative in outlook, requiring us to place all societies, our own as well as others, on the same plane of enquiry. Its point of departure is lived experience in the world here and now, although it seeks insights from all societies, however distant in space or time. It seeks to understand the rights and obligations that bind persons together, as well as the meanings they assign to the arrangements in and through which they live. It is watchful of the divergence between what people believe, or say they believe, about right, proper and desirable ways of living, and how they actually live. Finally, it is primarily a descriptive and an interpretive rather than a prescriptive discipline. In my conception, sociology is not a policy science: it can offer something to policy analysis but very little to policy prescription.

What of the relationship between sociology and social anthropology with which I started? It is undeniable that my enthusiasm for the unity of sociology and anthropology has cooled over the last thirty years. This is partly because of changes in my own professional experience and intellectual horizons, but also because of changes in the two disciplines themselves.

Let me return briefly to my professional experience both in India and abroad. In most universities, anthropology and sociology are taught in different departments, often, as in both Calcutta and Delhi, by different faculties. Where the two disciplines were started in a single department, they have not always remained together, as I have shown with the example of Manchester. Where they are in separate departments, as in Delhi, Calcutta, Cambridge or the London School of Economics, there is no close interaction—academic or social—between them. I have found it difficult to keep my faith in the unity of the two disciplines in the face of so much separation between them.

The institutional separation between sociology and anthropology is, in my limited experience, most marked in north American universities, and there is one aspect of it that has been a source of some annoyance to me. When a student of Indian society and culture goes to such a university, no matter whether he is a sociologist or an anthropologist in India, he is presented there as an anthropologist and not a sociologist. The established opinion in American, and to a large extent European, universities is that the study of Indian society and of other Asian or African societies is the province of anthropology and not sociology. I have myself resisted this perception of Indian sociology that it is in effect anthropology, or, as some have called it, 'ethnosociology' (Béteille 1974c), and not sociology, but that hardly affects the prevailing classification there.

It has been a matter of some regret to me that Indian sociologists accept without any hesitation the labels they are assigned in other countries, even when they are at odds with the ones they carry in their own country. I feel as a teacher that this must be somewhat unsettling, if not demoralizing, for our students. Many of the best products of our department now go abroad, particularly to the United States, for post-graduate work. But the majority of them slip into departments of anthropology; few seem to have the confidence even to apply for admission to departments of sociology.

Anthropology itself has changed much in the last three or four decades, and its concerns have moved away, at least to some extent, from what I consider to be the proper concerns of sociology. Two of the most important exemplars of anthropology in the 1940s and 1950s were Radcliffe-Brown in Britain and Redfield in the United States. Each was in his own way moving anthropology in a direction that made it very attractive to students of sociology in India. I had been introduced to the intellectual world of Redfield by Surajit Sinha in Calcutta just before I came to Delhi. Srinivas was, of course, greatly influenced by Radcliffe-Brown, and I, in turn, by Srinivas. It is true that even then the unity of sociology and social anthropology did not exist as a fact; but in 1959, it was, or appeared to me, a distinct and an attractive possibility.

But anthropology took a sharp turn some time in the 1960s or 1970s through the rise to prominence of Lévi-Strauss and what I would call the 'new structuralism'. To his admirers, the work of Lévi-Strauss appeared as a kind of Copernican revolution, and those who did not admire it were often browbeaten into silence. No two conceptions of anthropology could be further apart than those of Radcliffe-Brown and Lévi-Strauss. When Lévi-Strauss presented his paper on 'Social Structure' at the famous Chicago conference in 1952, most English-speaking anthropologists failed to see in it a signal of the shape of things to come (Kroeber 1953; Tax et al. 1953).

Lévi-Strauss has restored to anthropology some of its original concerns which Radcliffe-Brown, Redfield and others were trying to put behind. I believe that the enormous appeal of his work lies not so much in its structural method as in its marvellous evocation, from *Tristes tropiques* to *Le regard eloigné*, of the distant and the exotic. I now understand far better than I did thirty years ago that western social science has a perennial need for its 'astronomers among the social sciences', and no one has met that need with greater insight and imagination than Lévi-Strauss. His true precursor among anthropologists is neither Mauss nor Malinowski, but Frazer. There is no doubt that Lévi-Strauss' intellectual enterprise has been a splendid success, but then I have not felt the need, as a sociologist, to attach myself to that enterprise.

The radical turn, not to say reversal, in the orientation of anthropology towards sociology was plainly expressed by Rodney Needham who had identified himself closely with the work of Lévi-Strauss, as translator (Lévi-Strauss 1962), as editor (Lévi-Strauss 1969) and as expositor (Needham 1962). He used the occasion of his inaugural lecture at Oxford—incidentally, for the same chair whose first occupant had been Radcliffe-Brown—to explain where he thought anthropology stood in relation to other disciplines. He said, 'Our congeners therefore include philosophy, classics, philology, history (especially social history, the history of ideas, art history), theology (particularly the ancillary of biblical studies), and other non-mathematical kinds of study' (Needham 1978: 9). He then added, 'Sociology may seem an obvious relative, and it is true that we acknowledge common ancestors in the last century, but it is hard to cite titles in modern sociology that bear significantly on our problems' (Ibid.: 10). This may seem an unusual way of making a point, but Needham was not alone among anthropologists who sought to keep a distance from sociology. The change of orientation is clearly seen in the change undergone by the concept of structure (Sahlins 1976: 1–54). For Radcliffe-Brown, structure was, above all, a matter of social relations among persons or groups of persons in interaction with each other, whereas for Lévi-Strauss, structure dwells in the realm of ideas, especially unconscious ideas, rather than action. At any rate, there is, in the latter's work, very little concern with the rights and obligations among persons, or with the manner in which they are defined and redefined from one social situation to another. Nor is there the kind of concern that one encounters in anthropological studies based on intensive fieldwork with the meanings that persons assign to their actions.

All of this is not to say that Lévi-Strauss' work is deficient in comparison with that of Radcliffe-Brown or Redfield, but only that it has a different orientation and a different focus. Perhaps the former has a better claim to the title of anthropology than the latter. To the extent that a great deal of contemporary anthropology takes its orientation from Lévi-Strauss rather than Radcliffe-Brown or Redfield, anthropology and sociology have moved further apart and not closer together. I have certainly changed, but the times have also changed.

I do not wish to leave the impression in the end that for someone who embarks today on the kind of career that I entered in 1959, the choice has to be between Radcliffe-Brown and Lévi-Strauss, for I know only too well that there are few today who would prefer the former to the latter. I myself find it difficult to recapture the enthusiasm that I had felt for Redfield and Radcliffe-Brown when I moved from Calcutta to Delhi in 1959. But if next to Lévi-Strauss both Radcliffe-Brown and Redfield appear thin and insubstantial in today's light, surely the same cannot be said about Weber. In Weber, we have an intellectual figure who occupied a commanding position before Lévi-Strauss appeared on the scene and whose influence can be counted to last at least as long as the latter's.

It would be puerile to try to bring Weber and Lévi-Strauss into public competition with each other. My purpose in drawing attention to Weber's work has been twofold. First, I wanted to show that the classical tradition of sociology still has a very great deal to offer to a contemporary student of sociology in India or anywhere. Second, it appears obvious that Weber's work, and, beyond that, what I consider central to the enterprise of sociology, is in many ways closer to the economic writings of Schumpeter, the political writings of Duverger and the historical writings of Braudel than it is to the anthropology of Lévi-Strauss. Sociology must surely remain receptive to the ideas of great anthropologists—Malinowski and

Evans-Pritchard, and also Frazer and Lévi-Strauss—but I find it difficult to pretend that it has today a special relationship with anthropology that it does not have with history, economics or politics.

References

Béteille, A. 1965. *Caste, Class and Power: Changing Patterns of Stratification in a Tanjore village*. Berkeley: University of California Press.

————. 1974a. *Six Essays in Comparative Sociology*. Delhi: Oxford University Press.

————. 1974b. *Studies in Agrarian Social Structure*. Delhi: Oxford University Press.

————. 1974c. 'Sociology and Ethnosociology'. *International Social Science Journal*. 27, 4: 703–704.

————. 1977. *Inequality among Men*. Oxford: Basil Blackwell.

————. 1991. *Society and Politics in India. Essays in a Comparative Perspective*. London: Athlone Press.

————. 1992. 'Religion as a Subject for Sociology'. *Economic and Political Weekly*. 27. 35: 1865–70, see chapter 7, this volume.

————. 1993a. 'Amartya Sen's Utopia'. *Economic and Political Weekly*. 28. 16: 753–6.

————. 1993b. *Empirical Meaning and Imputed Meaning in the Study of Kinship*. University of Delhi: Department of Sociology, Working Paper No. 6 (mimeo).

————. (ed.) 1983. *Equality and Inequality: Theory and Practice*. Delhi: Oxford University Press.

Durkheim, É. 1966. *The Rules of Sociological Method*. Glencoe: The Free Press.

Goldenweiser, A.A. 1915. 'Review: Émile Durkheim—*Les formes élémentaires de la vie religieuse*. *American Anthropologist*. 17: 719–35.

Homans, G.C. 1962. *Sentiments and Activities*. London: Routledge and Kegan Paul.

Kroeber, A.L., (ed.) 1953. *Anthropology Today*. Chicago: University of Chicago Press.

Lévi-Strauss, C. 1962. *Totemism*. Harmondsworth: Penguin Books.

————. 1969. *The Elementary Structures of Kinship*. Boston: Beacon Press.

Motwani, K. 1961. *Integration. A Programme of Education*. Madras: Ganesh and Co.

Needham, R. 1962. *Structure and Sentiment*. Chicago: University of Chicago Press.

————. 1978. *Essential Perplexities*. Oxford: Clarendon Press.

Sahlins, M.D. 1976. *Culture and Practical Reason.* Chicago: University of Chicago Press.

Sen, D., G.S. Ray and A. Béteille. 1956. 'A New Palaeolithic Site in Mayurbhanj'. *Man in India.* 26, 4: 233–46.

Tax, S., L.C. Eiseley, I. Rouse and C.F. Voegelin, (eds). 1953. *An Appraisal of Anthropology Today.* Chicago: University of Chicago Press.

Chapter
4

Some Observations on the Comparative Method*

I have chosen the comparative method as the subject of my lecture this evening because it seemed appropriate for an institution devoted to the study of society and culture in the countries of Asia. These countries have a great variety of institutions and ways of life, with different historical antecedents and different prospects for change, but they also share a number of things in common, so that the knowledge and understanding of each is bound to be deepened by comparison and contrast with the others. Moreover, the comparative method has been a favourite topic for sociologists and social anthropologists for at least a hundred years, and there is a large, though inconclusive, literature on it. My treatment of the literature will be highly selective, being confined mainly to the tradition associated with Durkheim rather than Marx or Weber.

I must state at the outset that I do not believe I can reach any definite

*This is the text of the inaugural Wertheim Lecture delivered in Amsterdam on 5 July 1990. I am grateful to the Centre for Asian Studies for inviting me to deliver the lecture, and I offer it as a small token of gratitude to Professor Wertheim for his kindness to me on my first visit to Amsterdam in 1966. The paper was written while I was a Fellow at the Wissenschaftskolleg zu Berlin in 1989–90, and I would like to thank the Kolleg for its generous hospitality and its excellent facilities. I am grateful in particular to Peter Burke for the patience and care with which he read and commented on all that I wrote, and I would also like to thank Elaine Scarry for helping me to improve the language of the text. Thanks are due also to Jack Goody who took time off on a brief visit to the Kolleg to read the text and comment on it.

conclusion about the correct use of the comparative method at the end of the lecture. That can hardly be expected for a subject with which so many able scholars have wrestled over such a long period of time. Yet the subject retains a great fascination, and one may even profit a little from a consideration of some of the false starts that have been made in the past. I will adopt in the main a historical approach, dwelling on the development of the subject, although this may appear somewhat paradoxical since the comparative method has in the past been set in opposition to the historical method.

Before entering into a historical examination, I would like to indicate very briefly a new development in our subject whose implications have not so far been seriously examined. Much of the appeal of the earlier use of the comparative method, particularly by social anthropologists, lay in the attention it devoted to the study of non-western societies. It can easily be shown that the conclusions drawn about family and marriage, or about economic processes, or about the relation between religion and society remain incomplete, or even misleading, so long as they are based on studies confined within the context of a single society or a single type of society. Here the work of the scholars associated with the *Année sociologique* set an example, for they attempted to examine within a single framework all the varieties of human society, both western and non-western, from the simplest to the most complex, or, in the language of those times, from the most primitive to the most advanced.

Although the full integration of the study of western and non-western societies still remains to be achieved in practice, scholars have since the end of the nineteenth century steadily extended the range of the societies they have investigated through broadly similar concepts and methods. However, the scholars who began to extend their observation to an increasing range of societies were themselves all members of the same society or the same type of society. It would not be unfair to describe the project of the *Année sociologique* as the study of all societies, western as well as non-western, by western scholars. At least for that generation of scholars, the question did not arise whether their project might alter significantly by extending to the limit not only the range of investigation but also the range of investigators.

That question has to be raised now, and I believe that it will acquire increasing salience in discussions of the comparative method. There are now scholars in India, Indonesia, Pakistan, Sri Lanka and elsewhere engaged in the study of their own societies. This began after the First World War when a handful of scholars, trained in the west, sought to apply the methods and techniques they had learnt there to the study of their own societies. The last few decades have witnessed an enormous growth of sociology and social anthropology in these countries, and a beginning has been made by scholars from there to study aspects of western society. This has introduced new perspectives and raised questions about the very concepts and categories used by earlier scholars, both foreign and indigenous, in the study of societies in Asia and Africa.[1]

Comparative Method and the Scientific Study of Society

I must now return to the comparative method as it was fashioned in its early phase. It was in a sense the great achievement of nineteenth-century sociology and social anthropology. The most extensive comparisons were attempted, not only of whole societies but also of particular institutions and practices: kinship systems, marriage practices, techniques of agriculture and pottery, magical practices, religious beliefs, and so on. The central place assigned to comparison was signalled by Durkheim (1982: 57) when he wrote: 'Comparative sociology is not a special branch of sociology; it is sociology itself.'

If we take a sufficiently broad view of comparison, then it will be obvious that all sociologists and anthropologists have to rely on it, and they would probably all agree that there has to be some method in the comparisons they make. But beyond this, one finds important differences, for there are those who are enthusiastic about the comparative method and those who are sceptical about it. Among the enthusiasts I would include Spencer, Tylor, Durkheim and Radcliffe-Brown; and among the sceptics, Boas, Goldenweiser and Evans-Pritchard. The great wave of enthusiasm for the comparative method belongs to the past, and today there are probably more sceptics than enthusiasts.

In the nineteenth century, the principal attraction of the comparative method lay in the belief that it could be used for discovering scientific laws about human society and culture. The strong advocates of the comparative method believed in the possibility of a natural science of society that would establish regularities of coexistence and succession among the forms of social life by means of systematic comparisons. It must not be forgotten that in nineteenth-century anthropology the study of social and cultural phenomena was typically combined with the study of the physical or biological aspects of human life. Both Spencer and Durkheim were greatly influenced by the organic analogy, and in Durkheim, in particular, we find not only a metaphorical but also a methodological use of that analogy.

Not only was the early use of the comparative method tied to the idea of a natural science of society, it was, more specifically, tied to the theory of evolution.[2] A large part of nineteenth-century anthropology was concerned with the origins of phenomena and the reconstruction of the stages through which they had evolved from their simplest to their most complex forms. The classification and comparison of the forms of social life became an indispensable part of this process of reconstruction. Many anthropologists and sociologists believed that they could achieve through the method of classification what the biologists had achieved through the method of taxonomy. If only they could arrange all the known forms of social life in a systematic order, from the simplest to the most complex, they would get from it an evolutionary sequence, since, in their view, every type of society represented also a stage of evolution.

The attempt to trace the origins of institutions and the successive stages of their evolution through the comparison of existing types of society was fraught with many hazards. Knowledge of the existing types of society was sketchy and fragmentary. There were no agreed rules for the classification of social types. Social types that had disappeared did not leave behind the kind of records that the palaeontologist could examine in fossil form in order to make his classificatory series complete. A very great deal was left to conjecture, and anthropologists took easy recourse to what may be called the artifice of inversion. In other words, they took the end point of evolution as the form current in western, principally Anglo-American, society, and then constructed the starting point by a simple inversion of the features known in advance to have prevailed in the end.

The difficulty of arriving at valid generalizations through the classification and comparison of societies on a worldwide scale made some anthropologists uneasy. Within a year of the publication of Durkheim's manifesto for the comparative method (Durkheim 1982), there appeared an essay by Franz Boas (1940), entitled, 'The limitations of the comparative method of anthropology'. Boas objected above all to the sweeping generalizations made through the use of the comparative method, and recommended studies on a more limited geographical scale and with a more careful attention to facts. He introduced the distinction, that was to appear in one form or another in the writings of his successors, between the 'comparative method' and the 'historical method', clearly expressing his preference for the latter over the former.

Boas did not declare himself to be in principle against the comparative method, but he put his finger on a weakness of that method that was to embarrass its users in the future. His point was simply that 'before extended comparisons are made, the comparability of the material *must be proved*' (Boas 1940: 275, emphasis added). Now it is one thing to recommend caution while making comparisons, but how can the comparability of the material be proved before the comparisons are made? The proof of comparability in advance can be used to undermine virtually any application of the comparative method.

No one can deny the hazards of reckless comparisons. Such comparisons, made characteristically in the service of some grandiose theory, jeopardize the serious study of society and culture in our own time as they did in the time of Boas. But then there are disadvantages also in moving to the opposite extreme. Boas and his successors felt most at ease with comparisons between what may be called 'neighbourly cultures'.[3] But how much caution do we have to exercise in ensuring the conditions of 'neighbourliness'? Neighbourliness is obviously not just a matter of geographical propinquity, although that was important to Boas. By making the conditions of comparability successively more rigorous, we might find ourselves limited to the study of a unique constellation of characteristics in a single society. It is in this sense that Boas's historical method might become opposed rather than complementary to the comparative method.

The work of Boas and his pupils, particularly Goldenweiser (1922) and Lowie (1960), did much to damage the scientific pretensions of the theory of social and cultural evolution. But the retreat from the reconstruction of the stages of evolution did not necessarily lead to the rejection of the idea of a natural science of society. That idea was vigorously advocated by A.R. Radcliffe-Brown (1952, 1958) who exercised great influence on anthropologists in the United Kingdom and the Commonwealth in the thirties, forties and fifties of the twentieth century.

Radcliffe-Brown borrowed a great deal from Durkheim, including the idea that societies were governed by laws that could be discovered by the application of the proper method. That method was the comparative method, based on the observation, description and comparison of societies as they actually existed. Radcliffe-Brown wrote at a time when fieldwork among the simpler societies was opening up new possibilities for the understanding of social life, and he sought to base his natural science of society on observation as against conjecture. Evolutionary speculations belonged in his view to the domain of 'conjectural history', which he categorically rejected in favour of what he called 'systems analysis'. Hence, the laws that he sought to discover related to the structure and functioning of societies rather than to their evolution (Radcliffe-Brown 1952).

Radcliffe-Brown chose the comparative method in social anthropology as the subject of his Huxley Memorial Lecture of 1951. He began by referring to the writings of Boas in the late nineteenth century, pointing out that two distinct aims—those of reconstructing the past and of discovering the laws governing social processes—had been mixed together in them. Comparisons of particular features of social life for the purpose of historical reconstruction were very different from comparisons for the purpose that he had in view. 'In comparative sociology or social anthropology the purpose of comparison is different, the aim being to explore the varieties of forms of social life as a basis for the theoretical study of human social phenomena' (Radcliffe-Brown 1958: 108). It may be noted that Radcliffe-Brown not only tried to separate social anthropology from ethnology, which he regarded as being concerned with historical reconstruction, but often used the term 'comparative sociology' as a synonym for social anthropology.

I have pointed out that classification was thought to be of fundamental importance to comparative sociology by Durkheim who tried, moreover, to formulate rules for the classification of social types. Radcliffe-Brown's thinking was along similar lines. In his famous Chicago seminar of 1937, he declared:

I would suggest that an examination of the other sciences immediately suggests that the first step in social science will be to undertake the task of taxonomy and classification, and in the first instance, the classification of social systems themselves. I propose that no scientific study of societies can get very far until we have made some progress towards a classification of social systems into whatever types, groups, or classes suggest themselves as expedient, that is, likely to lead to valid generalizations with respect to all societies (1957: 33).

Radcliffe-Brown's thinking at this stage was dominated by the idea of 'natural kinds' and the belief that societies are natural kinds.

What is a natural kind? A natural kind is given by a combination of properties that occur repeatedly in the same arrangement, for instance, a class of metals or a species of animals. If societies were natural kinds, we would be able to classify them in the same way in which zoologists classify animals. I believe that it is a fundamental mistake to think of societies in this way, for human societies are not like plants and animals in *either* their similarities *or* their differences. No two societies resemble each other in the way in which two birds of the same species do; and no two societies differ from each other in the way in which a bird differs from a butterfly.

Radcliffe-Brown tried later to rescue the comparative method from too close a dependence on the organic analogy. Towards the end of his career, he wrote, 'But forms of social life cannot be classified into species and genera in the way we classify forms of organic life; the classification has to be not specific but typological, and this is a more complicated kind of investigation' (1952: 7). He did not, however, show any way of dealing with the complication without abandoning the basic objective of arriving at general laws about social life.

Radcliffe-Brown's successor at Oxford, Professor Evans-Pritchard, chose the comparative method in social anthropology as the subject of his Hobhouse lecture in 1963. By that time, the idea of a natural science of society that would discover universal laws of social life had fallen into disfavour, at least among anthropologists in Britain, and Evans-Pritchard was merely driving the last nail into the coffin. The general tone of his address was critical, not to say querulous, for, although he admitted the indispensability of 'observation, classification and comparison in one form or another', he went on to comment, 'But it is over two hundred years since *L' Esprit des lois* was written, and we may well ask once more what has been achieved by use of the comparative method, in whatever form, over this long period of time' (1965: 31–2). Evans-Pritchard reserved his severest censure for what he called the 'statistical use of the comparative method'.

Evans-Pritchard pointed out that, despite all its scientific pretensions, the comparative method as used by Radcliffe-Brown and many others was little more than the illustrative method, or what may be called the method of apt illustration. What the social anthropologist in search of general laws in fact did was quite different from the practice of any natural scientist. There was a wide gulf between Radcliffe-Brown's practice and his declared objective; and 'his version of the comparative method was in practice mainly a return to the illustrative method' which consists of 'thinking up some plausible explanation of some social phenomenon and then searching round for illustrations which seem to support it and neglecting the rest of the material relating to the topic under consideration' (1965: 23).

With Evans-Pritchard, we are back to the distinction between the historical method and the comparative method, with the preferences of Radcliffe-Brown reversed. The historical method views everything in its context; the comparative method takes things out of their context. Evans-

Pritchard is even more mindful than Boas of preserving the richness of context in writing about social institutions and practices. Where comparative studies are insensitive to this richness, as they invariably are when statistical techniques are used, they are to be treated with suspicion.

For a start, Evans-Pritchard would recommend a sort of intensive comparative investigation in a limited area because 'it might well be held that the small-scale comparative studies have been more rewarding than the large-scale statistical ones' (1965: 29). But he is sceptical even about that. 'Even when I have attempted to make a comparative study of only the northern and best-known Nilotic peoples, I have not succeeded in establishing any correlations I have thought important enough to record' (1965: 28). So finally,

One might go even further and assert that the intensive study of a single society may prove more illuminating than literary comparisons on whatever scale, if only because, as all who have had the experience must have discovered, a theory which can be well tested by observations in the field can seldom be so rigorously tested by literary research (1965: 29–30).

For those engaged in the study of large and complex societies in India or in Indonesia, this may appear as a counsel of despair. If it proves difficult to make valid generalizations about the Nilotic tribes, it might prove impossible to make them about Indian tribes which are more numerous, more dispersed and more heterogeneous; and the tribes constitute only one of the many components of Indian society. Those who study, let us say, migrant labour in India or the conflict of religious groups in Indonesia, will find it difficult, not to say impossible, to reproduce the total context within which the particular phenomena they study have their place.

It may of course be argued that comparisons *within* the same society stand on a different footing from those *between* different societies. But this raises the question of what we mean by a society. Is the Munda tribe of south Bihar a society, or is it only a component of the larger society of Bihar, or the still larger society of India? From Boas to Evans-Pritchard, anthropologists dealt primarily with simple societies, or what used to be called primitive societies, and they tended to assume a high degree of unity and coherence in those societies. Now, they also write about large and complex societies, what are generally called civilizations, and they tend to carry the assumptions of coherence and organic unity into the study of these societies as well. What I wish to point out is that the use of the organic analogy was not confined to the advocates of the comparative method such as Durkheim and Radcliffe-Brown; the assumption of organic unity is deeply embedded also in the writings of those who stress the uniqueness of civilizations and advocate the historical as against the comparative method.

Difference and Otherness

I now turn to the question of similarity and difference in comparative studies. What should be the aim of comparison in sociology and social anthropology? Should it be to identify similarity or to discover difference? Should our aim be to show that all societies are alike or that each one is unique? These questions may appear trivial, but people have responded differently to them, and their responses reflect differences of aesthetic, moral and political judgement.

It is obvious that when anthropologists make comparisons, they find both similarities and differences, and I do not know of a single anthropologist whose comparisons have in fact brought to light *only* similarities or *only* differences. It is nevertheless the case that some anthropologists have argued that the principal aim of comparison is to discover difference, although the forms of their arguments and the reasons behind them have not all been the same. Very broadly speaking, one can distinguish between the view that the societies studied by anthropologists all differ among themselves, and the view that they are all different from the anthropologist's own society, viz. western society. Again, the two views reflect differences of aesthetic, moral and political judgement, but they are closely intertwined with each other.

Returning briefly to Evans-Pritchard's essay on the comparative method, it expresses dissatisfaction with anthropologists from Frazer to Radcliffe-Brown for their search for universality which, according to him, 'defeats the sociological purpose, which is to explain differences rather than similarities'. Evans-Pritchard expresses his own bias for differences somewhat tentatively, thus:

I would like to place emphasis on the importance for social anthropology, as a comparative discipline, of differences, because it would be held that in the past the tendency has been to place the stress on similarities, as conspicuously in *The Golden Bough*, whereas *it is the differences which would seem to invite sociological explanation* (Evans-Pritchard 1965: 25, emphasis added).

Evans-Pritchard's stress on difference, as he himself indicates, is partly to redress the balance, but there seems to be more to it than that. It is hard to understand why difference should invite sociological attention more urgently than similarity. The stress on difference does not have any obvious methodological advantage, and seems to me the outcome of an unstated, and perhaps unconscious, aesthetic preference. Such a preference for the exotic, not at all uncommon among anthropologists, can lead to serious misrepresentation. No doubt an equally serious misrepresentation can result from an unstated aesthetic preference for sameness.[4]

For a hundred years since the days of Boas and Haddon, anthropologists from Europe and America have travelled to distant places to study the customs and institutions of the peoples of the world. They have not done so solely for the purpose of discovering the laws of social life through the application of the comparative method. Many of them have travelled to Asia, Africa and, now increasingly, Melanesia in search of a different experience and a different way of life. Something of the explorer's outlook has become a permanent part of the anthropologist's habit of mind; or, as Lévi-Strauss (1963: 378) has put it, combining romance with science, the anthropologist is 'the astronomer of the social sciences'.

It is, however, one thing to indulge a taste for what is different and another to try to make a distinct scientific discipline out of the study of other ways of life. One of the most popular textbooks of anthropology in Britain in the sixties and seventies, written, incidentally, by an Oxford colleague and former pupil of Professor Evans-Pritchard's, was entitled *Other Cultures* (Beattie 1964). Its author, like most of his Oxford colleagues of that period, had done fieldwork in Africa where, moreover, he had served in the colonial administration. Based on his own fieldwork and that of his colleagues, he had written the textbook *Other Cultures*. Assuming that the title was meant to be taken seriously, one wonders what the significance of such a textbook would be for students and teachers of anthropology in Africa.

To some extent, every discipline constructs its own object, and it has been said that the object that western anthropology has constructed for itself is the Other. The social anthropologist's preoccupation with otherness is justified by Evans-Pritchard (1951: 9) in the following characteristic terms: 'Moreover, it is a matter of experience that it is easier to make observations among peoples with cultures unlike our own, the otherness in their way of life at once engaging attention, and that it is more likely that interpretations will be objective.' As one would expect, there is an ambivalent attitude in the anthropologist towards his object, and the ambivalence has deepened over the years. The strong emphasis on the 'otherness' of other cultures has sometimes been only a pretext for stressing the uniqueness of the anthropologist's own culture. As a recent critic has put it, with perhaps a trace of dramatic emphasis, 'The We of anthropology then remains an exclusive We, one that leaves its Other outside on all levels of theorizing except on the plane of ideological obfuscation, where everyone pays lip service to the "unity of mankind"' (Fabian 1983: 157).

Perhaps the construction of the object as 'Other'—the view from afar—necessarily entails a certain amount of foreshortening and distortion. Much depends on the extent to which the anthropologist distances himself from his object of study, and the intellectual and political intent with which he does so. It would be a mistake to suppose that those who talk about the 'unity of mankind', or the fundamental similarity of all societies, even when they do so sincerely, become immune to the risks of foreshortening. For they might represent other societies and cultures as copies, more or less imperfectly formed, of their own.

Here I may refer very briefly to Malinowski, the great contemporary and rival of Radcliffe-Brown, whose fieldwork gave a new depth and richness to the discipline of anthropology. Whereas Radcliffe-Brown was the tireless advocate of the comparative method, Malinowski was the master of the single case study. He looked into every detail of society and culture among the Trobriand Islanders, and brought their complex interrelations to light. Malinowski's fieldwork set an example for the next generation of anthropologists in Britain, of whom Evans-Pritchard was perhaps the most outstanding.

Although not a comparativist in Radcliffe-Brown's style, Malinowski (1925,1948) was a great believer in the fundamental sameness of human beings everywhere. He used his mastery of Trobriand ethnography to expose the shallowness of the stereotypes of primitive man current in his day. Primitive man did not follow the dictates of custom blindly, nor was he driven solely by blind and irrational impulses. There was roughly the same mixture of reason and sentiment behind the actions of primitive as of civilized man. The image of primitive man becomes merged with that of 'man in general' who, in the end, looks suspiciously similar to the goal-oriented pragmatist of capitalist society (Leach 1957).

The point to stress here about those who made a dogma of the unity of mankind is that, in their comparisons, other societies often come out not simply as copies, but as imperfect or unformed copies, of their own society. This is seen most clearly in the nineteenth-century evolutionary theory which took it for granted that western societies had attained the highest levels of institutional advancement in every respect, and that other societies would follow them, also in every respect, in due course of time. I have explained how nineteenth-century evolutionary theory fell out of favour in the twentieth century. But its spirit was revived in our own time by what has come to be known as 'development theory'; that, however, is a whole subject by itself into which I cannot enter here.

What I would like to stress is that in making comparisons we must try to deal even-handedly with similarity and difference, and avoid making it a dogma that either the one or the other is the more fundamental of the two. This may sound like a counsel of perfection, and somewhat banal at that. But the point needs to be made because of the change now taking place in the context of comparative studies.

As I pointed out at the beginning, in the early use of the comparative method, from Durkheim to Radcliffe-Brown, scholars from one part of the world were studying societies in all parts of the world, their own as well as others. Speaking as recently as forty years ago, Evans-Pritchard (1951: 84) observed: 'However much anthropologists may differ among themselves they are all children of the same society and culture'.[5] When such a scholar studied his own society, he was regarded as a sociologist and when he studied another culture he was regarded as an anthropologist. A kind of objective distinction between 'ourselves' and 'others' was built into the comparative method. All this is rapidly changing, and we will need to weave into our comparative studies a far more sensitive treatment of similarity and difference than has been in evidence so far. As an Indian interested in comparative studies, I have found it frustrating to move in a world in which what is sociology for one person is anthropology for another.

Typification vs Classification

I drew attention a little while ago to the problem that arises when we treat the Other as a copy of ourselves. I must now say something about the practice, common among anthropologists who study civilizations, of treating the Other not as a copy but as an inversion. This practice is rooted in the belief, widely held and sometimes expressed, by western scholars in the uniqueness of their own civilization. It leads to a distortion of the non-western civilization being studied because those aspects of it that differ most from western civilization receive exaggerated attention and those that differ least from it receive scant attention.

Jack Goody has observed that wherever a strong anthropological bias has invaded comparative sociology, there has been 'a tendency to primitivise the Oriental civilisations'. In a recent comparative study, he has shown with a wealth of illustrative material that marriage and the family in India and China have often been wrongly represented by anthropologists in the image of their counterparts in African and other tribal societies from which they differ substantially. Goody's argument is that where a line needs to be drawn between industrial and pre-industrial societies, it is drawn instead between 'the West and the Rest' (Goody 1990: 11).

In this kind of comparative method, which proceeds more by contrast than by comparison, not only are differences between civilizations—China, India, etc.—flattened out, but the past and the present of each civilization tend to be treated as one. Here the contrast is between western civilization which is dynamic and ever-changing, and other civilizations in which change is so slow that it need not be taken into account.

If I may dwell for a moment on the Indian case, a kind of privileged position is assigned to India's past in the comparison, or rather the contrast, made between Indian and western civilizations. Indian civilization is represented by a structure of values that is viewed as relatively stable or unchanging, so that one can speak of the same structure whether one is speaking of India at present, or in the recent past, or in the distant past. These accounts of the structure of Indian society, although sometimes informed by fieldwork of a very high quality, take their orientation from the representation of it in classical Indian literature. I have elsewhere (Béteille 1990) described this approach as the 'Indological approach' whose ablest contemporary exponent is Professor Dumont, who has had a great influence on Indian studies through his own writings and through the journal, *Contributions to Indian Sociology*, established by him in 1957. A marked emphasis on the unique significance of the Indian religious tradition may also be found in the ethnosociological approach of the Chicago School of anthropologists as represented in particular in the work of McKim Marriott (Marriott 1976; Marriott and Inden 1974).

Dumont (1967) has spoken of his own work as representing a 'typifying' approach to which he has opposed the 'classifying' approach to be found in the work of Barth, Berreman and others. The classifying approach derives, in his view, from the natural sciences, and it leads to a comparison of part with part on a superficial assumption of their similarity, and without due regard to the meaning of each part in the whole of which it is a part. The typifying approach is, by contrast, a comprehensive approach, for in discussing any aspect of a society it always keeps the whole in view. Underlying all this is a very strong assumption of the ogranic unity of a civilization.

Dumont has used his typifying approach to formulate a comprehensive contrast between Indian and western (or modern) society. Such a contrast has been made repeatedly by western students of Indian society from the middle of the nineteenth century onwards. But Dumont's contrast is, in the judgement of many, at once the most forceful and the most subtle, and I would like to make a few observations on it in order to clarify my own position on the typifying approach.

Dumont's contrasting types are indicated by the titles of his two books, *Homo hierarchicus* for India, and *Homo aequalis* for the west (Dumont 1966, 1977, 1987; Béteille 1987). These types are constructed on the basis of the values said to be predominant or paramount in the two societies in question. Hierarchy, which characterizes Indian society in all its aspects, is itself an aspect of holism, according to which the part (that is, the individual) is subordinated to the whole (that is, society). Conversely, in western society, equality is an aspect of individualism which has established itself as the paramount value. In India, hierarchy animates every aspect of life and gives it meaning; in western, that is, modern society, hierarchy is fundamentally meaningless.

No doubt, there are collective identities in western or modern society based, for instance, on race and ethnicity, and no doubt there is ranking of both individuals and groups in it; but these, Dumont would maintain, exist on the plane of facts and not values, which are his main concern. As he has put it, 'Differences of rank run contrary to our dominant ideology of social life, which is equalitarian. They are for us fundamentally meaningless' (Dumont 1967: 28). One cannot talk about hierarchy in the West but only about stratification, whereas it is misleading to talk about stratification in India which is a hierarchical society. In a similar vein, the individual has no value *within* society in India; in order to be an individual in India, one has to renounce society and become a *sanyasi*.

In going over the full range of Dumont's work, one is struck over and over again by the neatness of the contrasts and the symmetry of the inversions. India is hierarchical, the west is egalitarian; the west values the individual, in India it is only the group that counts. These apparent commonplaces are hammered into the form of profound and ineluctable truths by a massive array of fact and argument put together with unsurpassed intellectual vigour.

A careful reading of the books, *Homo hierarchicus* and *Homo aequalis,* will show that the arguments have been constructed somewhat differently in the two cases. The book on India, although it takes its orientation from the past, is an exercise in anthropology, making extensive use of the data of ethnographic fieldwork. The book on the West is an exercise in the history of ideas, based on a different kind of empirical material (Béteille 1987). It is not that no one has done ethnographic fieldwork in the west, not to speak of the enormous body of sociological work on ranking and stratification in Europe and the United States. One will look in vain for a discussion of this literature although the book was designed to be a counterpart to the volume on hierarchy in India. If one decides in advance that differences of rank are 'fundamentally meaningless' in western society, one will naturally pay little attention to the literature on social ranking in the west.

Professor Dumont's book on India tells us a great deal about hierarchy, and even if it is not all new, it presents many new insights. His book on the west tells us nothing about inequality which exists in every western society, though declared by him to be 'meaningless'. What is more, it tells us very little about equality, although the title of its French version is *Homo aequalis* (in English it is called *From Mandeville to Marx*). The book is about individualism rather than equality, and there is a presumed correspondence between the two that is nowhere seriously discussed (Dumont 1987; Béteille 1987). Nor is there any serious discussion of the different meanings assigned to equality, some of which are less consistent with individualism than others (Hayek 1980). A classifying approach may lead to superficial comparisons, but a typifying approach can lead to misleading contrasts. It is not always easy to stay on the right side of the thin line between the scholarly art of typifying and the popular practice of stereotyping.

There is an ambiguous use of history characteristic of the typifying approach of Dumont and others. There are two kinds of contrasts used, between Indian society and western society on one hand, and between Indian society and modern society on the other, and the two contrasts tend to be merged. 'Holism' and 'hierarchy' are associated unambiguously with India; but 'individualism' and 'equality' are treated as defining features, now of western society and again of modern society, so that India is contrasted sometimes with western society and at others with modern society. It is as if India (and other non-western societies) were denied modernity by definition.

In some ways, Dumont's contrast between *Homo hierarchicus* and

Homo aequalis is a restatement of Tocqueville's contrast between aristocratic and democratic societies (Béteille 1983). But Tocqueville's contrast was a historical one, whereas Dumont's is, if the distinction be permitted, a typological one. Tocqueville was interested in showing how aristocratic societies were being transformed into democratic ones in the western world. In Dumont's scheme, there is very little room for the passage from *Homo hierarchicus* to *Homo aequalis*. Yet it is precisely with this acutely problematic passage that sociologists in India and other societies inheriting a hierarchical order from the past have to contend.

There is no doubt that Indian society had a markedly hierarchical structure in the past and that much of it continues to exist in the present: one encounters hierarchy at every turn in contemporary India. But there have also been important changes since the middle of the nineteenth century and, more particularly, since the middle of the twentieth. A new constitution has assigned a central place to equality and the rights of the individual. Adult franchise, agrarian reforms and positive discrimination have become important ingredients of the contemporary Indian reality. They may not have succeeded in establishing equality here and now, but they have seriously undermined the legitimacy of the traditional hierarchy. An enquiry into the meaning and significance of all this comes up against the wall established by the typifying approach.

The typifying approach used by Dumont has put all its emphasis on the enduring traditional structure, and paid little attention to newness and change. It has had a great appeal for those who have watched contemporary India from afar. But it has been out of tune with the perceptions of many Indian sociologists engaged in the study of their own society, for whom disorder and change have been a part of everyday experience. I would like to repeat again that the whole context of comparative sociology is being altered by the fact that not only are the same people studying different kinds of societies but that the same society is being studied by different kinds of people.

Conflicting Forces and Counterpoints

I have now come to that part of my discussions where I must introduce into it the eponymous hero of the present occasion, Professor Wertheim, after whom this lecture is named. As an enthusiast for the comparative method, I have always been uneasy about the typifying approach, its exaggerated contrasts and its stress on difference. Professor Wertheim's work has given me a basis for articulating my misgiving. I have in mind his view of society as a field of conflicting values and also the idea of the counterpoint, adapted by him from the work of the Dutch historian, Jan Romein (Wertheim 1964, 1967).

In a paper first written almost forty years ago on 'Society as a composite of conflicting values', Wertheim (1964) had drawn attention to the co-existence of disparate elements in all human societies. He developed the same theme at a seminar in Delhi in 1965. Drawing attention to the different approaches prevalent in sociology, he said, 'In my view, we should look for the common denominator in the realm of values.' But he then went on to say, 'I would suggest that, in any society, more than one value system is to be found as a determinant of human behaviour and judgement' (Wertheim 1967: 182–3). I would go further and speak of a field of conflicting forces, because in dealing with any society, whether in Asia or Europe, we have to deal not only with values, important though they are, but also with interests (Béteille 1969).

Even where certain values are dominant, there are others that act as counterpoints. Conflicting sets of values may function as a kind of counterpoint to the dominant set. They may be dormant and hardly noticeable, but their existence and latent acceptance among certain individuals or groups forms, from the outset, is a potential threat to the stability of the system (Wertheim 1967: 183). Here we have a different way of looking at societies, including the so-called traditional societies, with the eyes open to evidence of contradiction and change.

Those who adopt the typifying approach no doubt acknowledge the existence in any society of elements other than its paramount values. But these other elements do not receive the attention due to them. Either they are relegated to an inferior domain, that of 'mere facts' as opposed to values; or they are treated as values that are 'subordinated to' or 'encompassed by' the paramount values (Dumont 1980). The advantage with the idea of counterpoint, as I understand it, is that it acknowledges the coexistence of divergent values without seeking necessarily to place them in a hierarchical arrangement. In a hierarchical arrangement, the 'encompassing' and the 'encompassed' elements are in a stable equilibrium; no necessary assumption of a stable equilibrium is required by the idea of the counterpoint.

The great attraction of a model of society based on a single hierarchy of values, with the encompassing and the encompassed elements in their appropriate places, is that it provides the investigator with familiar land-marks that help him to find his way through a large and complex society.

The idea of society as a field of conflicting forces takes us away from the security of a well-ordered intellectual universe to one in which there are few clear signposts. It is a challenging exercise intellectually, but also one in which there are a great many risks.

Let me explain briefly why I consider it so important, in defining society as a field of conflicting forces, to take both values and interests into account. As I have indicated, the contrapuntal conception of values is fundamentally different from the hierarchical conception. In the latter, values arrange themselves according to their own internal logic, the inferior being encompassed by the superior. But as we know, and as Wertheim has suggested, different and even incompatible values may be characteristically associated with different groups, classes and categories in the same society, such as upper and lower castes, landowners and landless, or men and women. It becomes easier to understand these contrapuntal values when we keep in sight the divergent interests of the groups, classes and categories that are their characteristic bearers.

It is far from my intention to suggest that societies are carried along solely by the conflict of interests, and that we have no need to take values into account except as reflections of those interests. Indeed, I have tried to repudiate strongly that view in my work (Béteille 1974, 1987). Every society has, if not one single paramount value, at least its own distinctive equilibrium of values which, moreover, is often an unstable equilibrium. All I would say is that we need to understand the dynamics of this equilibrium and that we cannot effectively do so without taking interests into account.

Wertheim (1974) has used the idea of the counterpoint to construct a theory of social change in both its evolutionary and revolutionary forms. Without following him all the way in that direction, I would like to stress the need to take both continuity and change into account in making comparisons between societies. The advantage of viewing society as a field of conflicting forces and in terms of its contrapuntal elements is that it invites us to examine not only the facts of change but also the potential for change inherent in every society. A common abuse of the comparative method is to represent some societies (modern societies) as if they were destined to move forward all the time, and others (traditional societies) as if they were destined to remain forever embedded in their ancient moulds. One can show, on the other hand, how a society that has remained 'backward' for long can be moved ahead of a more 'advanced' society by the accumulated tensions inherent in its conflicting elements (Wertheim 1974).

It is true that many of the so-called traditional societies maintained broadly the same structure of values over long periods of time. This continuity is evident in all the societies of South Asia where old modes of perception and evaluation have survived major innovations in law and politics. But these innovations in law and politics have also introduced new modes of perception and evaluation. It is impossible to determine in advance which of these will prevail where, and it cannot be an established principle of method to subordinate new elements of value to old ones simply because the latter have had a longer life than the former.

To revert for a moment to the Indian example, its traditional structure was for centuries dominated by the hierarchical order of castes. It was a society in which inequality in both principle and practice prevailed in most spheres, and one, moreover, in which the individual was subordinated to the group. The long period of Muslim rule introduced some new elements, but these did not alter substantially either the old morphology or the old scheme of values. The impact of British rule was of a different magnitude, partly because it came in on the crest of capitalist expansion which was introducing new economic arrangements and new social values on a worldwide scale. It generated a nationalist movement, of which there are parallels everywhere, that sought to forge its own ideology by combining new elements of value with old ones. The nationalist movement was critical not only of the colonial power but also of many elements of value inherited from the past, including those associated with caste.

India became independent in 1947 after two centuries of colonial rule. It adopted a new constitution in 1950 which embodies very different values from those that prevailed in the past, and where the stress is on equality between individuals in place of the hierarchy of groups. I do not mean to suggest that the old values disappeared as soon as the new constitution was adopted; they are, as mentioned earlier, in evidence everywhere in contemporary India. At the same time, they now operate in an altered moral, political and legal environment in which they have to contend with other values that act as their counterpoints.

If we are to take seriously the view of society as a field of conflicting forces, we have to renounce the organic analogy—or the idea of the organic unity of societies—which has vitiated the comparisons made by the proponents of the classifying approach as well as the contrasts maintained by the proponents of the typifying approach. There are indeed similarities and differences among societies, but as I have pointed out earlier, these are not at all like the similarities and differences that we encounter in the world of plants and animals. Although societies differ among themselves, they are not separated from each other by the kinds of boundaries that separate organisms. Nor is there in the animal kingdom anything like the interpenetration among societies that has become such a common feature of the contemporary world. It is this interpenetration that makes it more appropriate to speak of societies as fields of conflicting forces than as discrete and bounded units. I am, of course, speaking of society in the broad sense and not just about the nation state.

It appears to me that if we treat societies as fields of conflicting forces, rather than as discrete and bounded units, the classification of social types according to the rules of taxonomy may not be a very rewarding exercise. Those rules require that comparisons should proceed on a strictly graduated scale, first between the nearest neighbours, then between groups of near neighbours and so on, just as in biology one first compares species within the same genus, then genera within the same family, and so on. Societies are implicated in each other to such a large extent in the contemporary world that one will find it hard to construct any simple scale of neighbourliness with which to assess the interpenetration, in terms of ideas, beliefs and values of, let us say, Britain and India, or the Netherlands and Indonesia.

The above difficulty is not avoided but in a way accentuated by the typifying approach. By stressing the organic unity of each society, and by dwelling on what it owes to its own past and ignoring what it owes to others, it tends to represent societies as mutually impenetrable substances.

To typify means to engage in a 'one-sided accentuation', and we know, since Max Weber, that a one-sided accentuation can be of the greatest use methodologically, under appropriate conditions (Shils and Finch 1949: 90). But what is a use under certain conditions becomes a misuse under others. It is one thing to construct ideal types of, say, 'rational action' or 'ethical prophecy' through one-sided accentuation, and quite another to typecast whole societies as being 'hierarchical' or 'egalitarian'. I doubt if that kind of typecasting can ever become an aid to the comparative method.

The Comparison of Whole Societies

A hundred years and more after Spencer, Tylor and Durkheim, it cannot be said that sociologists and social anthropologists have a method that they would all agree to describe as the comparative method. There is as much disagreement among them about it now as there was in the past, even though they have trimmed their ambitions considerably about what they can expect from such a method in the study of society and culture. One of the main problems—or perhaps it is merely the symptom of a deeper problem—is that while they make all sorts of comparisons themselves, they judge the comparisons that others make by excessively severe standards.

It is difficult to see how sociology and social anthropology can justify their existence without making comparisons extensively and continuously. The very fact that we are able to talk about matrilineal descent, or patron-client relations, or occupational mobility shows not only that we are inexorably dependent on comparisons, but, more importantly, that the comparisons made in the past, no matter by what method, have yielded some results. Nor is it true that the best results have come only when the comparisons were narrow and never when they were broad.

Where, then, does the problem lie? Part of the problem is that, in the absence of any definite method, comparisons are used to illustrate an argument arrived at in advance without careful attention to the available and relevant facts. This is what Evans-Pritchard called the illustrative as against the comparative method, and its most notorious exponent in anthropology was Frazer. However, it is not altogether easy to devise a clear test to distinguish the two methods; and Radcliffe-Brown, who was a strong advocate of the comparative method as well as a critic of Frazer, was himself criticized by Evans-Pritchard for using the illustrative in place of the comparative method.

What was wrong with Frazer's comparisons was not that they were broad and extensive but that they were made with little serious attention to the facts of the case. I believe that there is nothing wrong in comparing institutions that exist in widely dissimilar contexts, provided one keeps in mind the dissimilarity of their contexts. After all, comparisons between Dravidian and Kariera kinship have yielded interesting insights despite the vast differences between South Indian and Australian Aboriginal societies (Dumont 1983). Above all, I do not believe that the defects of Frazer's comparisons can be made good by a rule that requires us to establish first and foremost comparisons (or contrasts) between whole societies.

The idea that the comparison of whole societies constitutes the core of the comparative method accounts for many of the difficulties faced by that method. That idea was at the bottom of Durkheim's preoccupation with social types and the rules for their constitution and classification; it was also at the bottom of Radcliffe-Brown's preoccupation with natural kinds. In both cases, it was associated with the belief that the comparison of whole societies was an essential part of the discovery of the laws of social life. The prospect of such discovery has been abandoned by most sociologists and anthropologists, but many of them continue to adhere to the belief in the importance of comparing whole societies; that belief often comes out in the criticisms they make of the comparisons attempted by others. While making a concession to classification, Dumont (1980: 215) insists, 'If classification is to be introduced further on, it will have to start from wholes and not from itemized features'.

The comparison of whole societies requires us to categorize and label each and every society, or at least the ones we seek to compare and contrast. This process of labelling is a part of ordinary discourse, and it is impossible to avoid it altogether in scholarly discussion. There is no great harm in speaking about agnatic and cognatic societies, or about hierarchical and egalitarian societies, although, strictly speaking, we should speak of the agnatic principle or the egalitarian principle, since each of these principles generally coexists in one and the same society with all kinds of other principles. The label may be a convenience, but to take it too literally may lead to serious misrepresentation.

Durkheim's labelling of social types was based on a conscious use of the analogy between societies and organisms, and he maintained that there were social species for the same reason that there were species in biology. The labels used by him—simple polysegmental societies, polysegmental societies singly compounded, etc.—have become obsolete, and were never seriously applied except in the most rudimentary comparisons. Such use as they had was limited to the comparison of the simplest types of societies, and Durkheim never used them systematically in comparing and contrasting complex states and civilizations.

When we deal with larger systems, the states and civilizations in Asia and elsewhere, we encounter the coexistence of several different types in one and the same social field (Béteille 1986). The organic analogy, on which Durkheim based his constitution of social types, breaks down because there are no clear boundaries and interpenetration is pervasive, if not universal. Moreover, the types differ so enormously in scale that it becomes difficult to determine what should be the proper units of comparison.

It is clear that the comparison of whole societies cannot be satisfactorily made on a morphological basis because human societies do not have the same kind of structure as animal organisms. In fact, the organic analogy is no longer very widely used by sociologists and social anthropologists.

The morphological conception of social structure, representing the disposition of groups and classes in a society, has been displaced by a different conception of structure in which ideas and values have pride of place. Can the comparison (or contrast) of whole societies be more satisfactorily based on an 'ideological' than on a 'morphological' conception of structure? I think not; the difficulties are even greater here because of the lability of ideas and values, and their inherent tendency, particularly marked in the modern world, to flow across boundaries.

It is doubtful that we will ever have a comparative method, like some ideal method of the natural scientists, about whose proper use sociologists and social anthropologists will reach complete agreement. At the same time, our deepest insights into society and culture are reached in and through comparison. We have to improvise and exercise our judgement as well as our imagination, and beyond that we can only hope that our comparisons—as well as our contrasts—will be illuminating and fruitful. At any rate, it will be futile to suspend our comparisons until the perfect classification or the perfect typology of human societies is placed within our grasp.

Notes

1. M.N. Srinivas (1966: 153–4) wrote a quarter century ago, 'It is evident, however, that a sociologist engaged in the study of his own society enjoys advantages as well as disadvantages, and pedagogically it is very important to ensure that the disadvantages are minimized while the advantages are retained. This problem is urgent as an increasing number of sociologists from developing countries are likely to be studying, in the near future, aspects of their own society.'

2. It is difficult to exaggerate the significance of the theory of evolution for the earlier conception of the comparative method and, indeed, of anthropology itself. R.R. Marett, one of the most influential British anthropologists of the early part of the twentieth century, wrote, 'Anthropology is the whole history of man as fired and pervaded by the idea of evolution. Man in evolution—that is the subject in its full reach'. And, a little further on, 'Anthropology is the child of Darwin. Darwinism makes it possible. Reject the Darwinian point of view, and you must reject anthropology also' (Marett 1914: 78).

3. Marc Bloch was known among historians as an advocate of comparative history. He contrasted two uses of the comparative method, a general and a restricted one. His own preference was for the application of the comparative method to the study of 'societies that are at once neighbouring and contemporary' (Bloch 1967: 47).

4. Evans-Pritchard's position on these questions has been characteristically ambivalent, and he has not spoken in the same voice at all times. While he has stressed difference in some contexts, he has underlined basic similarities in others. For instance, 'One has, of course, to act with great caution in seeking from a study of social phenomena in one society interpretative guidance in the study of similar phenomena in another society; but in fact, however much in some respects the phenomena may differ, in other and basic respects they are alike' (Evans-Pritchard 1951: 128). Nor has he always been averse to talking about universals: 'The social anthropologist aims also at showing, by comparing one society with another, the common features of institutions as well as their particularities in each society. He seeks to show how some characteristics of an institution or set of ideas are peculiar to a given society, how others are common to all societies of a certain type, and how yet others are found in all human societies—are universals' (p. 123). And it is well to remember what Geertz (1988: 71) has recently written about Evans-Pritchard's view of man: 'On the Akobe as the Isis, men and women are brave and cowardly, kind and cruel, reasonable and foolish, loyal and perfidious, intelligent and stupid, vivid and boring, believing and indifferent, and better the one than the other.'

5. He went on to add, 'Certain kinds of fact are noticed, and they are seen in a certain kind of way, by people of our culture. To some extent at any rate, people who belong to different cultures would notice different facts and perceive them in a different way' (1951: 85).

References

Beattie, J.R.H. 1964. *Other Cultures*. London: Cohen and West.

Béteille, A. 1969. 'Ideas and Interests'. *International Social Science Journal*. 21 (2), pp. 219–34.

———. 1974. *Studies in Agrarian Social Structure*. Delhi: Oxford University Press.

———. 1983. 'Homo Hierarchicus, Homo Aequalis'. In *The Idea of Natural Inequality and Other Essays*. Delhi: Oxford University Press, pp. 33–53.

———. 1986. 'The Concept of Tribe with Special Reference to India'. *European Journal of Sociology*. xxvii, pp. 297–318.

———. 1987a. *Essays in Comparative Sociology*. Delhi: Oxford University Press.

———. 1987b. 'On Individualism and Equality'. *Current Anthropology*. 28 (5).

———. 1990. 'Race, Caste and Gender'. *Man* (n.s.) 25, pp. 489–504

Bloch, M. 1967. *Land and Work in Medieval Europe*. London: Routledge and Kegan Paul.

Boas, F. 1940 (1896). 'The Limitations of the Comparative Method in Anthropology'. In *Race, Language and Culture*, New York: Macmillan.

Dumont, L. 1966. *Homo hierarchicus*. Paris: Gallimard.

———. 1967. 'Caste: A Phenomenon of Social Structure or an Aspect of Indian Culture?' In Reuck and Knight 1967, pp. 28–38.

———. 1977. *Homo aequalis*. Paris: Gallimard.

———. 1980. *On Value*. London: The British Academy.

———. 1983. *Affinity as a Value*. Chicago: University of Chicago Press.

———. 1987. 'On Individualism and Equality'. *Current Anthropology*. 28 (5), pp. 669–72.

Durkheim, É. 1982 (1895). *The Rules of Sociological Method*. London: Macmillan.

Evans-Pritchard, E.E. 1951. *Social Anthropology*. London: Cohen and West.

———. 1965. 'The Comparative Method in Social Anthropology'. In *The Position of Women in Primitive Societies and Other Essays*. London: Faber and Faber.

Fabian, J. 1983. *Time and the Other*. New York: Columbia University Press.

Firth, R. (ed). 1957. *Man and Culture*. London: Routledge and Kegan Paul.

Geertz, C. 1988. *Works and Lives*. Oxford: Polity Press.

Goldenweiser, A.A. 1922. *Early Civilization*. New York: Alfred Knopf.

Goody, J. 1990. *The Oriental, the Ancient and the Primitive*. Cambridge: Cambridge University Press.

Hayek, F. 1980 (1946). 'Individualism: True and False'. In *Individualism and Economic Order*. Chicago: University of Chicago Press, pp. 1–32.

Kapferer, B. (ed). 1976. *Transaction and Meaning*. Philadelphia: Institute for the Study of Human Issues.

Leach, E.R. 1957. 'The Epistemological Background to Malinowski's Empiricism'. In R. Firth (ed). 1957. *Man and Culture*. London: Rowledge and Kegan Paul.

Lévi-Strauss, C. 1963. *Structural Anthropology*. New York: Basic Books.

Lowie, R.H. 1960 (1921). *Primitive Society*. London: Kegan Paul.

Malinowski, B. 1925. *Crime and Custom in Savage Society*. London: Kegan Paul.

———. 1948 (1925). 'Magic, Science and Religion'. In *Magic, Science and Religion and Other Essays*. Glencoe: The Free Press.

Marett, R.R. 1914. *Anthropology*. London: Williams and Norgate.

Marriott, M. 1976. 'Hindu Transactions'. In B. Kapferer (ed). 1976. *Transaction and Meaning*. Philadelphia: Institute for the study of Human Issues.

Marriott, M. and R.B. Inden. 1974. 'Caste Systems'. In *Encyclopaedia Britannica*. 15th edn., Macropaedia. 3, pp. 982–91.

Radcliffe-Brown, A.R. 1952. *Structure and Function in Primitive Society*. London: Cohen and West.

———. 1957. *A Natural Science of Society*. Glencoe: The Free Press.

———. 1958. *Method in Social Anthropology*. Chicago: University of Chicago Press.

Reuck, A. de and Knight, J. (eds). 1967. *Caste and Race*. London: J. & A. Churchill.

Shils, E.A. and Finch, H.A. (eds). 1949. *Max Weber on the Methodology of the Social Sciences*. Glencoe: The Free Press.

Srinivas, M.N. 1966. *Social Change in Modern India*. Berkeley: University of California Press.

Wertheim, W.F. 1964. 'Society as a Composite of Conflicting Value Systems'. In *East-West Parallels*. The Hague: van Hoeve.

———. 1967. 'Sociology Between Yesterday and Tomorrow'. *Comparative Studies in Society and History*. 9 (2).

———. 1974. *Evolution and Revolution*. Harmondsworth: Penguin Books.

Chapter

5

The Comparative Method and the Standpoint of the Investigator*

Comparison and contrast are so commonly used in the study of human society and culture that their utility seems hardly to require special emphasis. In a sceptical essay on the comparative method, one of Britain's leading social anthropologists had pointed out that comparison is 'one of the essential procedures of all science and one of the elementary processes of human thought' (Evans-Pritchard 1965: 13). Yet social scientists never seem to tire of criticizing the comparisons and contrasts made by their colleagues.

While the extensive, not to say automatic, use of comparison may be natural to the processes of human thought, the same cannot be said about the conscious search for a comparative method with definite or at least defined rules of procedure. Here one will find characteristic differences among the various disciplines that together make up the social sciences. Some disciplines, such as economics and psychology, have focused largely on universal structures and processes common to all human beings everywhere, and paid little attention to characteristic and persistent differences between societies. Others, such as history in particular, have dwelt much more on the specific features of given societies without venturing too far

*An earlier version of this paper was presented at a seminar held in Bangalore in March 1995 under the auspices of the Indo-Dutch Programme for Alternatives in Development. I am grateful to the participants at the seminar, and in particular to Dipankar Gupta, Ramachandra Guha and Alan Macfarlane for their comments on the paper.

across their chosen boundaries in space and time. The comparative method as a tool of investigation, designed consciously to discover the general features of all societies (or cultures) without losing sight of the distinctive features of each, has been a particular obsession of sociology and social anthropology, and more specially, as we shall see, of a particular stream within these two related disciplines.

As I wish to describe the comparative method in somewhat more specific terms than is usually done, I would like to ensure that not too much is claimed on its behalf. Here it may be useful to draw attention to the distinction made famous—or notorious—by Edmund Leach between 'comparison' and 'generalization'. As he put it, 'Comparison and generalization are both forms of scientific activity, but different' (Leach 1961: 2). He quickly declared his own preference for generalization, and dismissed comparison as 'a matter of butterfly collecting—of classification, of the arrangement of things according to their types and subtypes' (Ibid.). But it must be noted that for Durkheim and Radcliffe-Brown (and many others), comparison itself was a step towards generalization, although such generalization was of a different kind from what Leach had in mind.

'Butterfly collecting' is a bad name for a great deal of what the naturalist does, and considerable insight into societies and cultures has emerged from the natural curiosity about the varieties of human life. At the same time, we must not lose sight of the differences of orientation between the different intellectual disciplines. In terms of Leach's distinction, a substantial part of the insights of sociology and social anthropology have come from systematic comparisons. Economics, by contrast, has been a generalizing rather than a comparative science in the strict sense. At the other end, history has been largely concerned with the distinctive features of human thought and action at specific times and places, although, no doubt, individual historians have also undertaken comparisons across space and time.

Cutting across the differences between disciplines, there have been differences between national intellectual traditions. In France, the appeal of the comparative method has been nourished by the stress on the unity of all the sciences, natural and social. In Germany, on the other hand, the division between the 'Naturwissenschaften' and the 'Geisteswissenschaften' has been a source of considerable disagreement among students of human society and culture. Those who maintained that the study of society and culture could not be incorporated into the natural sciences were on the whole sceptical about the comparative method, whose greatest successes had been in the biological sciences. For Dilthey, Rickert and Windelband, the principal focus of attention in the Geisteswissenschaften was tradition, a tradition which they not only made the object of their enquiry and under- standing, but one in which they in some sense participated. Hence they saw their task as being quite different from that of the Naturwissenschaften which did not relate to tradition at all in the same way.

In Britain, Radcliffe-Brown followed closely the French sociologists, and in particular Durkheim. He (1952: 1–14) drew attention to the differ- ence in aim and purpose between nomothetic and ideographic enquiries, maintaining that the comparative method in the proper sense was central to the former and not the latter. At least in anthropology, there has been a tension, sometimes manifest but more often latent, between the compara- tive and the historical methods (Boas 1940; Evans-Pritchard 1965; Béteille 1990).

Nevertheless, it was the sociologists and anthropologists who took the lead in examining within a single framework of description and analysis, the usages, customs and institutions observed and recorded among human beings in all parts of the world and at all times. It was they rather than the historians or the economists who made the first systematic attempts to understand and explain the practices and beliefs of the Australian Aborigines, the American Indians and the sub-Saharan Africans along with those associated with the more complex civilizations of Asia and Europe. This change of outlook was itself a major innovation, and it sometimes caused a scandal. Durkheim's argument that the study of totemism threw new light on all religions, including Christianity, appeared offensive to many believing Christians in France (Pickering 1975: 228–76).

The early sociologists—Herbert Spencer in England, Émile Durkheim in France and Max Weber in Germany—were comparatists in a much stronger sense than the one implicit in the statement that comparison is one of the elementary processes of human thought. They believed that society, culture, religion, family, marriage and so on gave shape to human life everywhere, and called for serious intellectual attention not only at home but also abroad. In this sense, the comparative method required in its practitioners a certain detachment from their own society and culture that was not required of the practitioners of the historical method. Many of the latter had been ardent nationalists. Since the comparative method does not admit, at least in principle, of privileged exceptions, it cannot as easily or as openly accommodate the spirit of nationalism.

The pioneers of the comparative method in sociology and social anthropology were all influenced to a greater or lesser extent by the theory of evolution.[1] Indeed, it was the search for the stages of evolution that largely shaped the comparative method of Spencer and Morgan. This imposed certain limits on the extent to which they did in fact assign equal value to all societies and cultures. It was tacitly accepted that western societies had reached the highest stage of evolution and that all other societies stood at graduated distances below them. This view seemed indisputable for technology and economic organization so that few would question the words of Marx (1959: 19): 'The country that is more developed industrially only shows, to the less developed, the image of its own future'. But the same view prevailed, with occasional and minor modifications, with regard to religion, family, marriage and other institutions as well. It would not be difficult to show that the comparative method was extensively, if not always consciously, used by western sociologists in the late nineteenth and early twentieth centuries to reinforce their belief in the superiority of their own society and culture. There were hardly any voices outside the west to challenge these settled opinions. Thus a gulf existed from the very beginning between the aspirations of the comparative method and its achievements.

A hundred years ago, the practitioners of the comparative method in sociology and social anthropology were all Europeans or Americans. This is now no longer the case. Not only are many different societies being studied throughout the world, but they are being studied by a greater variety of persons from many different angles. There are more facts available and more ways of looking at the available facts. It is easy in the light of these developments to detect a clear Eurocentric bias in even the most successful users of comparison and contrast, including Durkheim and Weber. This bias may be detected not only in the earlier theories of evolution but also in the more recent theories of development and under-development (Arora 1968). Today, the comparative method has to come to terms not only with diverse facts but also with diverse perceptions of the same facts viewed from different angles.

In his essay on the comparative method written more than forty years ago, Evans-Pritchard (1965: 13–16) pointed out that its achievements fell far short of the claims made on its behalf. He was on the whole inclined to attribute this to the insufficiency of the facts at the disposal of students of human society and culture. We can see today that the problem may arise as much from an abundance as from a scarcity of data. In a sense, the more facts there are, the more acute appears to be the problem of reconciling different interpretations of them. However greatly the social sciences might benefit from the methods developed in the natural sciences, those methods cannot by themselves solve the problems of interpretation—or even of observation and description—that are fundamental to the understanding of human society and culture.

* * *

It is no longer possible for practitioners of the comparative method to evade the problems that arise in the social sciences from the complex relations between judgements of reality and judgements of value. Sociologists and social anthropologists have been aware of their importance, but they have dealt with them differently in their formulation and use of the comparative method. These differences become clear when we compare and contrast Durkheim and Weber, the two great comparative sociologists of their generation. Both Durkheim and Weber placed great emphasis on method—and not merely on comparison—but there were striking differences in their views of it.

Of the two, Durkheim's comparative method is easier to describe since it is formulated very clearly and applied systematically. Indeed, for Durkheim it was the comparative method that in some sense gave to sociology its distinctive character as a discipline as against such disciplines as history and philosophy. Moreover, the method was carefully developed within the workshop of the *Année sociologique* by a band of able and dedicated scholars, and it had great influence both within and outside France. In Britain its most forceful exponent was A.R. Radcliffe-Brown who dominated anthropology in the late thirties and forties, and used social anthropology as another name for comparative sociology.

Perhaps I ought to state here itself that I believe Durkheim's (and Radcliffe-Brown's) attempt to formulate a canonically-valid comparative method that would provide the key to the scientific study of society was largely a failure. The failure, however, has many lessons to offer, and, although the attempt failed to reach its goal, it generated many by-products of lasting value. In retrospect, Durkheim appears to have been too complacent about the scientific validity of his own standpoint to take sufficient note of the diversity of standpoints from which societies may be observed, described and compared. Today, it is this diversity that forces itself on our attention and makes us realize that there simply may not exist any Archimedean point from which the comparative method may be applied by no matter which investigator.

Durkheim's ambition was to bring all human societies, simple and complex, within the purview of a single science having its own body of facts, its own concepts and its own methods. He was greatly impressed by the success of the biological sciences, and the organic analogy featured prominently in his formulation of the comparative method. Although he recognized that social facts are at the same time 'things' and 'representations', he believed that they could be investigated, like the facts of nature, without any significant intrusion of the preconceptions acquired by the investigator as a member of his own society. This would be guaranteed once it was recognized that social facts, being things, were characterized by 'exteriority' and 'constraint'. In this view, there is no difference, at least in principle, between studies of one's own society and of other societies.

Durkheim regarded the comparative method as the counterpart in the social sciences of the experimental method pursued in the other sciences. He recognized that social facts could only be observed and not artificially produced under experimental conditions. 'When, on the contrary, the production of facts is not within our control and we can only bring them together in the way that they have been spontaneously produced, the method employed is that of indirect experiment or the comparative method' (Durkheim 1938: 125). What was essential to the success of the method thus conceived was the careful observation and arrangement of facts.[2]

We can see in this light how Durkheim came to regard his study of totemism among the Australian Aborigines as the 'one well-made experiment' that could lead to a proof that was 'valid universally' (Durkheim 1915: 415). Although Durkheim concentrated on one single religion, he did not confine himself to one single society, but examined facts selected from societies of a certain type. He compared the totemic practices of the different Australian tribes among themselves, and those in turn with corresponding practices among the tribes of North America. What I wish to stress is that these were not simply comparisons of the kind that the human mind automatically makes, but comparisons—and contrasts— systematically pursued in accordance with a definite plan.

Durkheim's plan in this 'experimental' study was to establish the presence everywhere of a particular form of religion in a particular type of society. But he was not satisfied with merely establishing a general correspondence between religion and social morphology with regard to totemism as a whole. He was interested in examining variation and change among subtypes within the type. Hence he compared different Australian tribes with each other, and those again with tribes outside Australia. The broader objective was to show that variation and change in religious beliefs and practices could always be related to variation and change in social morphology. In an earlier study of primitive classification, Durkheim and Mauss (1963) had used the comparative method to great effect in demonstrating the correspondence between social morphology and collective representations.

The systematic use of comparison and contrast as a method of enquiry became widely accepted among sociologists and social anthropologists in the first half of the twentieth century. Radcliffe-Brown (1952: 117–32) sought to extend Durkheim's sociological theory of totemism by comparing and contrasting the relationship between social structure and religious practice among the Australian Aborigines (who had totemism) and the Andaman Islanders (who did not have it). Radcliffe-Brown (1952: 153–77) also proposed that a relationship could be established through systematic comparative study between ancestor worship and lineage structure.

Durkheim's plan for the comparative study of societies was ambitious. He did not believe that comparisons should in principle be confined to societies of the same type, but only that they should be made according to a plan. The comparisons that he made in his study of totemism dealt by and large with societies of a single type; in his study of suicide (Durkheim 1951), he compared different types of European societies; and in *The Division of Labour in Society* (Durkheim 1933), he compared forms of solidarity among all human societies. As he put it in his book on method, comparisons 'can include facts borrowed either from a single and unique society, from several societies of the same species, or from several distinct social species' (Durkheim 1938: 136). Here, as in much of Durkheim's work, the concept of 'social species' is borrowed from the biological sciences.

It appears that the more Durkheim reflected on the diversity of social types, the more cautious he became about the feasible range of comparisons that could be fruitfully attempted. Reacting sharply against the work of Frazer and what he called 'the anthropological school' he wrote, 'The comparative method would be impossible if social types did not exist, and it cannot be usefully applied except within a single type' (Durkheim 1915: 94). This need to restrict comparisons within clear limits was forcefully expressed by Evans-Pritchard (1965: 13–36) in his critique of the practices of many of his colleagues. It was for a similar reason that Marc Bloch (1967: 47) favoured comparisons of 'societies that are at once neighbouring and contemporary'.

Among Durkheim's successors, Radcliffe-Brown took the lead in promoting the view that detailed empirical studies of particular societies must be combined with extensive and systematic comparisons. He argued his case in the Preface he contributed to an influential collection of papers on African political systems (Fortes and Evans-Pritchard 1940: xi–xxiii). His argument was that the systematic comparison of segmentary and centralized political systems in sub-Saharan Africa was a first and essential step towards a better understanding of all political systems, simple as well as complex.

The comparative method developed and employed by Durkheim and his successors was designed to free the investigation from the investigator's own biases and preconceptions. The first step was the detailed and careful observation of facts. Durkheim specified the conditions for such observation. The development of intensive fieldwork on the one hand and of survey research on the other greatly extended the depth and range of observation. Not that ideas, beliefs and values were to be excluded from observation, but they were to be treated as facts existing independently of the moral and political preferences of the observer. Once the techniques of observation had been perfected, one would need only patience and care, and it would not matter who made the observation.

A second major step, and one that was crucial to the success of the comparative method, as both Durkheim and Radcliffe-Brown saw it, was the classification of facts. Radcliffe-Brown had put it thus: 'But we cannot hope to pass directly from empirical observation to a knowledge of general scientific laws or principles . . . The immense diversity of forms of human society must first be reduced to order by some sort of classification' (Fortes and Evans-Pritchard 1940: xi). Some sort of classification is no doubt implied in the very use of general concepts, but what was being proposed here was a kind of master plan that would at once reveal basic similarities and differences among societies and their constituent parts.

Durkheim provided a sketch for such a master plan in his rules for the classification of social types. He believed that the concept of social type or social species was essential for avoiding the extremes of nominalism on the one hand and realism on the other.

But one escapes from this alternative once one has recognized that, between the confused multitude of historic societies and the single, but ideal, concept of humanity, there are intermediaries, namely, social species. In the latter are united both the unity that all truly scientific research demands and the diversity that is given in the facts, since the species is the same for all the individual units that make it up, and since, on the other hand, the species differ among themselves (Durkheim 1938: 77).

Radcliffe-Brown (1957) later used the concept of 'natural kind', which is a variant of Durkheim's concept of social species, as a basis for arguing the case for a natural science of society whose essential steps would be observation, description, classification, comparison and generalization.

The comparative method developed by Durkheim and Radcliffe-Brown was based on a particular conception of society. A society had a life of its own that could be observed from outside and described objectively. Different societies could be easily distinguished from each other. They could be grouped together according to their similarities and differences in the same way in which plants and animals were grouped together by biologists. The comparative method could then be applied to arrive at general conclusions about the structure and functioning of societies, and to distinguish between the normal and the pathological according to objective criteria.

The approach to the comparative method through the classification of societies, though very widely used in the nineteenth century, faced problems from the very beginning. Various general schemes of classification were proposed, but each could be shown to have severe limitations. In the nineteenth century, it was common to attempt to classify societies in such a way that each *type* of society could also be seen as a *stage* of evolution.[3] Perhaps the most famous among these was the classification by Morgan (1964) into Savagery, Barbarism and Civilization, which fell into disrepute when evolutionary theories came under attack from British and American anthropologists from the 1920s onwards (Lowie 1960; Radcliffe-Brown 1952).

One of the most extensively used schemes of classification, derived from Marx and Engels, was the one which grouped societies under Primitive Communism, Ancient Society, Asiatic Society, Feudal Society and Bourgeois (or Capitalist) Society. This scheme, with minor variations, remained a part of the canon of Soviet social science for decades, but each of its major classes, with the possible exception of the last, was riddled with ambiguity. It is for specialists in the field to decide whether more good or harm was done by the efforts of a determined band of historians to fit pre-British India into the category of Feudal Society (Mukhia 1981, 1985; Sharma 1985; Habib 1985). In like manner, the discussion of the category of Asiatic Society and its place in the general scheme of classification taxed the ingenuity of a long line of Soviet scholars, again, to what effect it is difficult to say today (Gellner 1980).

Durkheim's classification of societies is of special interest, firstly, because it was consciously linked to his comparative method, and, secondly, because it was made in accordance with a set of rules. Although Durkheim maintained that 'one branch of sociology must be devoted to the constitution and classification of these [social] species' (1938: 76), his own effort in that branch did not proceed very far. His basic principle was first to identify the component elements of societies and then to arrange them according to '*the nature and number of the component elements and their mode of combination*' (Durkheim 1938: 81, emphasis in original). Perhaps the only thing of value that emerged from this effort was the concept of 'segmentary society' which in a modified form played an important part in the development of political anthropology. Beyond that, even the attempt to classify societies of the 'organized' type was not seriously pursued.

A problem that is bound to bedevil any attempt to pursue the approach described above is its presupposition that in dealing with societies we can easily distinguish the part from the whole, and one whole from another. It is not at all evident from the nature of things whether a certain unit which is conventionally called a society should count as a part or a whole. Not only do the parts of a society flow into each other—Durkheim recognized this for 'organized' societies—but whole societies are frequently, even typically, mutually interpenetrating.

The problem raised above did not escape the attention of Radcliffe-Brown even while he argued the case for comparisons between societies through their classification. In his Presidential Address to the Royal Anthropological Institute in 1940, he observed:

At the present moment of history, the network of social relations spreads over the whole world, without any absolute solution of continuity anywhere. This gives rise to a difficulty which I do not think sociologists have really faced, the difficulty of defining what is meant by the term 'a society'. They do commonly talk of societies as if they were distinguishable, discrete entities, as, for example, when we are told that a society is an organism. Is the British Empire a society or a collection of societies? Is a Chinese village a society, or is it merely a fragment of the Republic of China? (Radcliffe-Brown 1952: 193).

There is no great harm done when the same author talks of 'Munda society' and again of 'Indian society', but it does create problems for the classification of societies.

Not only does the concept of societies as discrete and bounded units appear less tenable than before, but some anthropologists have begun to question the utility of the very concept of society (Ingold 1986; 1990).

Arguments of different kinds have been made against the concept, particularly as it has been used in the scholarly literature of sociology and social anthropology: that it sets up false oppositions—as between 'individual' and 'society'; that it reifies an abstraction—as in the statement that society is a reality *sui generis*; and so on. Finally, it has been suggested that it is the uncritical use of the concept of society that has brought comparative anthropology to an impasse (Ingold 1990: 6).

* * *

'Max Weber,' it has been observed, 'was the one sociologist in the history of the discipline who saw beyond the boundaries of modern Western civilization' (Shils 1981: 292). But his approach to the comparative study of society was different from the approach of Durkheim and Radcliffe-Brown because he had a different conception of society and a different assessment of the limits and possibilities of sociological enquiry. Sociological enquiry in his view was concerned with causes and functions, but it was also concerned with meaning, and there the organic analogy was more a hindrance than a help: 'We can accomplish something which is never attainable in the natural sciences, namely the subjective understanding of the component individuals' (Weber 1978: 15).

What is lacking in the approach adopted by Durkheim and Radcliffe-Brown is focused reflection on the standpoint from which observation, description and comparison are made. Weber, on the other hand, was continually preoccupied by the standpoint of the scholar, acknowledging tacitly the legitimacy of a variety of standpoints. His work on the Protestant ethic has had enormous influence on the development of our subject, and comparisons have been made on its basis between western and other civilizations. But it must not be forgotten that Weber himself offered his work as a contribution from a particular standpoint. To be sure, he was thinking of the variety of standpoints available within the western intellectual milieu, but the observation may be generalized to include other intellectual and cultural milieus as well.

For Weber, even observation and description had to be different in the social as against the natural sciences since the investigator could not confine himself only to external characteristics. It was not enough to examine statistical tendencies in the course and consequences of social action, one had also to reach into its meaning and significance, since 'subjective understanding is the specific characteristic of sociological knowledge' (Weber 1978: 15). This no doubt opened up new possibilities for social and historical enquiry, but it also posed difficult, not to say intractable, problems for the comparative study of civilizations.

Weber made extensive use of historical (as against ethnographic) material, and therefore had to confront more fully the questions raised by the historians of his time about the understanding of human society and culture. He was unwilling to accept the limits generally imposed on historical enquiry by its orthodox practitioners but eager to take advantage of the insights into the human condition revealed by their work (Weber 1950, 1988). He insisted that historical material threw light not only on events and personalities but also on structures and processes that could be compared and contrasted across both time and space. One required new tools for making those comparisons and contrasts, but Weber did not find it fruitful to turn to the biological sciences for aid in their construction.

Weber made wide and extensive comparisons among human socie-ties in different places at different times, but those comparisons did not presuppose in either principle or practice any single scheme of classifica-tion covering all human societies. His principal strategy of comparison and contrast was through the construction of ideal types, which enabled the selection and use of facts to establish significant similarities and dif-ferences. The construction of ideal types, (unlike Durkheim's social types or social species) is not necessarily linked to the comparative method as such, but Weber harnessed the device for making the most extensive historical and sociological comparisons and contrasts.

As is well known, Weber constructed ideal types of a great variety of phenomena, ranging from social action to whole institutional complexes such as bureaucracy and capitalism. He saw these ideal types as constructions of the mind rather than 'social species' or 'natural kinds' having some sort of independent existence outside the investigator's mind. As he himself put it, 'An ideal type is formed by the one-sided *accentuation* of one or more points of view . . . In its conceptual purity, this mental construct (Gedankenbild) cannot be found empirically anywhere in reality' (Shils and Finch 1949: 90, emphasis in original). Further, he took pains to distinguish between 'ideal types' and 'average types', the former being designed to bring out qualitative differences rather than differences of degree (Weber 1978: 20–1).

In a trenchant critique of Weber's mode of procedure, Carl Friedrich (1952: 28–9) pointed out that Weber used, with a great deal of attendant confusion, ideal types in both an 'individualizing' and a 'generalizing' manner. The ideal types of social action were clearly designed for use in every kind of social and historical context. The ideal type of Calvinism, on the other hand, was used to focus on distinctions within a single historical context. Again, some ideal types may serve well simply as heuristic instruments whereas others appear to be designed to bring sharply into focus a particular historical object. They may then be used as labels for marking out one society or one type of society from another, such as 'Occidental' and 'Oriental' societies.

Weber's ideal types give priority to 'representations' over 'morphology'. In that way, he was able to bring differences into prominence, sometimes at the cost of important similarities. A contemporary critic of Weber has pointed out that 'his attention was focussed on the over-all tendencies *distinguishing* one civilization from another rather than on the extent to which accommodations of theology and popular practice might tend to *diminish* these distinctions' (Bendix 1968: 500, emphasis in original).

The comparisons made by Weber have a free-ranging character that make them quite different from those that aim systematically to arrive at laws of increasing generality. These comparisons have illuminated many dark corners of human activity and experience. But one must always remember that Weber's primary historical object was western civilization. A recent commentator has noted: 'While Durkheim's main interest was in what all societies have in common, in what a society *is*, Weber's was in how societies differ' (Lockwood 1992: 15–6, emphasis in original). Much of Weber's work was animated by the desire to identify the unique characteristics of western civilization, and especially those characteristics that gave it its unusual dynamism and 'which (*as we like to think*) lie in a line of development having *universal* significance and value' (Weber 1976: 13, some emphasis added). In this sense, his comparative approach may be described as a 'typifying' rather than a 'classifying' approach. The ideal types used by him exaggerated, with a particular purpose, the contrasts between western and other civilizations. But the very act that brought into relief the defining features of the former often obscured significant differences among the latter.

One of the early attempts at a comparative study of civilizations by a scholar of non-western origin began with the observation: 'Max Weber helped to perpetuate a Western misconception that Hindus, as well as Egyptians and Arabs, are Orientals. Weber considered the civilization of India to be but one branch of the Oriental civilization, of which two other branches are the Chinese and the Japanese' (Hsu 1963: 1). As we have noted, Weber himself was very conscious of the importance of the standpoint from which historical or sociological investigations are made, and his own standpoint appears in review to be very much that of the European scholar at the turn of the century.

It may be plausibly argued that Weber's *interest* in Hinduism or Confucianism was different from his interest in Calvinism. In his famous critique of Eduard Meyer, he had argued that something may become of interest to the historian in at least three distinct senses: (1) as an 'historical object'; (2) as a 'historical cause'; and (3) as an 'heuristic instrument' (Shils and Finch 1949: 156). In terms of these distinctions, only Calvinism was of interest to Weber in all the three senses, whereas Oriental religious traditions were of interest to him primarily only in the third sense. One might then say that Weber's aim was not so much to devise a single comparative method that could be used by one and all irrespective of substantive interest, but to use comparisons extensively to sharpen his 'heuristic instruments' in the interest of particular substantive enquiries. The question of 'fair comparisons' between cultures is then left unsettled.

* * *

The comparative study of human societies must take into account not only their morphology or external characteristics but also the ideas and values characteristic of them or their self-representation. This much would be acknowledged even by Durkheim, for he observed, 'A society cannot be constituted without creating ideals. These ideals are simply the ideas in terms of which society sees itself and exists at a culminating point in its development' (1974: 93). In studying plants and animals, we are concerned only with how they appear to us; in studying societies and cultures, our concern has also to be with how they appear to themselves. Thus, similarities and differences have to be recorded on several registers, and not on just one register. This makes it difficult beyond a point to adapt to the social sciences the procedures for comparison and contrast used with such success in the biological sciences.

The differential evaluation of societies and cultures has been implicit to a greater or lesser extent in the use of the comparative method even when it has been presented as objective and neutral. As we have seen, where the method went hand in hand with theories of evolution, it inevitably placed some societies and cultures ahead of others. It is true that Durkheim maintained that all religions should be investigated by the same comparative method, but he also believed that Christianity was more evolved and exalted than other religions. Likewise, Weber believed that the elimination of magical components through the process of rationalization had progressed further in Protestant Christianity than in any other religion. The same kind of slant in favour of monogamous marriage and the nuclear family may be noted in the schemes of comparison freely used in the past.

Both Durkheim and Weber were aware of the problems that arise when ideas, beliefs and values are made the objects of systematic enquiry, and each tried to solve them in his own way. Durkheim believed that objective evaluation became possible once the social basis of individual judgements was recognized, for, as he put it, 'Social judgement is objective as compared with individual judgement' (Ibid.: 84). While this might provide some ground for identifying the arbitrary nature of individual judgements, it does not show how different social judgements—those held to be valid in Indonesia as against the Netherlands—may be compared in an objective way. Indeed, while Durkheim did seek to understand representations and judgements as social facts, the comparative method that he tried to adapt from the biological sciences proved less than adequate to the task he took on hand.

Weber's keen historical sense made him more aware than Durkheim of the difficulty of extracting standards of evaluation and judgement from an examination, no matter how systematic or scrupulous, of social facts. The dictum that the normal type is the average type would be as alien to Weber's sociology as the analogy of societies with organisms. While striving continuously to separate value judgements from judgements of reality, Weber rarely underestimated the magnitude of the problem involved. 'Nor need I discuss further whether the distinction between empirical statements of fact and value-judgements is "difficult" to make. It is' (Shils and Finch 1949: 9). He did not believe that the investigator could, or even should, free himself from his own values; but he did insist on self-awareness in the investigation of a problem and self-restraint in the expression of one's viewpoint.

One of the principal tasks of sociological enquiry, and most acutely of comparative sociology, is to devise a method for treating 'subjective' evaluation in an objective way (Ibid.: 10–1). The problem is not confined to sociology. It is akin to that of dealing with what the famous jurist Hans Kelsen called 'norms in a descriptive sense' as against what may be called 'norms in a prescriptive sense'. How difficult it is to maintain the distinction consistently may be judged from the misrepresentation of the idea so lucidly explained by H.L.A. Hart (1983: 286–308). The problem becomes particularly acute when the values characteristic of different societies are being compared (or contrasted) by scholars from different standpoints and with different presuppositions.

Weber's observations on value judgements, ethical neutrality and objectivity, no matter how acute or incisive, related largely to questions of policy or politics (in German the same word serves for both) within one's own society rather than to comparisons between different societies. When he compared science and politics as vocations, he had in mind mainly western science and German politics. I have already referred to his concern for accommodating more than one standpoint. In a well-known intervention, Weber defended the appointment of anarchists as teachers of law on the ground that they can 'perceive problems in the fundamental postulates of legal theory which escape those who take them for granted' (Shils and Finch 1949: 7). But he nowhere discussed seriously the implications of examining the fundamental postulates of social theories prevalent in his time from standpoints outside the western intellectual tradition.

'To view history from the "standpoint" of a particular class,' it has been observed, 'is as damaging as viewing it from the "standpoint" of one's nationality or one's generation or one's village' (Shils 1981: 60). Weber was aware of the damage done by viewing history from the standpoint of a particular class, but it is doubtful that he reflected sufficiently on the implications of viewing it from the standpoint of a particular nationality.

The question that I am raising relates more specifically to comparisons, and to standards of judgement and evaluation that are consciously or unconsciously built into the comparative method itself. To what extent are the definitions, classifications and ideal types employed in the comparative method coloured by the categories of one's own society, and to what extent do they, therefore, devalue or otherwise distort the representations of other societies? If, as Durkheim says, a society cannot be constituted without creating ideals, then the comparison of societies is in a sense the comparison of their ideals. Is it possible to make that comparison without injecting the ideals of one's own society into the very framework of comparison?

Every society is marked by conflicting aims and tendencies. The actual differences between societies, as we have seen from Bendix's observations, are accentuated by the method of contrast through ideal types. Much depends on what kinds of ideal types are used, how and by whom they are constructed, and with what ends in view. The accentuated contrast between societies might appear appealing from one point of view but invidious from another. There is sometimes only a thin line between the ideal type and the stereotype. Where human values are engaged, as they are in such comparisons and contrasts, it is difficult to remove allegations of misrepresentation and suspicions of bad faith.

The two features that strike us most about the comparative sociology practised by the generation of Durkheim and Weber are: (1) that they made a genuine effort to bring all human societies—simple and complex, past and present—under its scrutiny; and (2) that those who developed its concepts and methods all belonged within broadly the same social and cultural tradition. It is the second that is now changing before our eyes, and calls for serious attention. It would be safe to say that neither Durkheim nor Weber gave much thought to the viewpoint of the investigator in sociological comparisons when that investigator belonged to a non-western society. They were aware that viewpoints might vary according to class or political affiliation, but they did not take much account of variations due to differences of national tradition. They took ideas and values in non-western societies into account, but only as objects of investigation and not as elements in the construction of method. This has become a source of some anxiety to scholars from Asian and African countries. It is seen, perhaps rightly, as a very serious limitation of the comparative method as it now stands; but the remedy for it cannot be found by recommending different methods for observation, description and comparison to persons rooted in different geographical locations.

* * *

Whether or not he adopts the comparative method of Durkheim, or the approach of Weber, or some other approach, the sociologist is condemned to making comparisons, and he cannot dispense with the requirement of making them rigorously and systematically. Nor can he sweep under the carpet the 'value problem' that arises in every comparison. Cultural anthropologists have learnt to appreciate the virtue of 'reflexivity' (Rabinow 1977; Clifford and Marcus 1986) which calls upon us to recognize that what we write about societies and cultures tells us something not only about those societies and cultures but also about ourselves. This is certainly a good thing so long as it does not turn into self-indulgence, for sociology and anthropology cannot be used as covers for autobiography.

Sociologists are inclined to seek in their own or other societies the values to which they are committed as persons, as scholars or as citizens. Individual and community, equality and hierarchy, the rational and the traditional are things about which most scholars care, one way or another; and if they are sociologists or social anthropologists, they discover or seek out societies that uphold, or disregard, or deny one or another of those values. Some sociological and much anthropological writing is about 'other' societies, but one's own society is always in the background, implicitly more often than explicitly, as a standard of comparison.

Today, some of these values have acquired a kind of universal significance in the sense that they are recognized and acknowledged, at least to some extent and by some individuals, in all parts of the world. Disagreements are bound to arise when societies are compared to determine the extent to which they embody, or fail to embody, one or another value, for those who make the comparisons are likely to care not only more about some values than others, but also, and perhaps inevitably, more about some societies than others. Scholarly disagreements over facts and their interpretations are sometimes underlain by suspicions that arbitrary and invidious moral judgements are introduced through the backdoor in the course of 'scientific' comparisons.

Suspicions of bad faith are bound to arise when comparisons that appear 'scientific' or 'objective' from one standpoint appear invidious from another. Such suspicions can never be eliminated, but they can at least be mitigated if there is willingness to moderate the claims made on behalf of not only one's favoured method but also one's favoured society. For it is a fact that the second kind of claim is occasionally introduced in the course of comparisons, albeit in a tacit or oblique way. It is not simply that sociologists might subscribe to the social values they seek to investigate comparatively, but they sometimes display a possessive attitude towards their own society in a way that jeopardizes their comparative method.

The set of ideas and values centering around 'individual', 'person' and 'self' has engaged the attention of many historians and sociologists with a marked interest in comparative studies. A very significant contribution to the understanding of the subject has been made by a succession of French scholars beginning with Alexis de Tocqueville (1956). The delicate balance of judgements required in comparisons involving such values may be seen in the opposition with which Tocqueville began between 'individualism' to which a positive value, and 'egoism' to which a negative value was attributed. Where societies are being compared, some bias in reading the evidence relating to them is likely to creep in where a prior judgement based on moral preference, conscious or unconscious, has been made about the basic qualities of the societies in question, so that similar facts are treated as evidence of 'individualism' in one case and of 'egoism' in another.

The ambivalent attitude towards the place of the individual or person in the plan of social life—wavering between scientific detachment and moral commitment—may be seen in the work of Durkheim. As a sociologist, he took the view—against both utilitarians and contract theorists— that the individual as an autonomous moral agent, enjoying respect and responsibility in his own right, was not the starting point of social evolution but its end product. Pre-modern societies were, in his view, based on mechanical solidarity in which the individual was subordinated to the group, legally and morally; modern societies, on the other hand, were based on the division of labour which assigned legal and moral primacy to the autonomy of the individual. By modern societies, Durkheim meant modern western societies with which he contrasted all other societies, past and present. In *The Division of Labour in Society* (1938), Durkheim traced with the methods of positive science the general demographic, occupational and other social factors through whose operation the individual had assumed primacy in modern as against pre-modern—that is, primitive, ancient and medieval—societies. The discussion of this transition included many comparisons but it gave no explicit account of his own value preferences for or against the individual.

Only a few years later, Durkheim wrote an essay on the significance of the individual in society and history. In that essay, which was written in support of those who were demanding the reinstatement of Alfred Dreyfus, he stated his value preference clearly and openly in support of the individual. But there he not only assigned great importance to Christianity (as against demographic and other material factors) as a source of individualism, but shifted its origin to a much earlier phase of history. 'It is thus a singular error to present individualist morality as antagonistic to Christian morality; quite the contrary, it is derived from it. By adhering to the former, we do not disown our past; we merely continue it' (Durkheim 1969: 124). This is a somewhat different story from the one presented earlier about the causes of the division of labour.

A similar argument was presented by Mauss in a comparative essay on the person delivered as the Huxley Memorial Lecture to the Royal Anthropological Institute in 1938. The essay was offered as a 'sample . . .

of the achievements of the French school of sociology' (Mauss 1979: 59). It provided a survey of a whole range of societies—the Pueblo Indians, the Northwest Coast Indians, the Australian Aborigines, the Indians of India, the Chinese, and, of course, the modern Europeans. It is clear that only the last constituted, in Weber's terminology, the historical object for Mauss, all the others serving as heuristic instruments. The treatment of the ancient civilizations of India and China was cursory and superficial. The conclusion of the essay was that the 'category of the person' as an autonomous moral agent, as against a mere sense of the person, was acknowledged and valued only in modern western societies, and nowhere else.

Although the essay was offered as a sample of the work of the French school of sociology, one will find in it very little regard for the rules of sociological comparisons laid down by Durkheim. The objective of the essay appears to have been not so much to demonstrate a sociological approach as to assert a claim to an ideal and a value to which Mauss, like Durkheim before him, attached the highest moral significance. Hence the essay concludes with the following exhortation:

Who knows even if this 'category', which all of us believe to be well founded, will always be recognized as such? *It was formed only for us, among us.* Even its moral power—the sacred character of the human person—is questioned, not only everywhere in the East, where they have not attained our sciences, but even in some of the countries where the principle was discovered. We have a great wealth to defend; with us the Idea may disappear. Let us not moralize (Mauss 1979: 90, emphasis added).

I may add that this essay, which some may regard as shallow and mawkish, has received the highest praise from anthropologists in Britain where two separate English translations of it were published within ten years (Mauss 1979; Carrithers, Collins and Lukes 1985).

Do all scholars who make sociological comparisons involving fundamental values show themselves, like Marcel Mauss, to be good patriots in the end? When the occasion demanded, Max Weber showed himself to be as true a German patriot as anyone (Mommsen 1984), and who can say that his commitment to Germany and to Europe did not colour the many comparisons that he made? Patriotism is now out of fashion among western intellectuals, but that does not mean that it has been laid to rest. It is still a great force in the countries of Asia and Africa among intellectuals and others, but perhaps we should all try to learn from the mistakes of Mauss and Weber instead of insisting on our right to repeat those mistakes in our turn.

Notes

1. Talcott Parsons (1966: 71) was perhaps the last great sociologist who attempted to unite the comparative approach with an evolutionary perspective.

2. The 'method of controlled comparisons', in one form or another, continued to be used for long by social and cultural anthropologists. Fred Eggan (1954) provides a useful account of the limits and possibilities of the method as used in social anthropology. It may be recalled that Eggan had been much influenced by Radcliffe-Brown.

3. This was continued until recent times by sociologists and anthropologists of the Marxist persuasion. See, for instance, Godelier 1977: 70–96.

References

Arora, S.K. 1968. 'Pre-empted Future? Notes on Theories of Political Development'. *Behavioural Sciences and Community Development*. Vol. 2. No. 2, pp. 85–120.

Bendix, R. 1968. 'Weber, Max'. In D.L. Sils (ed). *International Encyclopedia of the Social Sciences*. New York: Macmillan. Vol. 16, pp. 493–502.

Béteille, A. 1990. *Some Observations on the Comparative Method*. Amsterdam: CASA, see chapter 4, this volume.

Bloch, M. 1967. *Land and Work in Medieval Europe*. London: Routledge and Kegan Paul.

Boas, F. 1940 (1896). 'The Limitations of the Comparative Method in Anthropology'. In *Race, Language and Culture*. New York: Macmillan.

Carrithers, M., S. Collins and S. Lukes (eds). 1985. *The Category of the Person*. Cambridge: Cambridge University Press.

Clifford J. and G.E. Marcus (eds). 1986. *Writing Cultures*. Berkeley: University of California Press.

de Tocqueville, A. 1956 (1840). *Democracy in America*. New York: Alfred Knopf. Vol. 2.

Durkheim, É. 1915 (1912). *The Elementary Forms of the Religious Life*. London: Allen and Unwin.

———. 1933 (1893). *The Division of Labour in Society*. Glencoe: The Free Press.

———. 1938 (1895). *The Rules of Sociological Method*. Glencoe: The Free Press.

———. 1951 (1897). *Suicide*. Glencoe: The Free Press.

———. 1969 (1898). 'Individualism and the Intellectuals'. *Political Studies*. Vol. 17, pp. 114–30.

———. 1974 (1924). *Sociology and Philosophy*. New York: The Free Press.

Durkheim, É. and M. Mauss. 1963 (1903). *Primitive Classification.* London: Cohen and West.

Eggan, F. 1954. 'Social Anthropology and the Method of Controlled Comparisons'. *American Anthropologist.* Vol. 56. No. 5, pp. 743–63.

Evans-Pritchard, E.E. 1965. *The Position of Women in Primitive Societies and Other Essays.* London: Faber and Faber.

Fortes, M. and E.E. Evans-Pritchard (eds). 1940. *African Political Systems.* London: Oxford University Press.

Friedrich, C.J. 1952. 'Some Observations on Weber's Analysis of Bureaucracy'. In R.K. Merton et al. (eds). *Reader in Bureaucracy.* Glencoe: The Free Press, pp. 27–33.

Gellner, E. (ed). 1980. *Soviet and Western Anthropology.* London: Duckworth.

Godelier, M. 1977. *Perspectives in Marxist Anthropology.* Cambridge: Cambridge University Press.

Habib, I. 1985. 'Classifying Pre-colonial India'. *The Journal of Peasant Studies.* Vol. 12. Nos. 2 & 3, pp. 44–53.

Hart, H.L.A. 1983. *Essays in Jurisprudence and Philosophy.* Oxford: Clarendon Press.

Hsu, F.L.K. 1963. *Clan, Caste and Club.* Princeton: Van Nostrand.

Ingold, T. 1986. *Evolution and Social Life.* Cambridge: Cambridge University Press.

————— . (ed). 1990. *The Concept of Society is Theoretically Obsolete.* Manchester: Department of Social Anthropology, University of Manchester.

Leach, E.R. 1961. *Rethinking Anthropology.* London: Athlone Press.

Lockwood, D. 1992. *Solidarity and Schism.* Oxford: Clarendon Press.

Lowie, R.H. 1960 (1921). *Primitive Society.* London: Routledge and Kegan Paul.

Marx, K. 1959 (1867). *Capital.* Moscow: Progress Publishers. Vol. 1.

Mauss, M. 1979 (1950). *Sociology and Psychology.* London: Routledge and Kegan Paul.

Mommsen, W. 1984. *Max Weber and German Politics.* Chicago: University of Chicago Press.

Morgan, L.H. 1964 (1877). *Ancient Society.* Cambridge, Mass.: The Belknap Press.

Mukhia, H. 1981. 'Was there Feudalism in Indian History?' The *Journal of Peasant Studies.* Vol. 8. No. 3, pp. 273–310.

————— . 1985. 'Peasant Production and Medieval Indian History'. *The Journal of Peasant Studies.* Vol. 12. Nos. 2 & 3, pp. 228–51.

Parsons, T. 1966. *Societies: Evolutionary and Comparative Perspectives.* Englewood Cliffs: Prentice-Hall.

————. 1971. *The System of Modern Societies*. Englewood Cliffs: Prentice-Hall.

Pickering, W.E.S. 1975. *Durkheim on Religion*. London: Routledge and Kegan Paul.

Rabinow, P. 1977. *Reflections on Fieldwork in Morocco*. Berkeley: University of California Press.

Radcliffe-Brown, A.R. 1952. *Structure and Function in Primitive Society*. London: Cohen and West.

————. 1957. *A Natural Science of Society*. Glencoe: The Free Press.

Sharma, R.S. 1985. 'How Feudal was Indian Feudalism?' *The Journal of Peasant Studies*. Vol. 12. Nos. 2 & 3, pp. 19–43.

Shils, E. 1981. *Tradition*. Chicago: University of Chicago Press.

Shils, E. and H.A. Finch (eds). 1949. *Max Weber on the Methodology of the Social Sciences*. New York: The Free Press.

Weber, M. 1950 (1927). *General Economic History*. Glencoe: The Free Press.

————. 1976 (1904–5). *The Protestant Ethic and the Spirit of Capitalism*. London: Allen and Unwin.

————. 1978 (1922). *Economy and Society*. Berkeley: University of California Press.

————. 1988 (1924). *The Agrarian Sociology of Ancient Civilizations*. London: Verso.

Sociology and Area Study:
The South Asian Experience

Sociology may be viewed in a broad sense as the comparative and systematic study of social life, its processes, structures and institutions in all societies of every type throughout the world, with special attention to societies of the present time. I include social anthropology within this broad conception for, as Radcliffe-Brown (1952, 1958) said, social anthropology is only another name for comparative sociology. Since the linkage of social anthropology with sociology will figure prominently in the later discussion, I wish to make a note of it at the outset. Sociology and social anthropology are not or should not be bound by geographical constraints: together, they provide a body of concepts, methods and theories on which any scholar may draw, no matter which particular society or culture he or she wishes to investigate.

Area study is by its nature constrained geographically. Here attention is devoted to the population of a given geographical area, which may be presumed to have a certain measure of social, cultural and historical unity. The study of a particular area, South Asia for example, is by definition narrower in geographical scope than is the discipline of sociology taken as a whole. But it is broader in another sense, for area study includes the study not only of society but also of economy, history, languages, literature and so on. Area study is by definition multi-disciplinary, and sociology is only one of the disciplines contributing to it. In what follows, I will naturally look at area studies from the angle of sociology.

As an organized form of intellectual enquiry, area study is a relative newcomer. But we must remember that as specialized intellectual disciplines, sociology and social anthropology are themselves relatively new, particularly in the countries of Asia. In some of these countries, social anthropology and area study have had similar origins and similar patterns of growth, and they have influenced each other very markedly. Yet they are not disciplines of the same kind. For them to be able to contribute fruitfully to each other, the differences in their aims, objectives and orientations must be kept in mind.

Sociology had its origins in the nineteenth century in Britain, France and Germany, and by the beginning of the twentieth century, it had made a place for itself as a more or less distinct academic discipline in western Europe and the United States. Britain played a more important part than other European countries in the early development of anthropology, partly because it had more extensive colonies. A kind of informal division of labour gradually emerged among western scholars by which sociologists studied mainly their own, that is, European and American societies, whereas anthropologists studied other cultures in Asia, Africa, Oceania and among the aboriginal populations of America and Australia. On the Indian subcontinent, both sociology and social anthropology began to be studied as academic disciplines within a few decades of their being set up in western universities. But the division of labour between the two has followed a somewhat different course from the one generally followed in the west, and this I take to be a matter calling for some consideration.

Area study as a distinct academic discipline is of more recent origin. It is true that each country, with its own geography, history, culture, economy and polity, had been studied by scholars belonging to various disciplines earlier. But the creation of special programmes, first for research and then for teaching, in which a region or an area became the focus of attention for a number of disciplines acting in concert is barely fifty years old. It began with the process of decolonization, and the initiative for its development came mainly from the United States. With the withdrawal of the old imperial powers and the emergence of the United States as a major presence on the international scene, the need was felt there for a closer and more systematic knowledge of the countries of Asia, Africa and Latin America. Once area study programmes became established, their advantages began to be more widely appreciated, and they were set up in many parts of the world.

I wish to draw attention to the differences in origin and orientation between the specialized social science disciplines on the one hand and area studies on the other so as to be able to examine how they may develop best to their mutual advantage. My emphasis will of course be on one specialized discipline, namely, sociology (inclusive of social anthropology) and one area, namely, South Asia, but I will also make observations of a more general nature.

Sociology, whether defined broadly or narrowly, is an empirical discipline: it is, to adapt the language of one of its principal architects, the science of social facts (Durkheim 1982). Sociological enquiry proceeds less through introspection and speculation than through the observation, description, interpretation and analysis of facts. Human beings everywhere and at all times have thought and written about the social framework of their existence, but only from the middle of the nineteenth-century onward that the framework became the object of systematic empirical investigation, first by scholars in Europe and America, and then by scholars throughout the world. The twentieth century witnessed the growth of rigorous methods of empirical investigation, through participant-observation, survey research and other procedures.

In the last hundred years, sociologists and social anthropologists have brought together an enormous body of empirical material based on the methodical investigation of existing societies throughout the world. This material covers such diverse aspects of their lives as technology and economic arrangements; political processes and organizations; family, kinship and marriage; religious beliefs and practices; and so on.

The amount of systematic empirical material on social processes, structures and institutions that has accumulated in the last hundred years is enormous. All sociologists and social anthropologists are parasitical on this vast body of material. Whether they write about kinship or religion or stratification, they have to refer back to some part of it. Now it is impossible for any single sociologist or social anthropologist, no matter how skilful he may be analytically or theoretically, to collect by his sole unaided effort all the material that is required for his theoretical or analytical work. It has become difficult for him even to have full knowledge of the entire body of available empirical material, except in such clearly delimited fields as preferential kin marriage or the social grading of occupations. Yet sociology and social anthropology, as the general and comparative study of human societies, cannot move forward unless more reliable and more detailed empirical material is continuously accumulated.

Sociologists of the generation of Émile Durkheim and Max Weber wrote with apparent ease about the entire range of human societies from the simplest to the most complex. The two persons just mentioned were both scholars of outstanding ability, but it has also to be remembered that the body of reliable empirical material available in their time was sufficiently limited to at least tempt individual scholars to seek to master it as a whole. That became increasingly difficult with the passage of time, and a division of labour among scholars soon became inevitable. The emergence of area studies may be viewed in part as a response to the need for that division of labour.

The years between the two Wars witnessed tremendous advances in the methods and techniques of empirical research, and these advances continue unabated. They also witnessed the growing divergence between sociology as the study of western or advanced societies and social anthropology as the study of non-western or backward, not to say primitive, societies. This divergence gathered momentum despite the strong desire of scholars like A.R. Radcliffe-Brown to develop a single unified discipline embracing the study of all societies of every kind. Specialization in the methods and techniques of empirical enquiry played some part in accelerating the divergence. It has had unfortunate consequences to the extent that it has led to a fragmented understanding of human society and culture by underscoring the division of the world into 'the West and the Rest' (Goody 1990).

In the beginning and until World War II, research in both sociology and social anthropology was conducted largely, if not entirely, by European and American scholars, so that the division of labour between the two types of enquiry was mainly a division of labour among western scholars. In the west, sociologists were those who studied not only advanced societies but in effect their own society; and social anthropologists were not simply those who studied primitive or backward societies but in effect the societies of Africa, Asia and Latin America. But things began to change after World War II, and more and more Asian and other non-western scholars undertook the study first of their own and then of other societies and cultures. An intellectual division of labour that had arisen to suit the convenience of western scholars did not appear equally convenient for scholars in every part of the world. In India, those who study their own rural or urban communities generally describe themselves as sociologists; but unfortunately, these same scholars are often obliged to present themselves as anthropologists in the United States and other western countries.

Anthropological fieldwork played a very large part in the collection of systematic empirical material from all parts of the world. Systematic field investigation is expensive and time consuming, and scholars began to specialize not only in the themes they chose to study but also in the areas in which they did their fieldwork. Thus, in the thirties, forties and fifties, British social anthropologists did much of their fieldwork in Africa; not only that, anthropologists from Oxford worked in east Africa, those from Cambridge in west Africa, and their counterparts from Manchester in central Africa. This, I repeat, was largely a matter of convenience, and individual scholars worked outside the areas on which their colleagues concentrated when that appeared convenient or attractive. And of course in departments of sociology in Britain, empirical investigations were made mainly into British society.

The sociological tradition begun by Durkheim laid down certain procedures for the comparison of facts relating to different societies. Experience seemed to show that comparisons between facts drawn from societies of widely different types could be superficial and misleading. It was felt that comparisons had to be made first between neighbourly societies or those of the same type before wider comparisons could be safely attempted (Béteille 1990). Thus, segmentary and centralized political systems were first compared in Africa as a basis for attempting wider comparisons among political systems (Fortes and Evans-Pritchard 1940). Or again, patterns of social mobility were compared among western European societies to provide a basis for comparisons of a wider sort (Erikson and Goldthorpe 1992).

Durkheim and his successors stressed the importance of taking variations seriously and systematically into account while attempting the formulation of general statements about society and its institutions. Social reality as such could not be made a subject of systematic study; such a study had to be based on the observation and description of individual societies and on their classification into social types. Each type needed to be identified and its features systematically analysed before comparisons could be made between different types. To the extent that social anthropologists and sociologists were exploring systematically the distinctive features of societies and cultures in the different parts of the globe, they were already preparing the ground for the area studies programmes that were to become established soon afterwards.

The approach through the classification of social types proposed by Durkheim and Radcliffe-Brown, though convenient in some respects, has serious limitations in others. It has not proved easy to sustain Durkheim's (1982) assumption that there are social species just as there are biological species, or Radcliffe-Brown's (1957) proposition that human societies constitute natural kinds. Societies do not have at all the kinds of boundaries that organisms have, and what strikes us more and more about the contemporary world is not the separation of societies into watertight compartments but their mutual interpenetration. To be sure, we need to classify social facts, but that does not mean that we can have a single master plan of classification for use on every occasion. To take an example that will appeal at once to students of the Indian subcontinent, the classification of societies according to religion and their classification according to language, each important in its own way, cut across each other at significant points. Further, societies change places in systems of classifications: Japan was at one time grouped along with the less advanced countries of Asia, but now it is one of the most advanced countries in the world.

Area studies programmes have grown in the last fifty years to meet a combination of theoretical and practical demands. They have not grown in accordance with any single plan, and convenience has played a large part in the shape and form given to them. The areas covered by them differ a great deal in size and degree of homogeneity. The disciplines deployed for the pursuit of area studies have also been various, although language and literature, history and ethnography appear to provide a common core everywhere. Naturally, these are also practised outside of area study programmes. Some of the social sciences such as ethnography have depended more on area studies than have others such as psychology and economics, except for that branch of the subject known as 'development economics'.

The area is at bottom a geographical concept. In many cases, it has also a certain historical identity acquired through common and shared experience over time. It has, in addition, a certain political identity although that has been subject to fluctuation and change. The case of the Indian subcontinent illustrates the last point well. Its political map has been twice redrawn in the course of the last fifty years. The old India was first divided on the basis of religion in 1947, and that part of it which became Pakistan was again divided on the basis of language in 1971. Similar examples can be found in the twentieth century from Africa and from central and eastern Europe.

To the extent that area study reaches beyond existing political boundaries, it provides opportunities for exploring larger and deeper historical, cultural and social identities. There is a sense in which South Asia represents an enduring civilizational unity, transcending the political divisions and partitions of the recent past. To take a specific example, we get a better understanding of caste by seeing it not simply as an institution specific to Hindus in present-day India but, more broadly, as an expression of pan-Indian civilization which has left its marks also on Muslims, Buddhists and others in Pakistan, Sri Lanka and elsewhere (Leach 1960).

At the same time, we have to acknowledge that the geographical unity of an area, no matter how skilfully selected, can never do full justice to the complexities of history, society and culture. The population of each area will not only be internally divided in many ways, but there will always be important unities and linkages between populations in different, and not necessarily geographically adjacent, areas. If it is true that civilizations have boundaries, it is also true that those boundaries are highly porous. The fabric of society is made up of networks of relations that easily overstep geographical and political boundaries, and much more so at present than at any time in the past. In this context, to adopt a rigid geographical framework in the pursuit of sociological enquiry can lead to serious distortions.

From the viewpoint of comparative sociology, the description and analysis of empirical material in conformity with the organization of area studies are matters of convenience and not matters of principle. The argument that comparisons between territorially proximate societies are always more fruitful than those between distant ones, or even the argument that the first kind of comparison must necessarily come before the second can no longer be accepted as binding. Experience has shown that in the study of human societies, differences can be as illuminating as similarities, and hence there cannot be any stringent rule restricting comparisons to societies of the same kind or of different kinds.

The contribution of area study to the development of sociology and social anthropology in the last fifty years in South Asia has been very large and very widely appreciated. It has been of special benefit to scholars from overseas, particularly the United States, who have made South Asia their chosen area of investigation. South Asian Area Studies programmes offered to anthropologists opportunities for a rigorous training in the language and history of the area in which they undertook their research. They also helped in the creation of a genuine community of scholars belonging to different countries and practising a variety of related disciplines. This endeavour succeeded best where a certain flexibility was maintained between disciplines with a certain comparative bias such as anthropology and the area studies programmes.

* * *

In the larger context of intellectual enquiry, area study may be viewed either as an end in itself or as a means to an end. For many persons, both within and outside the area, a wider and deeper understanding of the languages and religions, and of the social, political and economic arrangements in the area is a desirable theoretical and practical objective in itself. By focusing on a delimited and relatively homogeneous field of enquiry and by bringing together a range of disciplines in a more or less co-ordinated way, South Asian Area Studies programmes have greatly enhanced the understanding of an important segment of the human population.

I would like to stress a little further the international aspect of area study programmes. While the initiative for the development of those programmes came from outside, scholars from South Asia themselves soon became involved in them directly or indirectly. Much has been said and written about the comparative advantages of the study of one's own society and the study of other cultures. The experience of South Asian studies in the last fifty years has shown the advantage of a multiplicity of perspectives in the study of any complex and changing social reality. A South Asian scholar who studies his own society brings to his study a certain perspective shaped by his lived experience; it is essential for him to see how that experience appears to others who come to study the same society from afar. For a long time, the scholars who came from abroad to study South Asia came only from western countries. Now there is a growing band of Japanese and other scholars who have begun to take a serious academic interest in South Asia. Their work is bound to bring in a new dimension to the understanding of that area and must therefore be actively supported.

I take it as a great deficiency that the majority of South Asian sociologists and social anthropologists study only their own society whereas their American and European, and now increasingly also their Japanese, counterparts study their own as well as other societies. I believe that the understanding of their own society and culture among Indian sociologists would be enriched if more of them studied African, European and other Asian societies at first hand. There are financial and other organizational constraints that are difficult to overcome in a poor country where funding for social science research is meagre. But there is also the established habit of work, a kind of mental inertia that keeps the attention of Indian sociologists focused on their own world to such an extent that few of them have ventured into other regions of their country than the ones to which they belong.

Area study may also be viewed as a means toward the general and comparative study of human societies, their structures, their processes and their institutions. It is not necessary for every sociologist to make a particular society or a particular geographical area the main focus of his attention. Instead of being interested primarily in South Asia, the Middle East or Central Europe, he may have a special interest in family, marriage and kinship, in status, class and inequality, or in some other aspect of society, and expect to further his understanding of it by means of general and comparative enquiry. It will not be good for the health of Indian sociology if all Indian sociologists study only their own society, and none studies some other societies or some particular aspect of human societies in general. My own interest has tended to oscillate between the understanding of Indian society of which I am a member and the study of the tension between the ideal of equality and the practice of inequality which I believe to be a feature of all modern societies everywhere.

Sociology, in the sense that I have given to the term, has two sides, an empirical and a theoretical side, the latter being taken to include concepts and methods in addition to theory in the strict sense. Sociological reasoning and argument proceed by the appeal to facts, and therefore the collection, selection and arrangement of facts is indispensable to the work of the sociologist. At the same time, facts do not speak for themselves. It is not enough to accumulate more and more facts; there also has to be a development and refinement of theory to enable those facts to be put to the best and most efficient use. As I have argued elsewhere (Béteille 1996), sociology is different from common sense, and what makes it different is not simply its access to more abundant facts but also its command over more systematic theory.

On the empirical side, there has been a steady advance in the last fifty years in the study of South Asian society in general and of Indian society in particular. As I have already indicated, these empirical studies were given added impetus by the establishment of the South Asian Area Studies programmes outside India, by the coming in of able and talented scholars from America and Europe, and by their association with their Indian counterparts. The influential journal, *Contributions to Indian Sociology*, which began publication in Paris in 1957, soon moved to Delhi, from where it has been published for the last thirty years.

There was a great wave of village studies in India in the decades immediately following independence. A large number of scholars from India and abroad began to undertake intensive case studies of individual villages in the different parts of the country. The anthropologists took the lead in this, but they were soon followed by political scientists, economists, geographers, historians and others. The village came to be seen as a microcosm in which the principal features of the macrocosm of the wider world were reflected. Although it provided a convenient unit of enquiry and investigation, the Indian village is not and never was a completely isolated or self-sufficient unit; and social anthropologists began to explore the networks through which villages were linked to each other and the world beyond.

A major advance in Indian studies came about as a result of the shift from the 'book-view' to the 'field-view' of Indian society and culture. This shift was strongly advocated by M.N. Srinivas who regarded fieldwork as indispensable not only for collecting reliable empirical material but also for training young scholars in the craft of sociology. India has a very old and a very impressive intellectual tradition, but that tradition assigned very unequal values to the formal and the empirical disciplines. While India's intellectual achievements in such disciplines as mathematics, grammar, logic and metaphysics were outstanding, there was no comparable achievement in history, geography, or disciplines based on the systematic observation and description of facts. The field-view of Indian society was in that sense a new departure in the intellectual life of the country.

The field-view created a new perception not only of the Indian village but also of caste and the joint family. It challenged the received wisdom about these important features of Indian society and destroyed long-established stereotypes. The book-view of Indian society presented an idealized picture of its institutions—marriage, family, kinship, caste and religion—dwelling more on what they were supposed to be than on how they actually worked. The field-view revealed the gap everywhere between the ideal and the actual. By bringing to attention ambiguities, contradictions and conflicts, it paved the way for a better understanding of the dynamics of social change. The idea of an unchanging and immutable society began to give way, and the field-view changed not only the perception of India's present, but to some extent also the perception of its past.

The book-view had represented caste in terms of the invariant and immutable scheme of the four *varnas*. Field studies shifted attention away from the four-fold scheme of *varnas* to the operative units of the system which were the innumerable *jatis*. They also drew attention to the ambiguities of caste ranking and the very distinctive process of caste mobility. Through their field studies, social anthropologists and sociologists were the first to draw attention to the declining role of caste in religion and to its increasing role in politics. Empirical investigations also gradually altered the perception of the Indian family in the present as well as the past.

In this way, many different aspects of Indian society and culture began to be systematically explored. Rural and urban communities of different sizes and degrees of complexity were studied. The major institutions of kinship, religion, economics and politics were examined. In more recent years, attention has shifted to modern organizations and institutions such as factories, trade unions, schools, laboratories and hospitals. Virtually every aspect of contemporary Indian society has been brought under scrutiny by sociologists and social anthropologists. If we look at what we know about Indian society and culture today and compare it with what we knew about them fifty years ago, we cannot but be struck by the difference.

When they look at the empirical side of their work, Indian sociologists and social anthropologists feel a justifiable pride in the advances made in their discipline in the last fifty years. When, on the other hand, they look at the theoretical side of their work, they find that there has been little innovation in concepts, methods and theories during the period of the great advance in empirical work. As far as sociology is concerned, South Asian study has grown mainly as a field for the application of concepts, methods and theories developed in other places, generally for other purposes. This disjunction between the theoretical and the empirical sides of their work is a continuing source of anxiety to many Indian sociologists. It affects not only their research but also, and even more acutely, their teaching. In virtually every Indian university department of sociology, courses are offered in the sociology of India and in sociological theory, and there is almost everywhere a yawning gap between the two sets of courses.

Many Indian sociologists feel that the dependence on borrowed concepts, borrowed methods and borrowed theories has distorted their understanding of their own society and culture. Some of them would advocate the replacement of what they call the 'western' framework of sociology by an alternative framework more in tune with India's own intellectual tradition. I must make it clear that that is not how I view the matter. The tradition of sociological enquiry is a *new* tradition, not only in South Asia but also in Europe. In the world as it is today, all sociologists, no matter where they live or work, have something to contribute to this new tradition, provided they take their vocation seriously. It is now too late in the day to label the mainstream of sociology as western sociology, and to set about developing an Indian sociology for India, an Indonesian sociology for Indonesia, and a Japanese sociology for Japan.

It is impossible to find a recipe for being creative or innovative in the domain of theory. One may nevertheless attempt to identify the obstacles that stand in the way of finding something new in that domain. I will conclude by drawing attention to two such obstacles, of which the first has to do with the work practices of Indian and, more generally, South Asian scholars, and the second with the international division of labour between sociology, social anthropology and area studies.

As I have already indicated, very few Indian, or for that matter other South Asian, sociologists have ventured to make empirical studies of European or even other Asian societies. There have been a few exceptions, but they have been too few to have made a serious impact on the practices of the discipline in either their own country or outside. This almost exclusive concentration on the study of their own society has tended to make Indian sociologists at the same time diffident and aggressive. Because they have little direct familiarity with the operation of social processes and institutions in other countries, they are diffident in arguments about concepts, methods and theories that have a general as against a purely Indian source or application. But it also makes them aggressive in arguments with sociologists from other countries who, they say, can never really understand how Indian society works. Some take the extreme position that the Indian sociologist has to be an Indian first and then a sociologist; needless to say, I deplore such a position as being antithetical to the serious pursuit of the truth.

The international division of labour has on the whole acted against the unity of sociology and social anthropology, no matter how strongly that unity may have been asserted in principle. In this respect at least, the Indian practice has been more healthy than the European and American practices, for I believe very firmly that there should be one single general and comparative science of society. Unfortunately, some of the existing practices of sociology, social anthropology and area studies discourage the development of such a unified discipline devoted to the study of human societies everywhere by a community of scholars belonging to all parts of the world.

Centres for South Asian Area Studies in America and Europe bring together a variety of disciplines such as history, economics, political sciences, geography and anthropology. In my experience, the one discipline that is conspicuous by its absence, particularly in the United States, is sociology. It does not appear reasonable to me that inter-disciplinary programmes that bring together social anthropology and geography, or social anthropology and political science, should keep apart social anthropology and sociology. Despite its many advances in the methods and techniques of research, much of contemporary American sociology seems to be theoretically flawed by reason of its exclusive preoccupation with the study of one single type of society. One can only hope that the rest of the world will not follow this unfortunate example of putting into watertight compartments the study of advanced societies and the study of backward societies, or the study of one's own society and the study of other societies. If area study reinforces the tendency of Indian sociologists to study only Indian society, or if it encourages Japanese sociologists to study only Japan, leaving entirely to others the study of other societies, then it will have played only a limited and even a retrograde role. But there is no reason why it should do so, for it is open to sociologists and social anthropologists in each country to decide for themselves the terms of their own collaboration and of their collaboration with those engaged in area studies.

References

Béteille, A. 1990. *Some Observations on the Comparative Method*. Amsterdam: CASA, see chapter 4, this volume.

————. 1996. 'Sociology and Common Sense'. *Economic and Political Weekly*. Vol. xxxi. Nos. 35–7, pp. 2361–5, see chapter 1, this volume.

Durkheim, É. 1982. *The Rules of Sociological Method*. London: Macmillan.

Erikson, R. and J.H. Goldthorpe. 1992. *The Constant Flux*. Oxford: Clarendon Press.

Fortes, M. and E.E. Evans-Pritchard (eds). 1940. *African Political Systems*. London: Oxford University Press.

Goody, J. 1990. *The Oriental, the Ancient and the Primitive*. Cambridge: Cambridge University Press.

Leach, E.R. (ed). 1960. *Aspects of Caste in South India, Ceylon and Northwest Pakistan*. Cambridge: Cambridge University Press.

Radcliffe-Brown, A.R. 1952. *Structure and Function in Primitive Society*. London: Cohen and West.

————. 1957. *A Natural Science of Society*. Glencoe: The Free Press.

————. 1958. *Method in Social Anthropology*. Chicago: University of Chicago Press.

Chapter
7

Religion as a Subject for Sociology*

I would like to discuss in this essay the sociological approach to the study of religion. My purpose will be not so much to present the principal findings established by the sociology of religion as to examine the subject from the point of view of method. I believe that the sociological study of religion brings sharply into focus certain interesting questions of approach and method, and that a discussion of these may be of wider interest in the study of society as a whole, including the study of such subjects as class, gender, nation, and, more generally, politics. I have in mind particularly the comparative advantages of approaches that favour detachment, objectivity and value-neutrality as against those that favour commitment, engagement and partisanship.

We cannot take it for granted that simply because religion exists, it will be considered a suitable subject for sociology by all concerned. Some proponents of the materialist interpretation of history might treat it lightly on the ground that it can tell us little about the basic and hard realities of economic and political life; or, they might take it into account only in so far as it is implicated in politics, say, in the form of communalism. But others might deny a claim on it not because they consider religion unimportant but because they consider it too important a subject for sociology; that is sometimes the case in societies governed by a strong religious authority.

I have spoken of the sociological approach to the study of religion in the

*I am grateful to Rabi Ray and Ramachandra Guha for their comments on an earlier draft.

singular, but one can easily point out that there are several such approaches that differ among themselves. I would not like to narrow the scope of the discussion unduly, and would like, moreover, to take into account the works not only of sociologists such as Durkheim and Weber but also of social anthropologists such as Radcliffe-Brown and Evans-Pritchard.

There are many differences among the scholars who work within the field of the sociology of religion. One has only to mention together the names of Durkheim and Weber, the two most prominent figures in the field, to be reminded of these differences. The field has, moreover, expanded enormously since their time, and, with this expansion, further differentiation has come into being. Some scholars have devoted themselves to the study of 'world religions' such as Christianity, Hinduism and Islam;[1] others have studied religion among the simplest communities of hunter-gatherers, pastoralists and shifting cultivators (Radcliffe-Brown 1922, Evans-Pritchard 1956). There have been evolutionists, functionalists, structuralists and many others among the sociologists who have undertaken the study of religion. Nevertheless, certain common elements of approach and method are taken for granted when religion is made a subject for sociology. These common elements stand out when we compare the sociological study of religion with the study of it in other branches of learning.

* * *

Religion has been a subject of study and reflection for a very long time. The sociology of religion is, by contrast, a very young subject; or, if one prefers, a young branch of an old subject. It is necessary to stress the diversity of approaches to the study of religion in order to highlight the distinctive features of the sociological approach to it.

The oldest branch of study devoted to religion, and at least in the Christian tradition by far the most important one for many centuries, is theology. Divinity schools occupied a prominent place in medieval European universities such as Paris, Oxford and Cambridge, and continued to do so until recent times. Theological studies have occupied an important place also in the Judaic and Islamic intellectual traditions. The theological approach has undergone important changes in the twentieth century, particularly in the west, but it still retains a certain identity, and, in its pure form, it presents the sharpest possible contrast to the sociological approach to the study of religion.

Then there is the philosophy of religion which now occupies some of the ground held previously by theology. The philosophy of religion looks to theology on one side and the psychology of religion on the other. We have also the very broad and assorted body of work that carries the label of the history of religions.[2] We come finally to the anthropological and sociological approaches to the study of the subject; although they are treated separately by some, I will in what follows treat the two together.

In drawing attention to the varieties of approaches to the study of religion, it is not my intention to argue that there are or should be rigid boundaries between disciplines. Such boundaries do not exist, and are neither necessary nor desirable. David Hume, who wrote incisively on religion (Hume 1957, 1980), was not only a celebrated philosopher but also an historian. His contemporary and friend Edward Gibbon wrote about religion mainly as an historian (Gibbon 1910, esp. vol. 2), but what he wrote is permeated by philosophical and, indeed, sociological insight. *The Varieties of Religious Experience* by William James is a landmark both in the philosophy and in the psychology of religion (James 1961). Such examples could be multiplied almost indefinitely.

It is easy enough to arrange the various approaches on a continuum in such a way that one can pass from one approach to the next without any clear or noticeable break. But it is necessary also to make distinctions. I would like to begin with the distinction between normative and empirical—or, if one prefers, judgemental and non-judgemental—approaches to religious phenomena. The theologian is concerned primarily with questions of truth and rectitude in religious beliefs and practices. Such questions do not concern the sociologist in the same way; his primary concern is to observe, describe, interpret and explain the manner in which religious beliefs and practices operate. An important question from the viewpoint of method, to which I will return later, is how deeply it is necessary to be concerned with questions of truth and rectitude if one is interested in the description and analysis of religious beliefs and practices. The same question arises with regard to other systems of belief and practice, and the answers that we give to it must be consistent from one domain to another.

The distinction between the normative and the empirical orientations comes out most clearly in the contrast between the theological and the sociological approaches to the study of religion. It is no accident that, historically, the sociological approach came into its own with the decline of the theological approach. So long as the study of religion was governed by religious faith, there could be little room in it for sociology. The sociology of religion may in this sense be regarded as the offspring of religious scepticism and agnosticism, if not of atheism.

In a symposium on sacrifice, conducted jointly by anthropologists and theologians, the Jesuit priest M.F.C. Bourdillon put it thus,

When an anthropologist studies the moral values of a culture or a society, his aim is to try to understand them independently of the values of his own or any other culture. . . . It is, on the other hand, extremely rare to find a Christian theologian who does not hold that his discipline is concerned with ideals for living (In Bourdillon and Fortes 1980: 4).

The atmosphere of religious discussion, particularly in the Christian world, has altered enormously between the end of the nineteenth century and the present, so that theologians and social theorists are more prepared to learn from, or at least to listen to, each other. But this should not lead us to obliterate the distinction between an orientation to the subject that is grounded in religious scepticism and one that is grounded in religious faith. This distinction was presented sharply from the former viewpoint by Meyer Fortes, one of the two editors of the symposium volume (ibid.: v–xix).

There are two important features of the sociological approach—both common to sociology and social anthropology—on which I would like to make a few observations. The first is the extensive use of the comparative method, and the second is the investigation of religious beliefs, practices and institutions in relation to other aspects of society and culture.

The comparative method is central to the discipline of sociology and, as such, to the sociology of religion. As Émile Durkheim, one of the key figures in the subject, wrote, 'Comparative sociology is not a special branch of sociology; it is sociology itself' (Durkheim 1982: 157). Radcliffe-Brown, who was a follower of Durkheim, spoke of social anthropology as comparative sociology. This of course does not mean that sociologists devote themselves only to comparisons between different religious systems. In fact, most sociologists and social anthropologists spend most of their time in making detailed studies of particular religions, and both Durkheim and Radcliffe-Brown are best known for their case studies, of the Australian Aborigines by the first and the Andaman Islanders by the second (Durkheim 1915, Radcliffe-Brown 1922). But the case studies do not stand by themselves; they derive their significance from the comparative perspective that is characteristic of the discipline as a whole.

Both Durkheim and Radcliffe-Brown believed that the application of the comparative method would enable them to discover general laws about society and its institutions, including its religious institutions. They believed that sociology and social anthropology could be developed in the manner of the natural sciences. Their strategy was to proceed in a systematic way through observation, description and comparison to generalization (Durkheim 1982, Radcliffe-Brown 1957). We now have, as a result, a large body of data on religious beliefs and practices from all parts of the world.

The accumulation of such a large body of systematic data has certainly advanced our knowledge and understanding of religion, but it has not led to the discovery of the kind of general laws that Durkheim and Radcliffe-Brown had hoped to discover. What then is left of the comparative method? The comparative method remains of great value because it forces a certain discipline that does not come naturally to us when we examine the varieties of social life. It forces us to give equal consideration, at least in certain respects and for certain purposes, to all societies irrespective of our personal engagements. In that sense, the comparative method brings all societies on a level with each other; it does not admit of any privileged exception. This goes against our ingrained habits of mind when we are dealing with human societies, and particularly when our subject of study is religion. If fair-mindedness is a virtue in the study of society and culture, then the comparative method is an indispensable aid in the cultivation of that virtue.

We have to distinguish between the aspirations of the comparative method and its achievements. Where individual or collective biases were thrown out by the front door, they sometimes crept in through the back door. For Durkheim and his generation, the comparative method went hand in hand with a belief in the theory of evolution. Hence, while all religions might be investigated by the same method, some were regarded as more evolved or more elevated than others. Weber too differentiated among religions according to their degree of rationalization, placing primitive magical practices at one end and protestant Christianity at the other. Evolutionary theories are no longer as popular as in the past, but this does not mean that personal or ethnocentric bias has been completely eliminated from the sociological study of religion.

Theology stands at the opposite end of sociology in its orientation to the plurality of religions. At least in its classical form, its concern was with a particular religion which it singled out for special attention. There was thus Christian theology—and within it Protestant theology and Catholic theology—or Judaic theology or Islamic theology. Theology will defeat its original purpose if it places all religions on the same plane, for that purpose was to establish the truth of one religion and expose the errors of others. The theologian writes about religion from within; it is difficult to think of a Christian who is an Islamic theologian or of a Hindu who is a Christian theologian. Again, as Bourdillon has put it, 'Theologians are part of the tradition they study, and must be convinced that their rituals have the effects that they want them to have' (Bourdillon and Fortes 1980: 6). The sociologist, on the other hand, approaches religions from the outside even when he seeks to understand their inner meaning.

A second important feature of the sociological approach is that it studies the facts of religion in association with other social facts. The sociological approach, as I understand it, not only does not privilege one's own religion as against other religions, it also does not privilege the religious domain among the various domains of social life. In the sociological perspective, no matter how important the religious life may be in itself, it cannot be made fully intelligible without being brought into relationship with domestic life, economic life and political life. The interconnection among the different institutional domains is at the centre of sociological attention.

The position is different for the theologian. For him, the religious domain is pre-eminent, in a way the only one that has real significance. He is concerned, above all, with the inner meaning of religion rather than its external or institutional manifestation, which is what engages the attention of the sociologist. This does not mean that there can be no collaboration between the theologian and the sociologist. In fact, there has been such collaboration, with very fruitful results, as in the case of Ernst Troeltsch the theologian and Max Weber the sociologist. That collaboration deserves attention, for it brings to light not only the differences of perspective, but also the possibility of a reciprocity of perspectives.

Although their intellectual interests overlapped, Weber stressed the differences in orientation between himself and Troeltsch. Despite his considerable erudition in matters relating to Christian doctrine, he spoke of himself as a non-expert working at second-hand, and of Troeltsch as the expert best equipped to provide an authoritative view (Mommsen and Österhammel 1987: 221). But he obviously believed that the 'non-expert' had an important part to play in clarifying the relationship of religion to economy and society, and in examining that relationship comparatively. He probably felt that, as a sociologist, he could deal better with non-Christian religions than Troeltsch whose expertise lay in the field of Christian theology (Weber 1975: 331).

Weber also took an interest in the practical side of religion through his association with the Evangelical-Social Congress. He gave his time and counsel freely to Pastor Naumann who believed that in Germany the reform of religion could not succeed without the reform of politics and, in particular, the incorporation of the working class to full citizenship. What these relationships bring out is that there are not only many kinds of sociologists but also many kinds of theologians. Not all sociologists are militant atheists or ostentatiously irreligious, and Weber certainly was neither. Nor are all theologians intransigent dogmatists, concerned only with the letter of the creed, and, indeed, Troeltsch, who was a liberal from the beginning, moved in mid-career and on his own choice from a chair in theology to one in philosophy. The point is not that no sociologist can be a religious believer and no theologian a religious sceptic, but that there are characteristic differences of orientation between sociology and theology as disciplines.

Sociological studies of religious beliefs, practices and institutions vary enormously in scope and emphasis. Some are based on the analysis of literary material relating to large populations over long stretches of time; others are based on direct observation of life in small communities. Some deal mainly with religious phenomena; others deal with them only in so far as they bear upon some other aspect of life which is the primary object of attention. There are studies of the religious life of natural communities such as the village or the tribe, and studies of specifically religious associations such as the church or the sect.

A good example of the sociological approach is the study of religion and society among the Coorgs of South India by M.N. Srinivas (1952). The principal objective of the book is to give a coherent account of a system of religious beliefs and practices in its social context. As such, it begins with an outline of social structure and then proceeds to give an account of the ritual idiom of the Coorgs. The central part of the book deals with cults of the various social units, such as household, village and region, which constitute the principal components of Coorg social structure. The book concludes with some general observations on the relationship between religion and society.

Srinivas later elaborated the distinction between the 'book-view' and the 'field-view' of society. In terms of that distinction, his work on the Coorgs gives us a field-view of Hinduism. There are innumerable accounts in the ancient, medieval and modern literature of Hinduism that tell us how religious institutions ought to work. Srinivas was less interested in discussing how they ought to work than in showing how they actually worked. Such an account might be of considerable interest to a theologian, but it is not one that the typical theologian would himself write.

In studying religion, the sociologist or social anthropologist tries to observe and describe how people act as well as to understand and interpret the meanings they assign to their acts. There are important differences of emphasis here. Durkheim, for instance, believed in attending first and foremost to the external, observable characteristics of social facts before attending to their inner meanings. In much the same vein, Radcliffe-Brown wrote in his Foreword to the book by Srinivas, 'Social anthropology is behaviouristic in the sense that we seek to observe how people act as a necessary preliminary to trying to understand how they think and feel' (Srinivas 1952: vii).

Others have placed their emphasis elsewhere. For Weber, it was always important to enquire into the meaning the actor assigned to his action in every sphere of society: what did it mean for the priest or the prophet to choose and pursue a particular way of life? And, beyond that, what meaning did the world itself have from the viewpoint of a given religion? At the same time, Weber never neglected to compare and contrast, with the maximum possible detachment, the answers given to these questions in different religious traditions. He also examined systematically and with the greatest possible care the material and other external conditions associated with various religious beliefs and practices.

Collaboration between sociologists and theologians has never been free from problems since it is never very easy to reconcile the committed and the detached points of view. Among radical social theorists, Durkheim has been represented as a conservative who assigned too much importance to religion. It is true that Durkheim assigned great importance to religion in social life and rebuked his empiricist colleagues, particularly in the Anglo-Saxon world, for treating it lightly. But for Durkheim, religion is important not because it is true but because it is useful, whereas for the theologian, the importance of religion lies in its truth and not in its utility.

The Catholic church in France viewed Durkheim's work quite differently from the way in which it has come to be viewed among sociologists. His book was attacked in a long review article by Gaston Richard, entitled 'Dogmatic Atheism in the Sociology of Religion'. Richard maintained, 'In the end, it is incontrovertible that this sociology of religion (*sociologie religieuse*), as it is called, is incompatible not only with Christian faith, but even with philosophical theism, and indeed with any belief that recognizes, hypothetically at least, a divine personality' (Richard 1975: 229). Gaston Richard was not a theologian, but had begun his career as a member of Durkheim's *Année sociologique* circle. He was, however, a believing Christian who, though born in a Catholic family, had converted to the Protestant faith. Many years later, a similar attack against Durkheim's sociology of religion was launched by another former admirer, E.E. Evans-Pritchard. Evans-Pritchard had in his religious life travelled the same road as Gaston Richard, but in the opposite direction; his father was a minister of the Protestant church, but he had found his faith by embracing Catholicism.

One of the arguments of both Richard and Evans-Pritchard was that Durkheim had overreached himself, that he was claiming too much for his sociology of religion. Evans-Pritchard, himself the author of one of the finest anthropological monographs on religion, addressed himself to this very difficult question at the end of his book. After describing what the social anthropologist is able to observe and how far he is able to proceed towards an understanding of the inner meaning of what he observes, he concluded, 'At this point the theologian takes over from the anthropologist' (Evans-Pritchard 1956: 322).

But Evans-Pritchard did not rest content for very long with the division of labour that he seemed to be proposing between anthropology and theology at the end of his book on Nuer religion. With the passage of time, he became increasingly sceptical about the contribution that social anthropology and sociology could make to the understanding of religion. In his Aquinas lecture, delivered before a Catholic audience, he launched an attack on anthropological studies of religion, accusing their authors of bad faith (Evans-Pritchard 1962: 29–45). A little later, he repeated the same attack on sociological theories of religion, accusing Durkheim of having roughly the same perspective on religion as Marx and Engels (Evans-Pritchard 1965: ch 3).

Evans-Pritchard's later writings on religion reveal a very great anthropologist in a very poor light. I allude to them not out of ill will, but in order to suggest that there might be a possible connection between his increasing attachment to the Catholic faith and his growing disaffection with the sociology of religion. His own early essay, 'Zande Theology', of 1936 was a masterly demonstration of how such a meticulous observer as the Dominican priest Mgr. Lagae had arranged his ethnographic facts to fit a theologically convenient argument, creating a religious doctrine where none existed (Evans-Pritchard 1952: 162–203). He had begun from the position that social anthropologists and sociologists must not claim that they can tell us everything about religion; in course of time, he found such claims as they were making to be increasingly intolerable; in the end, he came very close to the position that they can tell us nothing about religion in the true sense of the term, or at least nothing of any real value.

The sociology of religion always, and perhaps necessarily, comes to grief when it moves beyond its proper empirical concerns under the urge to decide on the truth or otherwise of a religious doctrine. Whether or not Ram was the ideal man; whether Mohammed was a true or a false prophet; and whether Christ died in vain or for the redemption of mankind are questions that are beyond the purview of the sociology of religion in the sense given to it here. But that does not mean that it has nothing of interest to say about the place of religion in man's social life.

* * *

I now return to Max Weber and, in the light of his work, make some general observations on approach and method in social enquiry. It is Max Weber's sociology of religion, more than anyone else's, that has lessons to offer for sociology as a whole from the viewpoint of method.

There is something paradoxical about the life and work of Max Weber— his concern with meaning and understanding on the one hand, and with objectivity and value-neutrality on the other. Weber had very little patience for the kind of natural science of society that fascinated Durkheim; he argued untiringly for an interpretive sociology. He produced an enormous body of work on religion; yet he declared that he was 'absolutely unmusical religiously'.[3] Surely, it is not unreasonable to ask of a proponent of interpretive sociology how far a person who is religiously unmusical can go in the interpretation of religion?

No one who declares himself to be religiously unmusical can possibly claim that he understands the whole of religion. But is it necessary for the sociologist of religion to make such a claim? That kind of claim will be made only by those who maintain that we must first grasp the whole— or the totality—if we are to understand any of its parts. Weber, it seems to me, would be deeply mistrustful of such a claim. Most persons in fact understand some bits of life, but few would claim that they understand the whole of its inner meaning.

Weber's account of himself as 'absolutely unmusical religiously' has to be seen in the light of the stand that he took on objectivity and value-neutrality. Value-neutrality in the study of religion does not mean of course that one ignores the part played by values in social life; that would be quite contrary to the spirit of interpretive sociology. It only means that it should be possible, at least in principle, to understand religious institutions, religious beliefs and religious practices from the outside, without becoming personally committed to the values by which they are sustained within a given religious faith. The understanding and interpretation of, for example, Islamic, or Hindu, or Christian institutions does not require any moral commitment to the values of Islam or Hinduism or Christianity. Or, as Weber might put it, 'One need not have been Caesar in order to understand Caesar' (Weber 1978: 5).

Most contemporary social theorists would probably agree that one does not have to adhere to the tenets of a particular religion in order to understand the institutions of that religion; the work of Max Weber stands as a living testimony to that. Indeed, they would probably recommend a healthy dose of religious scepticism and detachment to those who would make religion a subject of sociology. The problem today does not lie there, but elsewhere. If it is possible to understand and interpret religious beliefs and practices while being 'religiously unmusical', is it also possible to understand and interpret political processes and institutions while being 'politically unmusical'? The great debates in social theory that divide those who subscribe to objectivity, detachment and value-neutrality from those who recommend commitment, engagement and partisanship are today not about religion but about politics. At the same time, the lessons that social theorists learn from the study of religion cannot be altogether without value for the study of politics.

No matter what sociologists might agree to about the study of religion, many of them would question the advantage to be derived from objectivity, detachment and value-neutrality in the study of such secular subjects as class, gender and nation. They would say that it is only through commitment to a specific set of moral values—and even a specific political project—that true insight into these problems can be attained. Commitment, according to their argument, is desirable not only from the moral and political, but also from the intellectual point of view. The attempt to separate 'methodology' from 'ideology',[4] they would say, is both disingenuous and self-defeating.

The theoretical foundations of the argument for commitment in social enquiry are to be found in the writings of Marx[5] and certain Marxists, such as Lukacs (1971), Korsch (1970), and Gramsci (1971), particularly in regard to the study of class. In all these writings, a kind of privileged place is assigned to the 'viewpoint of the proletariat'. The position adopted there is that other representations of bourgeois society are incomplete and, hence, distorted and false; only the viewpoint of the proletariat provides access to a complete and, hence, historically true picture of reality.

In an influential essay designed to demolish the foundations of 'value-free' social science, Lukacs put forward the case for a method whose central proposition was the unity of theory and practice (Lukacs 1971, esp. the first essay). Similar arguments were put forward at about the same time by Korsch, Gramsci and others.[6] Their approach offered new insights into class structure, consciousness and ideology, politics and a host of other subjects. More than that, they put many of the proponents of a value-free sociology on the defensive with their far-reaching claims about what could be achieved, both theoretically and practically, by the method they advocated.

Lukacs and others have maintained that there is no way in which true understanding of social processes can be reached except through an insight into the totality, an insight that comes, moreover, only when theory is combined with practice. Sociologists and social anthropologists have learnt to be wary of that kind of claim in regard to the understanding of religion. Why should they yield to its temptations in regard to the understanding of politics?

It can of course be said that in the modern world, politics is altogether different from religion in so far as no one can remain truly indifferent to the demands of politics whereas it is possible, and sometimes even desirable, to distance oneself from religion, although that point of view will hardly find favour with the theologian. The attack on detachment, objectivity and value-neutrality has often been made on the ground that the claims of their proponents are disingenuous since it is impossible in reality to be wholly neutral on fundamental political questions, and, therefore, those who profess to be so are in fact promoting a particular cause or a particular interest under the cover of neutrality. At the same time, I remain unconvinced that it is in principle either easier or more desirable to seek neutrality on matters of religious faith than on matters of political ideology.

It is undoubtedly the case that neutrality does not come naturally or effortlessly to us in the understanding and interpretation of our own beliefs, practices and institutions. Therefore, to require or expect the investigator to 'treat social facts as things' might indeed appear somewhat disingenuous. But that does not mean that the effort itself to achieve neutrality is misconceived. And if my argument is right, it is here that the sociology of politics—of the nation, class and gender—may have something to learn from the sociology of religion.

There are two lessons in particular to which I would like to draw attention in conclusion. The first is that value-neutrality, no matter how desirable in principle, is very difficult to achieve in practice, what is achieved being always incomplete. The exponents of value-neutrality do not all assert that the separation of fact and value is easy to maintain in a consistent way; some do and others do not. Here there appears to be a fundamental difference between what, for want of better terms, I will call 'scientific' sociology as against 'interpretive' sociology. The exponents of the former, among whom we may include Durkheim, or at least the author of *The Rules of Sociological Method*, tend to treat the problem lightly and to suggest that anyone can solve it provided he has the right 'method'. But the exponents of interpretive sociology do not in general take that view. They do not suggest that there is any simple recipe for success in the task which they rather see as being constantly at risk. Max Weber raised and answered the general question as follows: 'Nor need I discuss further whether the distinction between empirical statements of fact and value-judgements is 'difficult' to make. It is.' (1949: 9)

Not only is the practice of detachment, objectivity and value-neutrality difficult, but those who undertake it never achieve complete success in their endeavour. This is true no less in regard to politics than it is in regard to religion. It makes the proponents of value-neutrality permanently vulnerable to allegations of bad faith and duplicity. But failure to achieve complete success in practice cannot be a compelling reason for discarding a principle. Here I will quote what Maxime Rodinson, at one time a leading Marxist intellectual, wrote at the end of his celebrated biography of the prophet Mohammed: 'But even if pure objectivity is unattainable, it would be a sophism to suggest that it was necessary instead to be deliberately partial' (1973: 312–13). To me it does not seem accidental that a Marxist chose to be objective rather than partial when he made religion the subject of his study; but Rodinson was an exception, and not very typical of his generation of Marxists.

The second lesson that we learn from the sociology of religion is that sociology cannot provide a complete picture of the world as a whole in terms of either fact or value. Here again, sociology stands at the opposite end from theology, at least in its classical form. It is constantly at odds with all those who represent the world as a unity and maintain that there is a single key, within their reach if not in their grasp, to both understanding and action. As we have seen, sociology can say something about religious beliefs, practices and institutions in different places at different times, but very little, if anything, as to whether it is better to be a Hindu, a Muslim or a Christian, a believer or an unbeliever. Likewise, it can say something about political processes and institutions, but very little of practical utility as to whether it is better to be a liberal, a conservative or a radical in politics. These latter questions may be the most important ones for a particular individual at a particular point of time, but there is no social theory that can tell him which is the best political ideology just as there is none that can tell him which is the best religious faith.

I would not like my argument to be construed to mean that a Catholic or a Communist cannot be a sociologist or that he can at best be a poor one.[7] A Catholic may indeed have certain advantages when he studies religion and a Communist when he studies politics, but it is necessary to point out that these advantages can be easily abused. It is not unlikely that those who have direct experience of religion and politics have a certain advantage, at least initially, in making sense of symbols and processes that are not immediately accessible to the external observer. But religion, politics and other aspects of social life are not merely matters of experience, they are also subjects of doctrine. A doctrine is not always the best guide to experience and may indeed be an obstacle to it.

Evans-Pritchard had reason to castigate his predecessors to the extent that they, or at least some of them, appear to have decided in advance that all religions are equally false, for one might say that that too is a doctrine. But the matter does not rest there, for it is both complex and delicate. What really disturbed Evans-Pritchard was the relativism that followed from the successes of comparative studies of language, myth and religion. 'This pointed to a relativism in which Christianity was not the one true faith but just one religion among others, all equally false' (Evans-Pritchard 1962: 35). He paid a back-handed compliment to Max Muller for treading warily on that ground, presumably because he did not wish to fall foul of the Bishop of Gloucester who 'had already condemned attempts "to put into competition the sacred books of India and the Holy Scriptures"' (ibid.).

It should now be clear why I regard the matter to be both complex and delicate. While no one can hope to understand the meaning and significance of a religious belief or practice unless he approaches his subject with concern and sympathy, it is never very easy to decide how much of the concern and sympathy is due to the desire for understanding and how much of it to the fear of a bishop or some other religious authority. Parallels will not be difficult to find from the domain of politics. While studies of, say, the nation or the working class undoubtedly benefit from a sympathetic concern for the subject, it sometimes happens that the concern and the sympathy are mainly concessions to the demands of the state and the party.

Being religiously unmusical is not the same thing as being hostile or even unsympathetic to religion; being sceptical about the historical mission of the proletariat (or of oppressed minorities) need not deprive one of the capacity for concern and sympathy for their predicament. But sympathy and concern need not lead to the adoption of any particular doctrine in either religion or politics. Again, if one asks if it is easy to combine sympathy and concern for one's subject with detachment and objectivity, the answer is that it is not.

The demand for objectivity in the social sciences is most typically made in the name of intellectual rigour. To treat social facts as things is to place oneself on the same footing with them that the physicist or the biologist secures with respect to the facts that he or she investigates. Here objectivity is viewed as the separability of the investigator from the object of investigation, and the clearer the separation, the greater the presumed gain for intellectual rigour. But the facts of religion and politics are different, and have to be treated differently from the material facts investigated by the physicist or the biologist. In dealing with them, as in dealing with human beings generally, we have to be governed by considerations not merely of intellectual rigour but also of fairness.

The virtue of defining objectivity as fairness is most manifest in the comparative study of religion. The Catholic anthropologist has a right to demand of a person who studies Catholicism that he should approach his subject with respect; but he spoils his case by being peevish in the face of attempts to deal even-handedly with the Gita and the Bible.

Without any prejudice to what is due to rigour and precision, I would like to stress the perennial need in social enquiry for objectivity as fairness. It is this need for fairness in presenting, or at least taking into account, different points of view that gives to social enquiry its distinctive character. The hardest part of self-discipline in it is that which is due to the demand for fairness. For it is not simply that the same subject appears different when observed from different points of view, but, further, that the viewpoint of the observer must be constantly matched with that of the actor. The sociologist can at best bring these various points of view into the open, and present the case for each one of them to the best of his ability. He can be candid about his own values; but he cannot set himself up as a judge where questions of ultimate value, those of his subjects as well as of other observers, are at issue.

Notes

1. Max Weber is the most notable exponent. Apart from his well-known *The Protestant Ethic and the Spirit of Capitalism* (1930), there are *The Religion of China* (1951), *Ancient Judaism* (1952), and *The Religion of India* (1958).

2. This approach is well represented in the journal, *History of Religions*, published by the University of Chicago Press; see also Eliade; 1982.

3. In a letter dated 19 February 1909, quoted in Marianne Weber, (1975: 324), he wrote, 'It is true that I am absolutely unmusical religiously and have no need or ability to erect any psychic edifices of a religious character within me. But a thorough self-examination has told me that I am neither antireligious nor irreligious'.

4. Here I use the term 'ideology' in a broad sense; for an attempt to give the term a more precise meaning see, Béteille 2000: 11–33.

5. The most famous expression of this view is in 'The Theses on Feuerbach', written by Marx in 1845, first published by Engels in an edited form in 1888, and now available in various editions.

6. Outside of orthodox Marxism, but always sympathetic to it is Jean-Paul Sartre (1963).

7. The argument has been made in the past that a Marxist cannot or even should not be a sociologist. See for instance, Goldmann, 1957. See also Appendix II, this volume.

References

Béteille, André. 2000. *Autinomics of Society*. Delhi: Oxford University Press.

Bourdillon, M.F.C. and M. Fortes (eds). 1980. *Sacrifice*. London: Academic Books.

Durkheim, Émile. 1915. *The Elementary Forms of the Religious Life*. London: Allen and Unwin.

———. 1982. *The Rules of Sociological Method*. London: Macmillan.

Eliade, Mircea. 1982. *A History of Religious Ideas*. Chicago: University of Chicago Press, 2 vols.

Evans-Pritchard, E.E. 1956. *Nuer Religion*. Oxford: Clarendon Press.

———. 1962. *Essays in Social Anthropology*. London: Faber and Faber.

———. 1965. *Theories of Primitive Religion*. Oxford: Clarendon Press.

Gibbon, Edward. 1910. *A History of the Decline and Fall of the Roman Empire*. London: Dent, 6 vols.

Gramsci, A. 1971. *Selections from the Prison Notebooks*. New York: International Publishers.

Goldmann, Lkcien. 1957. 'Y a-t-il une sociologic marxiste?', *Les temps modernes*, no. 140: 720–51.

Hume, David. 1957. *The Natural History of Religion*. Stanford: Stanford University Press.

———. 1980. *Discourses Concerning Natural Religion*. Indianapolis: Hackett Publishing Co.

James, William. 1961. *The Varieties of Religious Experience*. London: Macmillan.

Korsch, K. 1970. *Marxism and Philosophy*. New York: MR.

Lukacs, G. 1971. *History and Class Consciousness*. London: Merlin Press.

Mommsen, Wolfgang J. and Jurgen Österhammel (eds). 1987. *Max Weber and his Contemporaries*. London: Allen and Unwin.

Radcliffe-Brown, A.R. 1922. *The Andaman Islanders*. Cambridge: Cambridge University Press.

———. 'Foreword'. In M.N. Srinivas. 1952. *Religion and Society among the Coorgs of South India*. Oxford: Clarendon Press.

———. 1957. *A Natural Science of Society*. Glencoe: The Free Press.

Richard, Gaston. 1975. 'Dogmatic Atheism in the Sociology of Religion'. In W.E.S. Pickering (ed.). *Durkheim on Religion*. London: Routledge and Kegan Paul.

Rodinson, Maxime. 1973. *Mohammed*. Harmondsworth: Penguin Books.

Sartre, Jean-Paul. 1963. *Search for a Method*. New York: Alfred Knopf.

Srinivas, M.N. 1952. *Religion and Society among the Coorgs of South India*. Oxford: Clarendon Press.

Weber, Marianne. 1975. *Max Weber, A Biography*. New York: John Wiley.

Weber, Max. 1930. *The Protestant Ethic and the Spirit of Capitalism*. London: Allen and Unwin.

———. 1949. *The Methodology of the Social Sciences*. New York: The Free Press.

———. 1951. *The Religion of China*. Glencoe: The Free Press.

———. 1952. *Ancient Judrism*. Glencoe: The Free Press.

———. 1958. *The Religion of India*. Glencoe: The Free Press.

———. 1978. *Economy and Society*. Berkeley: University of California Press.

Politics as a Subject for Sociology*

I n most contemporary societies, politics is a subject of general interest
to large sections of the population. Indeed, it is expected in a
democracy that the citizen should take an informed interest in politics,
at least when an election is announced, a government falls, or a cabinet
is reshuffled. Nowadays, even when the general population appears to
show signs of fatigue, the interest in politics is kept alive by the media.
Certainly in India, the press gives more coverage to politics than to most
other aspects of social life; and television has, within a short span of
time, created a new class of experts who may be aptly described as political
pundits.

My concern in the present essay is less with the occasional interest in
politics or with day-to-day commentaries on its course and development
than with the disciplined and systematic study of the subject over an
extended period of time. The kind of enquiry and investigation I have in
mind addresses itself to such questions as: What is politics, and what are
its various forms? What are the actions, relations and institutions in and
through which it operates in various places and at various times? Further,

*This paper is based on a lecture given at Chandigarh on 10 September 1999 at the
ICSSR North-Western Regional Centre. I am grateful to Professor Swarnjit Mehta, its
Honorary Director, for inviting me to give the lecture and to the many members of the
audience whose questions have helped me to clarify my own ideas. I am also grateful to
Dr Abhijit Dasgupta, Professor Vinay Srivastava and Professor Virginius Xaxa for their
comments on an earlier draft of the paper.

and even more crucial from my point of view: How far is politics an autonomous sphere of activity? How does it act upon the rest of society, and how is it in turn acted upon by it? What I wish to stress here is the difference of orientation between social and political theory on the one hand and political journalism on the other, although, to be sure, there have been writers such as Raymond Aron—and to some extent Max Weber before him—who have excelled in both.

In common parlance, the term 'politics' stands first and foremost for a certain process, what may be called the action in politics; it has also acquired a somewhat unsavoury connotation in current usage. But the term is used here in a broader sense and without any judgement as to the moral value of politics as a form of action. The emphasis is not so much on political action as such as on the social framework in which that action takes place. This is to some extent dictated by the very wide comparative perspective in which the field is surveyed. I certainly wish to avoid the impression that what I mean by 'politics' is to be found only in democratic or in 'advanced' societies.

Sociology is not the only academic discipline engaged in the study of politics, nor have all sociologists shown the same interest in its systematic study. For sociologists as against political scientists, politics is only one among several important subjects of study. Among the makers of modern sociology, Max Weber's interest in the study of politics was central and direct. Durkheim's interest was less direct, although he too had important observations to make about the moral basis of the authority of the state and about its contribution to the maintenance of the social order. Pareto, again, contributed substantially to the study of economy and polity as well as society.

Thus, when I speak of politics as a subject for sociology, I do not mean that all sociologists follow the same approach to its study or assign to it the same place in their general understanding of society. Sociology does not have a single body of theory or a single conception of its aims, objectives and methods, and it has often been pointed out that its subject matter is somewhat vague and at best loosely defined. Moreover, I propose to extend the scope of this discussion by considering in some detail the contributions of social anthropologists, for they have added something new to our understanding of politics in its social setting.

Compared with other disciplines engaged in the study of politics, s political philosophy and political history, sociology is a relative ner. Its beginnings as an academic discipline with a distinct orientation go back to the eighteenth century. The birth of sociology had to await the arrival of the modern age. The thinkers and writers of earlier ages had dwelt largely on such grand institutions as the church and the state, hence the greater antiquity of such disciplines as theology and political philosophy. Sociology had its first beginnings in the eighteenth century when some writers in France and in Britain decided to make society, or, if one prefers, civil society instead of the state the subject of their science.

Starting with the middle of the eighteenth century, the entire range of habits, customs, manners and institutions of human beings everywhere and at all times began to be made open for systematic enquiry and investigation. It is not that state and church were excluded from the purview of such studies, but, increasingly, they came to be treated along with the various other institutions of society in a naturalistic or matter-of-fact way. Although their own work was introspective and speculative to a large extent, the matter-of-fact approach of Montesquieu and the Scottish moral philosophers paved the way for more systematic empirical investigations by their successors in the nineteenth and twentieth centuries.

From the point of view of the present discussion, Montesquieu's most eminent successor in his own country in the nineteenth century was Alexis de Tocqueville. *Democracy in America* deals not only with state and government but also with society and its institutions. While fully recognizing the importance of laws, it stresses even more the significance of customs which are described in a memorable phrase as 'the habits of the heart' (Tocqueville 1956: I, 299). Even more important, the work was based on what may be described, without too much exaggeration, as a field-view of American society. Tocqueville was a keen observer of men and affairs, and during his stay of nine months in the United States, he missed few opportunities to see how society and politics actually worked in that country.

The nineteenth century also witnessed the birth of anthropology, which devoted itself mainly to the study of the customs and institutions of primitive or pre-literate societies. Here society and its institutions could be studied without much thought being given to state and politics, because many of the earlier anthropologists believed that primitive societies were governed by custom and not law, and that they did not have political institutions in the proper sense of the term. It was only with the publication in 1940 of *African Political Systems* (Fortes and Evans-Pritchard) that the serious study of politics in the simpler societies began.

* * *

By the beginning of the twentieth century, political science, sociology and anthropology had become established as academic disciplines in the universities of Europe and America. It is well to remember that in the west, these disciplines had grown over a long period of time outside the universities before becoming established inside them. Within a very short time of their becoming university subjects in Europe and America, they found places for themselves in universities outside the west, most notably in India.

The rapid, not to say explosive growth of universities in the twentieth century was accompanied by academic specialization and the differentiation of disciplines. Fifty years ago, when the great expansion in the social sciences was about to begin in the universities and centres of research in India, sociology and political science were taught and studied separately and in different departments. Where there was no department of sociology, as at the University of Calcutta, some sociology was being taught in the department of political science, but that was of a very rudimentary nature. In the same university, politics hardly figured in either teaching or research in the department of anthropology, where I was a student in the fifties.

In its early phase of growth, the main concern of sociology in India was with the distinctive features of Indian civilization and the Indian tradition. There was considerable reliance on the classical texts, including texts relating to statecraft, in the work of the early sociologists. The main emphasis in studies of contemporary India was on its traditional institutions, such as religion, family and marriage, and, above all, caste. These studies were often speculative and they did not have very strong empirical foundations. By and large, they presented what came to be described later as the 'book-view' of Indian society in which the dynamics of power and politics had very little place.

Political science as a discipline had a somewhat different orientation in Indian universities. If there was any meeting point with sociology, it was on the plane of Indian social and political thought, and that too mainly classical thought. Otherwise, the principal focus of study was on constitutions and formal political institutions, and on international relations. To a considerable extent, the emphasis was on government rather than politics, and that too at the national and provincial levels rather than the level of the village or the local community.

Things began to change after independence with the growth of empirical research on contemporary issues and problems. Sociologists and political scientists found that they had a number of common interests in examining the interface between society and politics at various levels of organization. The inception of village studies in the fifties marked a turning point in the empirical investigation of the relationship between society and politics. Here, the social anthropologists gave the lead, but they were soon followed by political scientists, economists, historians and others who were greatly influenced by the methods of empirical research, particularly fieldwork, developed by the former (Béteille 1996: 231–51).

Intensive field studies by anthropologists in the fifties and sixties overturned the image of the Indian village as a placid and unchanging little republic. Those who observed the village at close quarters, in no matter which part of the country, generally noted the divisions and conflicts in it. They also noted that the village was in a state of ferment as a result of the changes that came in the wake of independence. Not everyone who studied the Indian village took a central interest in its political structure, but hardly anyone who lived in a village for any length of time could altogether ignore its influence on village social life.

When I went to do fieldwork in a Tanjore village in 1961, my aim was to provide an account of the system of social stratification in the village, its principal divisions and subdivisions, and their mutual relations. I did not have any specific plan to study its political life. But I soon realized that I could hardly do justice to the changing relations between caste and class without paying some attention to power and politics. In the event, the work I produced dealt at some length with the distribution of power and the pattern of politics in the village. Others who had set out to study other aspects of village life were also driven in the same direction. In addition, there were those, both political scientists and social anthropologists, who made village politics the principal focus of their studies (Retzlaff 1962; Nicholas 1968).

Social anthropologists had been trained to study all aspects of social life at the level of the small community. They had not been trained to study large-scale political systems at the regional or national level, or specialized political institutions such as legislatures and parties. Those among them who stumbled on to the importance of politics in the course of their fieldwork soon realized that, at least in India, village politics could not be understood in isolation from district politics and state politics. Some of them turned for counsel to the political scientists who had greater familiarity with state and national politics.

While all this was happening in sociology and social anthropology, a new generation of political scientists was bringing in a less formal and a more flexible approach to the study of politics. India had embarked on a new and an ambitious venture in democracy, and it was natural for some of them to ask how the venture was faring. It did not take them long to recognize that state politics could not be understood without looking at district politics, and district politics without looking at village politics. Thus, sociologists, social anthropologists and political scientists discovered complementarities in their work as they sought to explore the articulations between the different territorial levels of the political system (Bailey 1960).

Sociologists and political scientists, both Indian and foreign, found a common interest in exploring the operation of the democratic process in a distinctive, not to say unique, social environment. The democratic process not only operates at different territorial levels, but it has to work through a social structure that exercises manifold constraints on it. Those who were seriously interested in seeing how democracy worked in India could not help noting how the political process was being refracted by the social structure. And those whose objective was to record the enduring features of that social structure could not help noting the tremors introduced into it by democratic politics.

While introducing the Draft Constitution to the Constituent Assembly on 4 November 1948, Dr Ambedkar had said, 'Democracy in India is only a top-dressing on an Indian soil which is essentially undemocratic' (Constituent Assembly of India 1989: 38). He had in mind the hierarchy of caste with the practice of untouchability as an integral part of it. The study of caste and politics provided a significant and, at the same time, a very concrete subject matter for mutual interchange between sociologists and political scientists. Here I will mention only two among many important authors: M.N. Srinivas (1962) in sociology and Rajni Kothari (1970) in political science.

In the last ten years, the idea of civil society seems to have caught the attention of many social scientists in India. As I have already indicated, the idea itself is not new but goes back to Hegel in the nineteenth century, and before him to the Scottish moral philosophers in the eighteenth-century. But it has acquired a new appeal in the context of a troubled political environment in India. Ironically, it is the political scientists who have taken the initiative in opening up the subject, although sociologists too have something to say about the relations between citizenship, state and civil society (Mahajan 1999; Béteille 1999).

* * *

I have said enough to indicate that there has been a great deal of interchange between sociologists and political scientists in the last fifty years to the advantage of both and of the general understanding of society and politics. Nevertheless, some differences remain, and there is no good reason why all differences of orientation, approach and even subject matter should disappear between the various disciplines.

Politics has to be almost by definition the central, if not the sole, concern of a distinct discipline, no matter what name we give to it, whether political philosophy, political theory or political science. It is also one of the major concerns, but cannot be the sole concern, of sociology, conceived broadly so as to include social anthropology. The majority of sociologists devote much of their time to topics other than politics, such as family, marriage and kinship; religion and ritual; education and occupation; social stratification and social mobility; and so on. It is desirable to have a general science of society, for that makes it possible to place politics in a larger social context than would ordinarily be done in a discipline devoted solely to the study of politics.

A prominent French political scientist pointed out in a widely read textbook that there were two different conceptions of his subject matter, as being, firstly, the science of the state, and, secondly, the science of power (Duverger 1966: 14–6). He himself opted for the second conception, although many political scientists prefer to work with the first one which is more restrictive. It would be fair to say that to the extent that they do engage in the study of politics, the majority of sociologists use the broader and not the narrower conception of it.

It is one thing to opt for the broader conception of politics and quite another to find an acceptable definition of power. The topic has been dealt with in many different ways in disciplines ranging from ethics to sociology. It has also provided endless occasion for moralizing for those who believe, or say they believe, that power is inherently evil, and can and should be eliminated from the conduct of human affairs. The moral and not merely the cognitive ambiguities surrounding the concept of power in social theory have been brought to light in a brilliant essay by Raymond Aron (1964). Despite many disagreements, most sociologists believe that power is constitutive of human societies, and that inequalities in the distribution of power and conflicts over its distribution are general and widespread, if not universal (Béteille 1977: 48–72). The equal distribution of power is the limiting and not the typical case, and the balance of power within and between societies is inherently unstable.

The conception of power that has had the most sustained influence on the work of sociologists in the twentieth century is the one due to Max Weber. Further, its influence has extended beyond the boundaries of sociology. Weber's much quoted definition of power is as follows: 'In general, we understand by "power" the chance of a man or a number of men to realize their own will in a social action even against the resistance of others who are participating in the action' (Weber 1978: 926). This is an extremely wide definition which can serve a useful purpose only when it is related to a concrete social situation. What is important therefore is not simply the definition of power, but also the specification of the social setting in which it is distributed and exercised.

Because social settings are infinitely various, the forms in which power is held and exercised are also various. Many attempts have been made by sociologists and others to classify the forms of power. In a classic study, Goldhamer and Shils classified power into three major forms: force, domination and manipulation (Shils 1975: 239–48). More recently, the British sociologist Michael Mann classified it into ideological, economic, military and political power (Mann 1986). It would take us too far away from our present purpose to review all the available classifications of power proposed by social theorists.

In the political sociology of Weber, power is the broadest and most general concept. He dealt more specifically with domination (*Herrschaft*) which he regarded as a special case of power (*Macht*). But domination itself was in his view of very wide and general significance in social life. As he wrote, 'Domination in the most general sense is one of the most important elements of social action. Of course, not every form of social action reveals a structure of dominancy. But in most of the varieties of social action domination plays a considerable role, even where it is not obvious at first sight' (Weber 1978: 941). As an example of domination, he pointed to the elevation of one language or dialect—one might just as well choose a religion or a sect as an example—above the others by authoritative fiat.

Weber recognized that the concept of domination could be rendered scientifically infructuous by defining it so broadly as to accommodate every situation and every relationship, from 'the social relations in a drawing room as well as in the market, from the rostrum of a lecture-hall as well as from the command post of a regiment, from an erotic or charitable relationship as well as from scholarly discussion of athletics' (Ibid.: 943). In his own work, Weber tended to concentrate on domination by virtue of authority, that is, 'power to command and duty to obey', but recognized other forms of domination, in particular economic domination.

Max Weber's treatment of power, though highly influential, is by no means the only possible treatment of it. Talcott Parsons sought to develop a modified version of it in which power is viewed as the capacity to be effective in collective action (Parsons 1963). A more radical conception of power as permeating every human situation and every human relationship, openly or insidiously, has been put forward by the French philosopher and historian of ideas, Michel Foucault (1977; 1980). Anthony Giddens (1981) has provided a brief but very useful comparison and contrast of the approaches to power of these two highly influential authors.

* * *

The broader conception of politics as the science of power opened up many new fields for systematic enquiry and investigation. This broader conception was in fact forced upon sociologists and social anthropologists as they encountered social situations, processes and relations that had a manifestly political component but could not be accommodated within the classical definition of politics. The great impetus for the reformulation of the idea of politics was provided by the growth of empirical enquiry through direct observation in the different parts of the world. It is far from my intention to suggest that all those who became engaged in this kind of enquiry shared the same conception of politics or employed the same definition of power.

The sociological study of politics is concerned in its most general sense with the distribution of power in political communities. Weber assigned crucial importance in this distribution to classes, status groups and parties, although there are other aspects of it that are equally important, for instance, the distribution of power among castes in India or among races and ethnic groups in other societies. The distribution of power does not show in any society a completely static or fixed pattern. To the extent that there is continuity—and there is often considerable continuity—it is a dynamic and not a static continuity. But there are also changes—sometimes swift and dramatic, more often gradual and incremental—in the distribution of power between parties, between classes, between castes, and between communities based on race, language and religion.

A large part of the empirical work undertaken by sociologists and social anthropologists consists of the observation, description and analysis of associations, organizations and institutions. Here a distinction has to be made between what may be called specifically political associations, such as state legislatures, town councils and political parties, and other associations such as schools, banks and temples whose aims and functions are not primarily political. To be sure, the distinction between the two is not always easy to maintain, although the differentiation of institutions is a long-term evolutionary tendency and a notable feature of all modern secular democracies.

As I have already indicated, political science concentrates on the study of specifically political institutions whereas sociology studies non-political institutions as well. Moreover, whereas political scientists have devoted considerable attention to the relations between states and between nations, sociologists have dwelt primarily on the internal arrangements within a nation or society. There have no doubt been exceptions among sociologists, such as Raymond Aron (1962) who maintained a keen interest in the relations among nations.

With some oversimplification, it may be said that what sociologists study are the social aspects of political associations and the political aspects of other social associations. Specifically, political associations are of many different kinds, and they have not all received equal attention from sociologists. Every political association is also a social association in which human beings interact with each other in accordance with rules that define their rights and obligations. Close examination of any social association, whether political or otherwise, reveals that it rarely works in the manner specified by the explicit or formal rules of its organization. Sociology has contributed much to the understanding of the informal or implicit rules by which a large part of the internal life of every association is regulated.

Not all political associations are accessible to direct or first-hand observation by the sociologist. Sociologists, and particularly social anthropologists, have made valuable contributions to their understanding at the local level through the study, for example, of village, town and district councils. Here they have investigated not only the formal distribution of power, but also the processes through which political decisions are actually made. These studies reveal the complex nature of the matrix within which political decisions are made, and how those decisions are affected by the social matrix and how they affect it in turn (Banton 1965).

The study of local-level politics shows that the distinction between specifically political associations and other associations, though important in principle, is difficult to maintain consistently in practice. There are what have been called para-political systems, whose study has illuminated the interface between society and politics in significant ways (Bailey 1969). There are, again, quasi-political associations of which the faction is a characteristic example. Unlike municipal corporations or even village councils, factions are not formally constituted authorities, but they operate actively, and sometimes decisively, in the contest for power within and between such authorities at every level of the political system, from the village to the nation (Lewis 1954; Brass 1984).

Although it is not a formally constituted body, the faction has a structure of its own which corresponds with, although it does not fully replicate, the structure of the society in which it operates. Factions have their own cycles of birth, expansion and decay, although the patterns of their operation are not always easy to detect and describe because, unlike parties, they tend to lead a subterranean existence. They are different from parties, but sometimes they are more important, not just in local politics but even in national politics. Factions are also lodged in associations other than specifically political ones whose activities and purposes are then altered under their influence.

A school, a temple, a hospital, a bank or a factory is not a specifically political association. Every society has a number of associations for the regular conduct of its various activities, although the extent to which these activities and the arrangements through which they are conducted is differentiated varies from one society to another. All modern societies have associations, organizations and institutions of many different kinds, performing a variety of functions that are often of a highly specialized nature. Each of these has a structure of authority and is a field for the operation of political forces.

A hospital or a school could not conduct the activities specific to it on a regular or continuing basis without a certain structure of authority. To be sure, in a well-conducted organization, people generally know what they have to do, and do not need to be issued commands at every step. But the multifarious activities of the organization need to be co-ordinated, and that co-ordination cannot be sustained without a structure of authority. Max Weber's idea of domination or Herrschaft—'the power to command and the duty to obey'—has its concrete social setting in the Herrschaftsverband or 'the imperatively co-ordinated association' (Dahrendorf 1959).

No structure of authority can be effective or stable unless it enjoys a degree of legitimacy, that is, unless it is acknowledged and accepted, at least in some measure, by those who obey and not only by those who command. The co-ordination of activities solely through the use of force and guile may work in some cases and for some time, but it is not typical of enduring social associations in general. But it is also true that the structure of authority in an association is not perceived in the same way by all its members; some embrace it actively while others resign themselves to it fatalistically.

It is generally not very difficult in a given concrete situation to distinguish between the person who commands and the one who obeys. But even though superordinate and subordinate positions may be readily distinguished in most contexts, it does not follow that they constitute mutually exclusive categories. In most associations, there is a graded distribution of authority so that the same person is superordinate to some and subordinate to others.

In the sociological study of institutions, it is important to keep in mind the distinction between the formal distribution of authority and the actual exercise of power. The two are related but they are not the same. How much power someone is actually able to exercise in an institution depends not only on his formal position in it but also on his political skills and what may be called his general social capital. The power to move the system—as well as the power to bring it to a standstill—does not flow strictly along the lines of constituted authority.

In India, some of the best insights into the distribution of power and the political process have come from case studies conducted in a variety of settings. I will refer here, and only very briefly, to three such studies conducted by sociologists from the Delhi School of Economics in the sixties and seventies. These three studies, along with many others of their kind, led to a decisive shift in the image of Indian society as eternal and unchanging.

The first study to which I would like to refer was conducted in a village in the Jaipur district of Rajasthan. The main aim of the study was 'to show how political relations in the community had been affected by various measures initiated in the wider political society, such as land reform, adult franchise, and democratic decentralization' (Chakravarti 1975: 21). The development of new political skills, including what the author described as 'political entrepreneurship', encouraged by the changing social and economic environment, helped to weaken to some extent the traditional advantages of caste and class.

Baviskar's study was set in rural Maharashtra, but in a sugar co-operative instead of a village. A co-operative society cannot be accurately described as a specifically political association, but there are many political aspects to its internal life, and its links with the outside world have many political strands. 'The linkages between the various structures of power and the interlocking positions of power occupied by the leaders sharpen the cleavages between the factions and lead to their organized articulation' (Baviskar 1980: 183). This study shows how economic development and political participation go together. It also provides a graphic account of the operation, at the grass roots level, of a major national party.

A trade union comes closest to being a specifically political association. The study by E.A. Ramaswamy (1977) of a trade union in a textile town in Tamil Nadu addresses itself to the relationship between democracy and oligarchy in a concrete social and political setting. A trade union is meant to promote industrial democracy by neutralizing, at least to some extent, the power of the employers through the collective political action of the workers. But in order to act effectively, the trade union must have a strong organization, and that introduces the 'iron law of oligarchy' into its own internal life.

From what I have said above, it will be clear that the distribution of power in a political community extends beyond the structures of domination in associations, organizations and institutions having distinct social identities. There are networks of social relations linking individuals and groups with each other that play a crucial part in maintaining as well as altering the balance of power in society and in its various segments. Wherever the distribution and exercise of power can be placed in a more or less definite social context, it becomes a subject for study by the sociologist.

As already indicated, the long-term evolutionary tendency has been for societies to become progressively differentiated. Some believe that differentiation leads to fragmentation and disorder, and others that it leads to better integration. Both have obviously happened at various places and various times, but the fact remains that human societies have on the whole managed to endure the process of increasing differentiation with reasonable success.

Political structures and processes are less differentiated from other social structures and processes in simple and small-scale societies than in complex and large-scale ones. In the latter, they are less differentiated at the local level than at he national level. The differentiation and integration of societies is an important part of general sociological enquiry (Luhmann 1982), and the study of political structures and processes contributes something of importance to that enquiry.

In many of the simpler societies there is a large measure of overlap between the political system and the kinship system (Gluckman 1965). The political group is often a kin group, or at least has a kin group as its core, and political networks follow, at least to some extent, the lines on a genealogical chart. Relations in such a society have a multiplex or many-stranded character, such that one interacts largely with the same sets of persons over a range of activities that are at the same time economic, political and ceremonial. Even in large-scale and complex societies, a similar lack of differentiation between the different types of activity may be seen at the level of the local community.

With the differentiation of society, political processes, relations and institutions begin to be more clearly discernible as such within the general social matrix. The emergence and growth of the modern nation state with its highly differentiated organs of government and politics created the conditions for treating the political system as an independent subject of study with its own concepts, methods and theories. I have already referred to the place of political science as a specialized and autonomous discipline in our universities and other centres of study and research.

Even in the most highly differentiated of modern states, the autonomy of the political system is only relative and not absolute. Here I would like to point to two distinctive features of the sociological approach to the study of politics. Firstly, the political system is viewed as a social system, on the same level as other social systems such as those relating to kinship, religion and economics. Secondly, the relationship between the political system and other social systems is given detailed and systematic attention. This remains true no matter how we characterize the political system, whether in terms of the means peculiar to it or in terms of the functions specific to it.

A social system, of whatever kind, has certain general properties. These properties are not conceived in the same way by all sociologists. Some define it as a system of meaningful action; others as a set of roles and relations; and yet others as a structure of rights and obligations. In so far as politics operates through social arrangements, the sociologist asks about those arrangements questions of the same order that arise in investigating the social arrangements through which economics, religion and kinship operate.

The various social arrangements through which politics, economics, religion and kinship operate may become differentiated, but they nevertheless remain interconnected. Tracing these interconnections, bringing them to light and analysing them are major objectives of what may be considered to be the specifically sociological approach to the study of politics. Kinship, religion and economics all influence politics at various levels and in various ways, but their influence is neither always open nor always direct. The outcome of a political contest is sometimes determined, and determined decisively, by forces that are external to and apparently unconnected with the political system as a differentiated and specialized system.

Democratic systems of government and politics have been adopted by many countries throughout the world in the last fifty years. Although the fundamental principles of democracy may be the same, democratic practice varies enormously from one country to another. Political science attends mainly to variations that are internal to the political system, such as the relations among the organs of government, the electoral system, the structure of parties, and the balance of powers between federal and state governments and between different sovereign states. The main aim of the sociologist is to see how the democratic process is refracted by the social system which includes not only the major institutions of society such as those of religion and kinship but also such major social divisions as those based on class, caste, ethnicity, race and gender.

* * *

In studying politics, the sociologist casts his net wide. He seeks not only to study the relationship between politics and other social institutions, but also to study that relationship in all human societies from the simplest to the most complex, from the least to the most highly differentiated. If we include social anthropology in our conception of sociology, as I have argued we should, then it has the widest comparative scope among all the social sciences. Comparative politics has conventionally operated within a somewhat restricted band of systems, partly because its basic thrust has been on the prospects of democratic political systems. The comparisons on which it has focused mainly, if not solely, are between democratic and totalitarian regimes, and between the different types of democratic regimes.

The political systems to which social anthropologists have mainly devoted their attention are far removed from both democratic and totalitarian regimes. Political anthropology made its beginnings about sixty years ago with the study of what may be broadly described as tribal political systems, at first in Africa. It has since then covered different types of political systems in virtually every part of the world, and has made significant contributions to the general understanding of political systems and the distribution of power in simple as well as complex societies.

The distinction with which political anthropology began was between segmentary and centralized political systems. A book by a group of social anthropologists published sixty years ago under the title of *African Political Systems* presented case studies of eight political systems from the different parts of sub-Saharan Africa. The concerns of the authors were far removed from democratic theory, or any kind of normative political theory. The editors of the volume distinguished their approach sharply from the approach of those political theorists whose concern was with 'ought questions' rather than 'is questions'. They wrote, 'We speak for all social anthropologists when we say that a scientific study of political institutions must be inductive and comparative and aim solely at establishing and explaining the uniformities found among them and their interdependencies with other features of social organization' (Fortes and Evans-Pritchard 1940: 5). Not all sociologists who study politics would today make such a sharp distinction between judgements of reality and value judgements.

The distinction between the two main groups of political systems is based on the presence of centralized authority, administrative machinery and judicial institutions in the first and their absence in the second. In presenting their classification, the editors noted, 'Those who consider that a state should be defined by the presence of governmental institutions will regard the first group as primitive states and the second group as stateless societies' (Ibid.: 5).

The same year in which the collection of eight studies appeared also saw the publication of a full-length monograph on the political system of a stateless society (Evans-Pritchard 1940). Then followed a succession of studies of such systems. The empirical study of stateless societies introduced something new into the understanding of politics. No doubt political philosophers had written with conviction about the withering away of the state and about possible worlds in which there would be no oppression, no domination and no conflict. But those accounts were speculative, whereas what we had here were exact and reliable accounts of actually existing societies which had been studied at first hand by trained social scientists. The authors of these studies were not impelled by any desire to show that the societies about which they wrote had attained any kind of moral or ethical perfection.

I have paid special attention here to the contributions to political anthropology of a group of British social anthropologists, for they were the pioneers in the field. Their work had worldwide influence, not least on the work of Indian sociologists studying their own society. The contributions of French scholars to the field who were broadly influenced by them is ably represented by the work of Georges Balandier (1967). A somewhat distinctive approach was developed in the sixties and seventies by a younger group of French anthropologists under the influence of Marxism (L'Homme 1978).

How can a society maintain any kind of unity, stability or continuity in the absence of an authority whose decisions are binding on all? Stateless societies have been described as existing in a condition of ordered anarchy, and the order behind the anarchy has been subjected to careful and systematic analysis. There is conflict, violence and bloodshed, but the very rudimentary technology of warfare limits the extent of destruction. More important than that are the established social mechanisms through which they are kept under control. Firstly, there is the balanced opposition of segments which restrains the elimination of one part of society by another; then there are cross-cutting alliances, based on kinship, marriage and residence, that put brakes on the intensity of hostilities; and, finally, there are rites and ceremonies indispensable for the collective well-being that require the participation of friends and foes alike.

These mechanisms whose real significance was brought to light through the study of segmentary political systems also operate, though in combination with other mechanisms, in larger and more complex political systems. It was Durkheim's belief that the study of the most elementary form of religion, namely, totemism would reveal the fundamental characteristics of all religions, including the most highly organized. Durkheim achieved only partial success in his venture, and those who came after him have been more modest in their claims. It may nevertheless be said that the study of segmentary systems did for political sociology what the study of totemism had done for the sociology of religion.

As a result of the work done in the last fifty years, we know that even the simpler societies show a variety of political types. There is first of all the distinction between segmentary tribes and tribal chiefdoms (Sahlins 1968). Segmentary tribes such as the Nuer are often, though not always, characterized by well-developed lineage systems. Even more rudimentary than such segmentary tribes are bands which subsist by food gathering rather than food producing, as for instance among the Bushmen and the Bergdama of southern Africa (Schapera 1956; Service 1966). At the other extreme are the tribal states, as among the Nupe of Nigeria, with their complicated, some would say Byzantine, structures of power and authority (Nadel 1942).

Further, the distinction between segmentary and centralized systems is not as clear-cut on the ground as it is in the typology. One and the same political system may accommodate a segmentary as well as a centralized mode. This was brilliantly demonstrated in a study of the political systems of highland Burma. There, among the Kachins, there was a regular pattern of oscillation between the *gumlao* (or egalitarian) and the *gumsa* (or hierarchical) modes of organization. In addition, the *gumsa* organization might sometimes move away altogether from the Kachin socio-political ambit and become incorporated into the larger, more centralized and more hierarchical Shan political order (Leach 1964).

Centralized and segmentary political systems have coexisted in near or distant association with each other in large parts of the Islamic world over a very long stretch of time. Evans-Pritchard's classic study of the Sanusi of Cyrenaica has provided a vivid account of the relationship between religion and politics in a very distinctive social setting (Evans-Pritchard 1949). More recently, the relationship between tribe and state has been studied by anthropologists in Iran and Afghanistan (Tapper 1983). These studies show the continuing vitality of the segmentary principle in political systems that are by no means insignificant in their extent and reach.

When we look at political systems in countries such as India and Indonesia, we are struck by the extent to which they are what Soviet sociologists used to call multi-structural formations. Small-scale formations do not simply give up all their social and political characteristics when they seek or are granted accommodation within the larger nation state. The different parts of such a system do not all move in accordance with the same rhythm; what we witness instead is a process of uneven development. Because these formations retain some of their older characteristics, the linkages between the different levels of the political system are generally complex and sometimes tenuous.

The democratic theory that has been used and developed by most modern political scientists is too narrowly focused, both empirically and normatively, to attend to many of the problems discussed above. Political sociology, as I have described it, lacks the sharpness of focus of political theory. Its intellectual aims are, relatively speaking, ill-defined and un-coordinated; it tends to move in many directions and at various levels. For these reasons, it succeeds occasionally in revealing unsuspected con-nections between the different components of political life, and between political life and other aspects of social life.

*   *   *

In the opening pages of his monumental *Economy and Society*, Max Weber placed sociology among the empirical sciences of action with which he contrasted dogmatic disciplines 'such as jurisprudence, logic, ethics and aesthetics, which seek to ascertain the "true" and "valid" meaning associated with the object of their investigation' (Weber 1978: 4). As I have indicated earlier, not all sociologists take the same view of the relationship between facts and values, but they have been on the whole more hesitant than political theorists to declare their opinions unequivocally on the rights and wrongs of what they study.

I have already alluded to the fact that political theory—or even political science—has a sharper focus than sociology. It concentrates on one set of institutions—political institutions—and devotes special attention to one type of political regime—the democratic type. It is perhaps easier there to form a judgement on what is right and what is wrong—or what is valid and what is not—than it is in the case of sociology which straddles many different institutions and many different regimes.

It may be natural to suspend judgement where whole societies, with the entire range of their beliefs, practices and institutions, are concerned, but is it possible to remain indifferent as between alternative forms of government? Also, it is relatively easy to suspend judgement where politi-cal regimes in remote and alien societies are concerned, but far more difficult to maintain the same detachment towards political regimes in one's own immediate environment. As an intellectual discipline, sociology belongs to the modern world, and every sociologist is also a citizen which is a distinctively modern phenomenon; how can the sociologist, as a citizen, avoid forming judgements of value about his own political envi-ronment?

It has been said that in order to be fully comparative, sociology must treat all societies alike, and not admit any privileged exceptions. In the past, adherence to a particular religious faith made the comparative study of religion a difficult if not an impossible task. The sociology of religion began to emerge as a distinct discipline only a little over a hundred years ago, although its concerns are foreshadowed in the writings of eighteenth century historians such as Edward Gibbon and philosophers such as David Hume. The fact that the social theorists of today are by and large 'religiously unmusical' has helped them to understand the relationship between religion and society in a very distinctive way. Should we require them to be also 'politically unmusical' in order to reach the same kind of understanding of the relationship between society and politics?

I am certain that most political sociologists, Max Weber included, would reject the requirement of being 'politically unmusical' as a condition for the successful scholarly analysis of politics. I am also certain that most of them would maintain, if not proclaim, a preference for the democratic type of political regime over all other types of it. Does this render inoperative the distinction between value judgements and judgements of reality where politics becomes a subject for sociology? I believe it does not, although it does place a special burden on the sociologist to remain clear about the standpoint from which he approaches his subject, to make it clear to others, and to be willing and able to consider with patience and care observations made from standpoints other than his own.

It may not be out of place here to point out that the practice of sociology itself rests on values that have a much closer affinity to the values of secular democracy than to those of any of the established religions. This practice calls for equal consideration of, if not equal respect for, all societies; it questions established views on kinship, religion *and* politics, but does not claim any finality for its own conclusions; and it accepts the position that the same problem may be viewed from more than one standpoint and lead to more than one solution.

The sociological study of politics is concerned not just with political practice but also with political ideals, both of which it treats as social facts. It is concerned above all with the disjunction between political ideals and political practice in one's own society as well as in other societies, in one's favoured political regime as well as in other regimes. Its main task is to observe, describe, analyse, interpret and explain the disjunction between ideal and practice rather than to prescribe remedies for it. It is in this sense that sociology is an empirical rather than a dogmatic or a normative discipline.

More than in most other domains of society, the interest in politics is linked with considerations of policy. As Raymond Aron pointed out, there is in the French language only a single word which stands for *both* policy and politics: 'The first ambiguity is that which results from the fact that the word "politique" serves to translate two English words each one of which has a precise connotation. In effect, the French word "politique" translates at one and the same time what the Anglo-Saxons call *policy* and what they call *politics*' (Aron 1965: 21, my translation, emphases in original). The same is the case with German. When Max Weber gave his celebrated address, 'Politik als Beruf'—translated into English as 'Politics as a Vocation'—he was referring to both at the same time.

Some scholars would classify economics, political science and even sociology as what they call the policy sciences (Lerner and Lasswell 1951). Because of its interest in a wide range of institutions and practices, and an equally wide range of societies and cultures, sociology has had less to do with matters of policy than have some other disciplines. There are very many issues of direct interest to the sociologist that simply do not fall within the ambit of policy in the ordinary sense of the term. And since decolonization, anthropologists who study social and political systems of which they are not members have become increasingly hesitant in taking positions on matters of policy. Those who sought to advise governments in the initial phase of decolonization soon found that their advice was either disregarded or put to uses that were very different from the ones they had in mind.

A British social anthropologist who studies local-level politics in India or in Africa may avoid taking a position on matters of policy, but can an Indian sociologist who makes politics in his own society the subject of his study be expected to do the same? Such a sociologist can hardly sustain the pretence that he is 'the astronomer of the social sciences', or that he takes 'the view from afar'. He may strive to achieve the maximum possible detachment and objectivity, but he cannot disregard either the social origins or the social consequences of the policies of the day.

The question in the end is not whether the sociologist who makes politics the subject of his study should or should not pay attention to matters of policy. After all, policies are also social facts; they arise in particular social environments through the operation of particular social forces and have particular social consequences, intended as well as unintended. They are forms of social action that call for the same kind of scholarly attention as other forms of meaningful social action. That having been said, it must be added that there is a fundamental distinction between policy analysis and policy prescription. It is policy analysis and not policy prescription that has brought out the best in sociology as a scholarly discipline.

References

Aron, Raymond. 1962. *Paix et guerre entre les nations*. Paris: Calman-Levy.

———. 1964. 'Macht, Power, *Puissance*'. *European Journal of Sociology*. Vol. V, pp. 27–51.

———. 1965. *Democratie et totalitarisme*. Paris: Gallimard.

Bailey, F.G. 1960. *Tribe, Caste and Nation*. Bombay: Oxford University Press.

———. 1969. *Stratagems and Spoils*. Oxford: Basil Blackwell.

Balandier, Georges. 1967. *Anthropologie politique*. Paris: PUF.

Banton, Michael (ed). 1965. *Political Systems and the Distribution of Power*. London: Tavistock.

Baviskar, B.S. 1980. *The Politics of Development*. Delhi: Oxford University Press.

Béteille, André. 1977. *Inequality among Men*. Oxford: Basil Blackwell.

———. 1996. *Caste, Class and Power*. Delhi: Oxford University Press. 2nd edition.

———. 1999. 'Citizenship, State and Civil Society'. *Economic and Political Weekly*. Vol. XXXIV. No. 36, pp. 2588–91.

Brass, Paul R. 1984. *Caste, Faction and Party in Indian Politics*. Delhi: Chanakya. (2 vols.)

Chakravarti, Anand. 1975. *Contradiction and Change*. Delhi: Oxford University Press.

Constituent Assembly Debates. 1989. *Official Report*. New Delhi: Lok Sabha Secretariat. Vol. 7.

Dahrendorf, Ralf. 1959. *Class and Class Conflict in Industrial Society*. London: Routledge and Kegan Paul.

Duverger, Maurice. 1966. *Sociologie politique*. Paris: PUF.

Evans-Pritchard, E.E. 1940. *The Nuer*. Oxford: Clarendon Press.

———. 1949. *The Sanusi of Cyrenaica*. Oxford: Clarendon Press.

Fortes, Meyer and E.E. Evans-Pritchard (eds). 1940. *African Political Systems*. London: Oxford University Press.

Foucault, Michel. 1977. *Discipline and Punish*. Harmondsworth: Penguin Books.

———. 1980. *Power/Knowledge*. Brighton: Harvester Press.

Giddens, Anthony. 1981. *A Contemporary Critique of Historical Materialism*. London: Macmillan. Vol. 1.

Gluckman, Max. 1965. *Politics, Law and Ritual in Tribal Society*. Oxford: Basil Blackwell.

Kothari, Rajni (ed). 1970. *Caste in Indian Politics*. Delhi: Orient Longman.

Leach, Edmund R. 1964. *Political Systems of Highland Burma*. London: Bell.

Lerner, Daniel and Harold D. Lasswell (eds). 1951. *The Policy Sciences*. Stanford: Stanford University Press.

Lewis, Oscar. 1954. *Group Dynamics in a North Indian Village*. New Delhi: Planning Commission.

L'Homme. 1978. *L'Homme, Revue française d'anthropologie*. Vol. XVIII. Nos. 3–4.

Luhmann, Niklas. 1982. *The Differentiation of Society*. New York: Columbia University Press.

Mahajan, Gurpreet. 1999. 'Civil Society and Its Avatars'. *Economic and Political Weekly*. Vol. XXXIV. No. 20, pp. 1188–96.

Mann, Michael. 1986. *The Sources of Social Power*. Cambridge: Cambridge University Press. Vol. 1.

Nadel, S.F. 1942. *A Black Byzantium*. London: Oxford University Press.

Nicholas, Ralph W. 1968. 'Structures of Politics in the Villages of Southern Asia'. In Milton Singer and Bernard S. Cohn (eds). *Structure and Change in Indian Society*. Chicago: Aldine, pp. 243–84

Parsons, Talcott. 1963. 'On the Concept of Political Power'. *Proceedings of the American Philosophical Society*. Vol. 107. No. 3, pp. 232–62.

Ramaswamy, E.A. 1977. *The Worker and His Union*. Bombay: Allied.

Retzlaff, Ralph H. 1962. *Village Government in India*. Bombay: Asia Publishing House.

Sahlins, Marshall D. 1968. *Tribesmen*. Englewood Cliffs: Prentice-Hall.

Schapera, Isaac. 1956. *Government and Politics in Tribal Societies*. London: Watts.

Service, Elman R. 1966. *The Hunters*. Englewood Cliffs: Prentice-Hall.

Shils, Edward. 1975. *Center and Periphery*. Chicago: University of Chicago Press.

Srinivas, M.N. 1962. *Caste in Modern India and Other Essays*. Bombay: Asia Publishing House.

Tapper, Richard (ed). 1983. *The Conflict of Tribe and State in Iran and Afghanistan*. London: Croom-Helm.

Tocqueville, Alexis de. 1956. *Democracy in America*. New York: Alfred Knopf, 2 vols.

Weber, Max. 1978. *Economy and Society*. Berkeley: University of California Press, 2 vols.

Chapter
9

Economics and Sociology*

1. Institutional Setting

I t is scarcely possible for me to cover the relationship between economics and sociology in its entire range, and I doubt that many persons in the present audience will expect me to do so. There are many different ways of studying economics, and I cannot claim any special competence in judging which of these is the most central, the most significant or the most fruitful. There are also many different ways of studying sociology; and, in this case, although I may not be the best judge, I do have my own judgement about the scope, and the aims, objectives and methods characteristic of the discipline.

The focus of attention in the present exposition will naturally be on sociology; it is indeed a part of a long-term endeavour to discover and describe the nature and significance of sociology. It always helps to understand something by comparing, contrasting and relating it with something else. Sociology and economics are by common consent neighbourly disciplines, and two of the most significant figures in the development

*This is an expanded version of the Golden Jubilee Lecture delivered at the Delhi School of Economics on 21 January 2000. I am grateful to Professor Badal Mukherji, the Director, and to Professor K. Sundaram, the head of the department of economics, for inviting me to deliver the lecture, and to the members of the departments of economics and of sociology for their encouragement. I would also like to thank Professor B.S. Minhas for presiding over the occasion which was for me a memorable one.

of sociology, Max Weber and Vilfredo Pareto, retained an active interest in economic science, or what they would call political economy, over a long period of time. But sociology has other neighbours, such as history, political science, psychology, cultural anthropology and linguistics. How one thinks of one's own discipline determines in part which among the neighbourly disciplines one chooses for the most active interaction. Not all sociologists choose the same neighbours, and this choice is governed by many different factors, including, of course, the opportunities for material and symbolic rewards.

The movement of knowledge, it has been said, is a disorderly movement. Many factors contribute to it, and they do not always work towards the same end. Individuals of outstanding intelligence and imagination contribute a great deal to the development of scholarship, but the institutions in and through which they work contribute no less. Today the work done in the department of which I was a member for more than forty years is well known both within and outside the country. I have no doubt in my mind that the achievement of its individual members and, even more, their academic reputation owe a great deal to the location of the department of sociology in the Delhi School of Economics.

While it is true that during much of the nineteenth century, both economics and sociology grew largely outside the universities, it is difficult to see how this could have happened in the second half of the twentieth century in India, or for that matter anywhere else. David Ricardo, John Stuart Mill and Karl Marx were not university men; nor were Auguste Comte and Herbert Spencer. Very soon the two disciplines, first economics and then sociology, began to find places in the universities which themselves underwent rapid expansion from the end of the nineteenth century onwards. With expansion came differentiation and specialization, and both economics and sociology got adopted as more or less specialized intellectual disciplines in the Indian universities not long after their adoption in the western ones. A university is a place for the pursuit of specialized learning, but it is also a place which offers the most extensive scope for interchange between the different branches of learning.

The location of the department of sociology in the Delhi School of Economics was not by accident. Certainly, the founder of the School, Dr V.K.R.V. Rao believed that sociology had something to contribute to both economic science and economic policy, although his ideas on the subject were not always very clear or precise. The story of how he enticed Professor Srinivas to set up the department of sociology as a part of the

Delhi School of Economics is by now well known (Srinivas 1995; Fuller 1999), so I will not repeat it here. The founder of the department of sociology was of a more sceptical disposition than Dr Rao, but he too believed that the department of sociology would benefit by its location in the Delhi School of Economics.

The proposed alliance of economics and sociology in the Delhi School of Economics was based on a certain perception of the Indian economy and society, and the changes taking place in them. India had only recently achieved independence, and Indian social scientists believed not only that there ought to be change, development and progress but also that their disciplines had a positive role to play in the creation of a modern India that would be prosperous, democratic and secular. Both V.K.R.V. Rao and M.N. Srinivas took very seriously the social responsibility of the social scientist, although their views on the subject were not identical (Béteille 1995: 65–6). The economists of the fifties and sixties seemed to be quite comfortable with the idea of their discipline as a policy science whereas the sociologists had a more ambivalent attitude towards policy.

Although Srinivas's approach was always tinged with intellectual scepticism, he felt that sociology should contribute not only to the study of development and change but also to their advancement. He believed that India was on the move, and this belief is clearly expressed in the two books that he published while he was at the Delhi School of Economics, *Caste in Modern India* and *Social Change in Modern India* (Srinivas 1962, 1966); the inclusion of the word 'modern' in the titles of both the books was hardly an accident. The sociologists of his generation had not been gripped by any Angst about 'post-Enlightenment modernity'; they were by and large at one with the economists in their confidence in India's capacity to take its place in the modern world.

Srinivas's interest in the problems of modern India was evident even before he came to the Delhi School of Economics in 1959, in his involvement with what was then *The Economic Weekly*. He not only wrote for it but also actively encouraged other sociologists to do the same; two of my own earliest papers were published in it on his advice (Béteille 1962, 1963). The essays in the important collection on the Indian village edited by Srinivas (1955) were in fact first published in *The Economic Weekly* between 1951 and 1954. *The Economic Weekly*, now *Economic and Political Weekly*, has provided an outlet of a kind that has few parallels in the world for economists, sociologists and other social scientists to write on subjects of common interest. Several members of the Delhi School of

Economics, both economists and sociologists, have been actively involved in the conduct of its affairs.

Yet, the relationship between economists and sociologists, as I experienced it in the fifties, sixties and seventies, was by no means an easy one (Béteille 1995). I soon realized that this was generally the case throughout India and indeed in most other countries, at least in the English-speaking world (Swedberg 1990). In the decades immediately following independence, the universities and, after them, the research institutes entered a phase of expansion, and in the social sciences, the economists were always in the lead in this expansion. They were able to attract better talent and, what is more important, more funds.

The Chicago economist, George Stigler gave currency to the description of economics as 'the imperial science' (Stigler 1984). If economics was the imperial science anywhere in the world, it was in Delhi in the third quarter of the nineteenth/twentieth century. In the universities, in the research institutes, and in the government, the economists were more prominent than all other social scientists, and the Planning Commission, which enjoyed great prestige till the mid-seventies, always included economists but rarely other social scientists. The self-image of the economists was that they were like the natural scientists, precise and practical at the same time. They generally believed that development and change lay in the province of economic science, although they might on occasion take some account of 'non-economic factors'.

Today economics is no longer as secure as it used to be in its self-image as the imperial science. In any case, that image of economics did not at any time prevail in all parts of the world. In France, for example, philosophy, history and some of the cultural sciences have enjoyed greater pre-eminence throughout the post-War years. The French have been inclined to regard economics as a 'technical' rather than a 'humane' discipline. Perhaps they believe seriously what Keynes said only light-heartedly, that economists are like dentists, and the French certainly do not place dentists very high in their rating of intellectuals.

In India, the disenchantment with the Five Year Plans had something to do with the fall from grace of the discipline which was expected to provide the main intellectual instrument for the formulation and execution of those plans. There were other reasons as well. In the early years of independence, economics had been more closely identified than any other social science discipline with the agenda of modernization through the application of rational scientific knowledge. This agenda itself came under increasing scrutiny and attack after 1977. There was a search for alternative frameworks of knowledge, and in some quarters a plea for the wholesale rejection of 'post-Enlightenment modernity'. This has led some sociologists to turn to obscure, not to say obscurantist, pathways to knowledge. But sociology will only harm itself if it turns its back on the solid ground of knowledge established by economic science in the last two hundred years.

2. Framework of Constraint

Despite important differences in aims and method, which are perhaps more clear now than they were fifty years ago, economics and sociology have a great deal to contribute to each other. I will say little here of what sociology has contributed or can contribute to economics, but dwell instead on the contribution of economics to the development of sociology. Needless to say, the conception of economics, and to some extent also of sociology, on which I base my observations is a personal one; but that does not mean that it is either eccentric or quixotic.

The most important contribution of economics to the development of all the social sciences was the introduction of a new perspective on human affairs, based on the simple recognition that human action is constrained, and constrained inexorably, by material and social factors. Thomas Carlyle spoke for many when in 1850 he characterized economics as 'the dismal science'. This means above all that after the establishment of economics as a serious intellectual discipline, it became impossible to construct utopias in the old way.

This change of orientation is of great importance since I consider the sociological perspective to be the antithesis of the utopian. In a remarkable essay, Sir Isaiah Berlin (1991: 20–48) sought to establish a secular trend of decline in utopian thinking in the west, but it has not declined in the world as a whole. In India, it is a major obstacle to the development of sociology, and here economics can be a valuable ally, for it has been more successful than most social sciences in outgrowing utopian thinking. In the sociological perspective, human action is constrained above all by the division of labour, and there is no escape for the sociologist from the division of labour, just as there is none for the economist from scarcity. I am not speaking now of any particular form of the division of labour or of scarcity of any particular resource, but of the division of labour and of scarcity as such.

The passage from an unconstrained view of human action to one in which it is constrained by material and social factors may be illustrated from the writings of Marx who has been so influential in the development of both economics and sociology. The first text I choose for illustration is from *The German Ideology* (1968) written jointly with Engels in 1845–6 but not published in the lifetime of either. The second is from the famous Preface to *A Contribution to the Critique of Political Economy* (1970) published by Marx in 1859. Both texts are among the most widely quoted of the writings of any nineteenth-century social theorist.

The text from *The German Ideology* presents a memorable picture of a world in which

> nobody has one exclusive sphere of activity but each can become accomplished in any branch he wishes; society regulates the general production and thus makes it possible for me to do one thing today and another tomorrow, to hunt in the morning, fish in the afternoon, rear cattle in the evening, criticize after dinner, just as I have a mind, without ever becoming hunter, fisherman, shepherd or critic (Marx and Engels 1968: 45).

This is a world in which the individual is freed from all material *and* social constraints, from the constraints of the division of labour and, presumably, also of scarcity.

The work of Marx has been described by one of the foremost sociologists of our time as 'equivocal and inexhaustible' (Aron 1970: 355–77). What made it inexhaustible was the fundamental tension between his basic ideas. In the Preface we get a very different picture of society from the one in *The German Ideology*. Here we are told: 'In the social production of their existence, men inevitably enter into definite relations which are independent of their will, namely relations of production appropriate to a given stage in the development of their material forces of production' (Marx 1970: 20). The text underlines with a heavy hand the social framework of human action, and the constraints imposed by the social relations of production on what the individual can do.

What brought about this change of perspective within a span of a dozen years? Obviously, many different factors were at play, and, as we shall see, it is not clear that Marx turned his back once and for all on the utopian perspective presented in *The German Ideology*. At any rate, many of his followers have invoked that vision of an unconstrained world well into our own time.

It can scarcely be an accident that between 1845 and 1859 Marx had turned his attention to the serious study of economic science. What many have rightly regarded as the sociological perspective of the Preface could not have been derived from the writings of sociologists such as Comte and Spencer for whose ideas Marx had scant respect. Nor did they arise from his study of Hegel and classical German philosophy. They arose almost certainly from his engagement with the ideas of the classical political economists, that is, Smith, Malthus and Ricardo.

The idea that individual action is constrained by a material and social framework that has a definite and determinate structure was carried over into the works of the next generation of writers such as Weber and Durkheim who became the real founders of modern sociology. I hardly need to stress that Max Weber began his academic career as a professor of economics, and although he saw himself more and more as a sociologist, this does not mean that he ceased to describe himself as a political economist.

Marx was in my judgement a proto-sociologist rather than what I would describe as a sociologist in the full and proper sense of the term. At any rate, he was not a sociologist in the same mould as Pareto, Weber and Durkheim who came after him. More germane to the present discussion are the distinctions made by Schumpeter (1976) between Marx the economist, Marx the sociologist and Marx the prophet. If there is a tension between economics and sociology, there is a much deeper one between social science and prophecy. Even after he had mastered the economic science of his time, Marx never fully renounced the prophetic vision, and that vision is not easy to accommodate in the social sciences.

3. Constraint as Inherent in Society

I would now like to clarify the specific sense in which first economics and then the other social sciences introduced the idea of constraint in the understanding and explanation of human action. The idea of constraint itself was not new, only the nature and sources of the constraints on human action came to be viewed in a distinctly new light. Human beings had always believed their actions to be ruled by divine, mystical and metaphysical constraints. What the new sciences of population, economy and society did was to provide a secular basis for the understanding and explanation of those constraints. In their view, the constraints on human action were not imposed from above, they were inherent in the very conditions of collective existence.

The constraints that were most immediately apparent to the economic and social theorists of the late eighteenth and early nineteenth centuries were those relating to population and resources. The wealth of a nation was not a fixed quantity, and there were signs everywhere that it could be increased through human effort. But it was also evident that it could not be increased indefinitely, or at the will and pleasure of individuals, whether acting singly or in combination. Moreover, what increased was not simply the wealth of a nation but also its population, and the relation between the two needed to be examined through careful and systematic empirical enquiry.

It increasingly appeared that the action of men in production, exchange and consumption were governed by rules that were largely unknown to the actors themselves but that could nonetheless be discovered by systematic enquiry and investigation. Although the writings of Smith, Malthus and Ricardo were different in many respects from those of Comte and Spencer, they appear to have been driven by a common impulse. Firstly, they were contemporaries or near contemporaries. Secondly, they were all seeking to move from a 'metaphysical' to a more empirical or 'positive' mode of understanding and explanation. And thirdly, they all believed that there were discoverable regularities of coexistence and succession in the conduct of human affairs.

The disciplines devoted to the study of population, economy and society came to be gradually differentiated in the nineteenth century. Before that, Adam Smith, who had laid the foundations of economic science, and Adam Ferguson, with whom the study of civil society may be said to have begun, had shared a great many things in common. Throughout the nineteenth century, economists and sociologists often addressed themselves to problems of the same kind. It may be well to remember that the division of labour, which had attracted the attention of the founders of economics at the end of the eighteenth century, still provided at the end of the nineteenth century the subject matter for Durkheim's entry into sociology. Although Durkheim viewed the significance of the division of labour from a completely new angle, he assigned great significance to the relationship between resources and population in his explanation of the change from one type of society to another. A separate part of *The Division of Labour* was in fact devoted to that topic.

With Durkheim, we see the establishment of a new conception of the social order and the constraints imposed by it on individual action. Social facts, in his well known formulation, are things, and, as things, they are characterized by the two properties of exteriority and constraint. There is a social order in and through which individuals live and fulfil themselves.

That social order includes a great many things besides the technical apparatus of material production. It includes not only a structure of roles and relationships but, equally, the values and norms on which that structure is based. In this conception of the social order, whether one takes the former or the latter as one's point of departure is largely a matter of convenience. Both social morphology and collective representations are social facts, and they both exercise constraint on individual action.

Durkheim's idea of the constraints exercised by social arrangements was no doubt anticipated by Marx in the famous Preface from which I have already quoted. But it was Durkhiem, rather than Marx, who drew out the full implications of that idea. For one thing, Durkheim was more consistent and systematic in its application than Marx. It would be quite out of character for him to suggest that a stage would arrive when the constraints of society on the individual would cease to exist. For him they were inherent in the nature of society, although, no doubt, they changed their character from one type of society to another and from one phase in the life of a society to the next. Marx's views on the subject were more ambivalent, not to say inconsistent. He never gave up the belief in the leap from the realm of necessity to the realm of freedom with the termination of capitalism which he took to be the last antagonistic form of society.

Durkheim had not only a more consistent but also a more comprehensive view of society and its constraints. Marx believed that those constraints were rooted in the contradiction between the material forces of production and the social relations of production; and that once that contradiction was resolved, as it would be with the termination of capitalism, the constraints themselves would cease to operate. Marx himself, and certainly the majority of his followers from Kautsky to Lenin, assigned primacy to the economic structure of society—the 'real foundation' as he called it—in a way that would be quite inconsistent with the view of society held by Durkheim and by most sociologists who came after him. My own view is that the economic structure of society is of fundamental importance, but that it is neither determinant nor dominant in any absolute sense.

The view of constraint as being inherent in every domain of society—family, school, church, political party, and even the voluntary association—and not only, or even predominantly, in the economic domain or the domain of material production has given to sociology in the last hundred years its distinctive orientation to human action. We find it not only in Durkheim but also in Max Weber, who had a more intimate knowledge of economics and a more sustained interest in it. Weber never tired of pointing to the constraints of the economic order, but he insisted on the equal and autonomous significance of the symbolic order. He has been unjustly criticized, mainly by Marxists, for putting more stress on religion than on economics, on the superstructure as against the base, whereas for him, as for most sociologists since his time, the very distinction between base and superstructure is of doubtful value.

It is clear that on balance Marx assigned special and preponderant significance to the base which for him stood for the 'totality of the relations of production', or 'the economic structure of society'. This he did, not only on substantive but also on methodological grounds. For he believed that, unlike the changes in legal, political, religious and other forms, the material transformation of the economic conditions of production 'can be determined with the precision of natural science' (Marx 1970: 21). It was also his belief that the economic processes of capitalist production were governed by laws that work 'with iron necessity towards inevitable results' (Marx 1954: 19).

Marx was not alone in believing that the economic domain was privileged in being amenable to investigation by the exact methods of the natural sciences. I have already pointed out that the self-image of a great many economists is that their science is at the same time precise and practical, more akin to physics than to sociology. It is true that there have been sociologists who have sought to present their discipline as 'a natural science of society' (Radcliffe-Brown 1957), but their views have not prevailed for very long. My own view is that it is far more useful to regard society as a moral rather than a natural system, but this does not mean that the constraints of the moral order are less deserving of scholarly attention than those of the natural order.

4. Constraint and Agency

The preoccupation of sociologists with the constraints of society on individual action has not been without its costs. That preoccupation can lead to a fatalistic conception of the social order without any place in it for human agency. It would contradict our experience of the world in which we live where human beings make choices, circumvent obstacles, overcome all kinds of constraints, and through conscious and purposive action change the very conditions of their existence. If it were unable to take account of the constant flux of social life and the capacity of human beings to contend with the constraints of economy and society, sociology would scarcely count as a serious intellectual pursuit.

Not all sociologists have been preoccupied in the same way with the external constraints on individual action, whether due to the mode of production or the social order more generally. Max Weber's approach to the subject was in some ways fundamentally different from the approaches of both Marx and Durkheim. He did not believe that human life was regulated by anything like the laws that regulate the movement of the planets around the sun, and he found little attraction in the idea of a natural science of either economy or society. He characterized his own sociology by the rather ponderous term, 'Sinnverstehendesoziologie' which may be roughly translated as the sociology of the understanding of meaning.

In *The Rules of Sociological Method*, Durkheim had observed that the explanation of a social fact would be complete once both its causes and its functions had been determined (Durkheim 1938: 89–124). He argued that the causes of a social fact must be sought among other social facts and likewise its functions, and not in the needs, dispositions or desires of the individual. Weber took a somewhat different view. For him, a sociological account had to be not only causally and functionally adequate, but also adequate in terms of meaning. Statistical uniformities as such were not directly relevant to a sociological account; they became useful only when they could be related to a context of meaning.

For Weber, meaningful action in a given social situation was often the point of departure for a sociological enquiry. What does it mean for an entrepreneur, or a priest, or a scholar to do what he does, and to be what he is? What provides such a life with its distinctive orientation? Weber recognized the hazards of proceeding in this way. Intuition carried one some distance in the pursuit, but it was not always a reliable guide. The subjective interpretation had always to be verified, methodically and with the maximum attention to detail, by comparison with the concrete course of events as they actually took place. What the actor or agent thought or felt was important, but the sociologist could never dispense with the objective correlate. 'Sociology', as Weber himself put it, 'is a science concerning itself with the interpretive understanding of social action and thereby with a causal explanation of its course and consequences' (Weber 1978: 4). The causal explanation is no less important than the interpretive understanding.

As an economist-turned-sociologist, Weber remained acutely conscious of the presence of the external environment within which meaningful social action took place. No matter how much he might emphasize the symbolic components of this environment, he never disregarded its material components. As is well known, his first major work, *The Protestant Ethic and the Spirit of Capitalism*, began not with the inner meaning of either Calvinism or capitalism, but with a series of objective correlations between economic attainment and religious affiliation (Weber 1976: 35–46). It is true that his correlations have been questioned by later writers, but the fact remains that they provided the point of departure for the work.

Weber began his celebrated address at Munich on 'Science as a Vocation' with the following observation:

Now, we political economists have a pedantic custom, which I would like to follow, of always beginning with the external conditions. In this case, we begin with the question: What are the conditions of science as a vocation in the material sense of the term? (Gerth and Mills 1946: 129).

He made a detailed analysis of those external conditions in his own country and elsewhere, and of the changes taking place in them before asking what it meant for the scientist or the scholar to choose and to remain in the vocation of his choice. The scientist or scholar was for him not someone who simply pursued his own ideas single-mindedly and in splendid isolation; his work, like that of the banker, the civil servant or the engineer, had to be conducted in a specific institutional setting with its own distinctive material and social constraints.

Weber maintained a lifelong interest in economic science but his approach to it was different from the approaches of his most influential contemporary economists, though he did influence Schumpeter and Frank Knight who came after him. Economics, whether for Walras or for Marshall, was a generalizing science, whereas sociology, for both Durkheim and Weber, was a comparative science. I believe this to be a very important distinction. When he writes, whether about inequalities or about institutions, the economist seeks to identify their general or universal features, whereas the sociologist tends to look for the similarities and differences in their forms in various societies.

In their search for what is universally valid, economists have tended to neglect differences, whereas for the sociologist, differences are no less significant than uniformities. After all, it was Max Weber's lifelong intellectual endeavour to discover how something so peculiar as capitalism could have come into being and extend its hold so successfully.

By dwelling on the similarities and differences among societies, the comparative method reveals the weight of social constraints in a particularly striking way. We come to appreciate the real nature and significance of constraint only as we become acquainted with the inexhaustible variety of its forms. When we move from one society to another, or from one phase in the life of a society to the next, we learn that the constraints change but also that they do not disappear. We take the constraints of our own society for granted, or believe that when those particular ones are abolished, there will be no constraints any more. The comparative study of societies provides the best corrective to that way of thinking.

5. Class, Inequality and Stratification

I referred earlier to the great importance of the division of labour as a subject that attracted the attention of both economists and sociologists in the past. From the sociological point of view, the division of labour may be seen in the most general way as the differentiation of roles among the members of a society. The differentiation of roles is constitutive of human societies as such, although some societies have it in a very rudimentary and others in a very elaborate form. This is partly a matter of scale. Other things being equal, the more complex and dynamic a society is, the more highly differentiated its system of roles.

The division of labour and the differentiation of roles tend to be associated with inequality and ranking, although the association is by no means uniform. Two roles that are different need not necessarily be ranked as superior and inferior, but in a complex system of many roles, some are invariably ranked above others. Now, whereas many persons may be prepared to accept the division of labour and some of the constraints due to it, they feel less at ease in having to acknowledge that inequality too may be inevitable and inescapable. Liberals who welcome difference for its own sake are often opposed to inequality, but the weight of comparative sociology indicates that as far as human societies are concerned, differentiation tends to be accompanied, sooner or later and with unfailing regularity, by inequality.

Inequality, class and stratification have been subjects of common interest for sociologists and economists for more than a hundred years. The analysis of classes occupies a central place in the Marxian approach to the study of both economy and society. According to Marxist theory, much of what takes place in capitalist society is constrained by its class structure; not only what a person does, but even his perception of himself and others is governed by his location in that structure. At the same time, the class structure is a historical and not a universal feature of human societies. According to that theory, there have been societies in the past and there will be societies in the future free from the burdens of class.

Whereas the idea of a society free from the division of labour was never actively pursued by the Marxists, the idea of a classless society has had a much longer and more vigorous life. The Marxian idea of a classless society turned crucially around the definition of classes in terms of a particular criterion, that of private property. But, as Raymond Aron has put it, 'If you define classes with reference to private ownership of the means of production, nothing is easier than to make the former vanish by hoping to suppress the latter' (Aron 1964: 61, my translation). Fifty years ago, many left intellectuals, in India and outside India, believed that classes had been effectively abolished in the Soviet Union under Stalin, and were being abolished in China by Mao.

Even after we have defined classes out of existence, inequality and stratification remain, and they continue to be subjects of interest to both economists and sociologists. Until World War II, economists and sociologists who worked in the field had a great many things in common, and the names of Pareto, Weber and Schumpeter come readily to mind. The work of economists and sociologists in the last fifty years has, however become highly specialized and increasingly differentiated from each other, although here, in the Delhi School of Economics, some attempt has been made to keep the interchange alive (Béteille 1983). The divergence may be seen in the very terms used to characterize their respective fields of study: economists prefer to write about 'inequality', whereas the term favoured by most sociologists is 'stratification'. Some of the best technical work in sociology is now done on the related problems of social stratification and social mobility. The very distinctive approach to class pursued by the Marxists appears to have lost some of its ground.

When economists study inequality, they tend to concentrate on the distribution of income and wealth (Sen 1973; Atkinson 1975; Tendulkar 1983). This has certain obvious advantages. It gives their work a certain rigour, but it tends also to give it a narrow focus. Where reliable data are available, income distribution may be measured and compared with some precision, although neither the reliability of income statistics nor the utility of such measures as the Gini coefficient is above question. The other attraction of focusing on the distribution of income and wealth is that it can be related to policy. It is easier to formulate policies for reducing the disparities of income and wealth than for reducing other and more fundamental forms of inequality.

The belief that inequality is at bottom a matter of income and wealth is itself a part of the common sense of capitalism of which we are all prisoners to a greater or lesser extent. No doubt income and wealth confer status and power, but there are other sources of both status and power. The Soviet experience has shown that even when income disparities between manual and non-manual workers are reduced, the disparities of status remain. There are many occupations that enjoy higher esteem than other occupations where the pay is higher.

Again, while it may be possible to level out the disparities of income and wealth, at least for some time, it is doubtful that the inequalities of power can be levelled out in the same way. Pareto (1926) had warned in the early part of the last century that the socialist regimes would come to grief because the inequalities they hoped to eliminate were rooted ultimately in power and not in property, and one does not eliminate the inequalities of power by abolishing the rights of property. Who can deny today that the instruments for the suppression of inequality themselves generate inequalities that are sometimes more oppressive than the ones they aim to suppress?

While economists have focused on the distribution of income, sociologists have dwelt more extensively on the ranking of occupations. The differentiation and ranking of occupations is directly associated with that familiar subject of common interest to economists and sociologists, namely, the division of labour. In all modern societies, the individual's position in society—his social identity, his economic standing, his own self-esteem—is to some extent dependent on his occupation. A large part of his adult life is devoted to it, and much of his early life is a preparation for it. No doubt other attributes such as wealth, income and education, or race, caste and gender are important, but it is occupational differentiation, occupational ranking and occupational mobility that have dominated the sociological study of stratification, particularly in the advanced industrial countries, in the last fifty years.

The continuous differentiation of occupations is a common feature of all modern societies. It seems to be driven in part by the technical requirements of modern economic systems. Demographers and sociologists who study the occupational systems of advanced industrial societies such as the United States and the United Kingdom have to work with lists of tens of thousands of individual occupations (Blau and Duncan 1968; Goldthorpe and Hope 1974). These occupations are not only differentiated from each other, they are also ranked among themselves; the differentiation and ranking of occupations go together.

The social grading of occupations is a complex and laborious task, calling for much technical ingenuity, and not all sociologists are attracted to it. There are, as I have just said, tens of thousands of occupations, and millions of persons engaged in them. Nevertheless, there is a considerable measure of consistency in the ways in which, within the same society, these millions of persons rank the tens of thousands of occupations in which they are engaged. What is more, at least in industrial societies, the ranking of occupations tends to follow the same general pattern, although there are variations from one country to another, depending on technological, economic and cultural factors (Treiman 1977).

In every modern society, the occupational structure constrains the life chances of the individual to a greater or lesser extent, though not to the extent the Marxists believed the class structure to do so. These constraints are relative and not absolute; and the constraints of the occupational system act very differently from those of the caste system. Moreover, modern societies are characterized not only by occupational differentiation and ranking, but also by occupational mobility. In all such societies, there is some reproduction of inequality along with some individual mobility. This creates a peculiar tension within them. As Raymond Aron has observed about modern societies, they 'are both egalitarian in aspiration and hierarchical in organization' (1968: xv).

6. Institutions in Economics and Sociology

Like inequality, institutions have received attention from a number of different disciplines. But whereas the comparative study of institutions has been central to sociology, they have been studied only occasionally and fitfully by economists, except perhaps for economic historians.

Given the wide range of disciplines, such as law, political theory, history, anthropology, sociology and even economics, that have contributed to the study of institutions, it will be unreasonable to expect a single definition of the term on which all students of the subject agree. Sociologists themselves have shown little agreement on the use of the term. They have used it sometimes to refer to an association of persons with a distinct identity and continuity over time, and at other times to a regular and established pattern of activities among persons. Thus, the court may be described as an institution, but the law is also an institution; the school is an institution, but so too is education; again, the family is an institution, and so also is marriage. In the broadest sense, an institution is something that works according to rules, established or at least acknowledged by law or by custom, and whose regular and continuous operation cannot be understood without taking those rules into account.

It is a truism that economic transactions take place in and through social arrangements. To revert to Marx once again, 'In the social production of their existence, men inevitably enter into definite relations which are independent of their will.' The social relations through which economic transactions take place form part of a larger whole which is governed by distinctive principles that are not the same as the principles of the market. For the most part, the economist takes for granted the presence of the social framework which he treats as being external to his field of enquiry and analysis. When he takes account of it, he finds it most convenient to treat it as a constraint.

Douglass North begins his important work on institutions and economic performance with the following definition: 'Institutions are the rules of the game in a society or, more formally, are the humanly devised constraints that shape human interaction' (North 1990: 3). Arrow has a somewhat different emphasis, treating institutions as agencies 'for the enforcement of norms' (Swedberg 1990: 139).

North distinguishes between institutions and organizations in the following somewhat abstract terms: 'Institutions, together with the standard constraints of economic theory, determine the opportunities in a society. Organizations are created to take advantage of those opportunities, and, as the organizations evolve, they alter the institutions' (North 1990: 7). The main objective of his work is to show how institutions change— or fail to change—in response to the demands of economic performance.

It is in a sense natural for the economist to treat social institutions as constraints, along with 'the standard constraints of economic theory'. But not all those who have written about institutions have thought about them only, or even mainly, in that way. For while institutions undoubtedly impose constraints on the individual, they also provide him with facilities. Nor is this all. An institution may be viewed instrumentally as a constraint or a facility, or both; but it may also be viewed from another angle, as an end in itself. Millions of persons have for centuries viewed the family, the church, the state, or even the political party as an end in itself, and it goes against the grain of the sociologist to dismiss all of this as a delusion. It is this double nature of the institution, as a constraint (or a facility) and as an end in itself, that has made it a subject of perennial interest to the sociologist.

I would like to dwell a little on the double nature of institutions. I need not enumerate all the social and political philosophers who have waxed eloquent about the supreme value of such institutions as the family, the church and the state. But there are also others who have adopted a bleakly negative view of the subject, taking as their examples of institutions the prison, the clinic and the asylum. In a certain kind of emancipationist perspective, institutions are just bad news: the family stands for the exploitation of women, the school for the oppression of children, and the church for the manipulation of the credulous. These are both extreme philosophical positions, and neither does justice to the reality as most sociologists see it.

There is an established tendency in economic thinking whereby not only social institutions, but most things social, such as customs, conventions, ceremonials and manners in general, are viewed as just so many impediments to the unfolding of economic forces. We see this in the contrast made by Marx between the material forces of production and the social relations of production. The two might act in concert with each other, but the harmony does not last very long. Sooner or later, with the advance of economic forces, the existing social relations of production become fetters. They then have to be burst asunder to make room for further development of the material forces of production.

In India, the first quarter century after independence witnessed the high tide of development economics and economic planning. In my somewhat faded recollection of that period, the economists were the experts on development and the sociologists on the obstacles to development. Naturally, this way of looking at the world appealed more to the economists than to the sociologists, although it must be admitted that it struck a chord among large sections of the Indian intelligentsia.

As I see things, social institutions, for all the limits they impose, are far too important in the lives of human beings to be judged solely by what they contribute to the annual rate of growth. Certainly, one is entitled to turn the question around, and ask what economic growth contributes to the well-being of institutions, for there are many who value the well-being not only of individuals but also of institutions. It is far from my intention to put economic growth and institutional well-being into competition with each other, or to suggest that we can have the one only at the expense of the other. At the same time, it will be hard to deny that economic growth does sometimes damage institutions that are valued by people for their own sake and not for what they contribute to economic performance.

Part of the difference in orientation towards institutions arises from a difference of method between economists and sociologists. Economists are by and large proponents of methodological individualism: for them, the rational individual is the point of departure in the construction of theory, and this fits very well with the conception of economics as a generalizing science. Sociologists on the whole take a more sceptical view of methodological individualism, although some are more friendly, or at least less hostile to it than others. At any rate, institutions in one sense or another have figured either directly or indirectly in a great deal of sociological writing.

It may of course be argued that institutions are in the end created, sustained, altered and discarded by the actions of individuals. But the converse is no less true. No individual comes into the world with a preformed set of dispositions. His ideas, beliefs, tastes, preferences and prejudices are all acquired by him in the course of his life as he passes from one institution to another. Nothing reveals this more clearly than the comparative study of social institutions. A comparative science has a better chance of seeing how individual dispositions are shaped by social institutions than a generalizing or universalizing science.

In the sense in which I use the term, an institution has a corporate identity and a continuity over time that extends beyond the lives of its individual members. It comprises a system of differentiated roles with some inequality of esteem and authority among them. It is through its institutions that society as a whole maintains the continuity of its collective existence. Societies differ from each other because their institutions differ, in themselves and in their relations with each other. In the course of human history, there has been a continuous differentiation of institutions. We can see this easily by comparing the simpler, small-scale societies studied by anthropologists with the complex and large-scale societies characteristic of the modern world.

Economic and social change is accompanied not only by the differentiation of institutions but also by the displacement of certain kinds of institutions by others. Economic development requires the emergence of dependable social arrangements for the pursuit of new kinds of economic activity. Democracy requires stable social arrangements through which wider and more continuous political participation can be maintained.

This means not only that old social arrangements have to be discarded but also that new ones have to be created.

We cannot dispense with the rational individual which economic science takes as its point of departure. In India, the rational individual has been more successful in breaking down old institutions than in creating or sustaining new ones. The traditional institutions, based largely on kinship and religion, have been undermined and many of them are now in disarray. But new, open and secular institutions, essential for the sustenance of civil society, are yet to acquire secure foundations. The prospects for such institutions seemed hopeful at the time of independence. We gave ourselves a new constitution and set up ambitious agencies for planning and policy making. But somehow the new political, administrative, financial, educational, scientific and other institutions that were to spearhead the creation of a new society failed to fulfil their promise. We need, at the very least, a better understanding of why we have had such indifferent success in creating and sustaining open and secular institutions in the fifty years since independence.

References

Aron, Raymond. 1964. *La lutte de classes*. Paris: Gallimard.

———. 1968. *Progress and Disillusion*. London: Pall Mall Press.

———. 1970. *Marxismes imaginaires*. Paris: Gallimard.

Atkinson, A.B. 1975. *The Economics of Inequality*. Oxford: Clarendon Press.

Berlin, Isaiah. 1991. *The Crooked Timber of Humanity*. London: Fontana Press.

Béteille, André. 1962. 'Sripuram: A Village in Tanjore District'. *The Economic Weekly*. Annual Number, pp. 141–6.

———. 1963. 'Politics and Social Structure in Tamilnad'. *The Economic Weekly*. Special Number, pp. 1161–7.

———. 1995. 'My Formative Years in the Delhi School of Economics, 1959–72'. In Dharma Kumar and Dilip Mookherjee (eds). *D. School*. Delhi: Oxford University Press, pp. 53–67.

———. (ed). 1983. *Equality and Inequality*. Delhi: Oxford University Press.

Blau, P.M. and O.D. Duncan. 1968. *The American Occupational System*. Glencoe: The Free Press.

Durkheim, Émile. 1938. *The Rules of Sociological Method*. Glencoe: The Free Press.

Fuller, C.J. 1999. 'An Interview with M.N. Srinivas'. *Anthropology Today*. Vol. 15. No. 5, pp. 3–9.

Gerth, H.H. and C.W. Mills (eds). 1946. *From Max Weber: Essays in Sociology*. New York: Oxford University Press.

Goldthorpe, J.H. and K. Hope. 1974. *The Social Grading of Occupations*. Oxford: Clarendon Press.

Marx, Karl. 1954. *Capital*. Moscow: Progress Publishers. Vol. 1.

———. 1970. *A Contribution to the Critique of Political Economy*. Moscow: Progress Publishers.

Marx, Karl and Friedrich Engels. 1968. *The German Ideology*. Moscow: Progress Publishers.

North, Douglass C. 1990. *Institutions, Institutional Change and Economic Performance*. Cambridge: Cambridge University Press.

Pareto, Vilfredo. 1926. *Les systèmes socialistes*. Paris: Marcel Giard. 2 vols.

Radcliffe-Brown, A.R. 1957. *A Natural Science of Society*. Glencoe: The Free Press.

Schumpeter, J.A. 1976. *Capitalism, Socialism and Democracy*. London: George Allen and Unwin.

Sen, A.K. 1973. *On Economic Inequality*. Oxford: Clarendon Press.

Srinivas, M.N. 1962. *Caste in Modern India and Other Essays*. Bombay: Asia Publishing House.

———. 1966. *Social Change in Modern India*. Berkeley: University of California Press.

Swedberg, Richard (ed.). 1990, *Economics and Sociology*. Princeton: Princeton University Press.

———. (ed). 1955. *India's Villages*. Calcutta: Government Press.

———. 1995. 'Sociology in Delhi'. In Dharma Kumar and Dilip Mookherjee (eds). *D. School*. Delhi: Oxford University Press, pp. 31–52.

Stigler, George J. 1984. 'Economics The Imperial Science?'. *Scandinavian Journal of Economics*. Vol. 86, pp. 301–13.

Tendulkar, Suresh D. 1983. 'Economic Inequality in an Indian Perspective'. In A. Béteille (ed). *Equality and Inequality*. Delhi: Oxford University Press, pp. 71–128.

Treiman, Donald J. 1977. *Occupational Prestige in Comparative Perspective*. New York: Academic University Press.

Weber, Max. 1976. *The Protestant Ethic and the Spirit of Capitalism*. London: George Allen and Unwin.

———. 1978. *Economy and Society*. Berkeley: University of California Press, 2 vols.

Chapter
10

The Place of Tradition in Sociological Enquiry

Tradition enters into sociological enquiry in two distinct though related ways. The first concerns the nature of tradition as a set of beliefs and practices, and their various forms in different places and at different times. The second concerns the tradition of sociological enquiry itself, its unity and diversity, and its roots in one or another general cultural or national tradition. Given the fact that there are several cultural and national traditions, is it possible or even desirable to have one single body of sociological concepts and methods to be applied to the interpretation and explanation of the entire range of social phenomena the world over? Thus, the topic I have chosen relates to the content as well as the method of sociological enquiry.

Of the two, it seems to me that the issue of method is the more difficult and the more contentious one. It is also an issue that is in some sense inescapable in the discipline of sociology. For, unlike economics and some other disciplines, sociology is, along with history, closely concerned with the understanding and interpretation of tradition. But, unlike history, sociology is comparative by deliberate choice; it cannot confine its attention to any single tradition as a unique and self-contained system, but must examine the similarities and differences among traditions. It is therefore important to ask how far the sociological method can detach itself from given historical and cultural traditions so as to examine all traditions in an objective and unbiased way.

Like most modern academic disciplines, sociology had its origins in the west. Since it is a relatively new discipline even there, it found a place in teaching and research in India within a few decades of its being established in Europe and America. But whereas one could speak of a German or an American tradition of sociology by the 1930s (Mannheim 1953: 185–228), one cannot even now speak with much conviction of an Indian tradition in the discipline. This is largely because in their teaching and research, Indian sociologists have drawn upon concepts, methods and theories already in use in the West instead of developing their own.

What sociologists do in this regard is hardly different from what is done by physicists or biologists, or even economists. But they worry more about their predicament than do the natural scientists. The relationship between data on the one hand and concepts, methods and theories on the other is in the human sciences different from what it is in the natural sciences. Indian physicists freely draw their tools of investigation and analysis from the common pool, and when one of them formulates a general rule or principle, such as the Saha equation or the Chandrasekhar limit, he takes it for granted that it will be used by physicists everywhere and not just in India. The utility of a common stock of tools is not in question in the natural sciences; but in the human sciences, its very existence is in question.

No approach or method in any intellectual discipline can be satisfactory in every respect. The urge for continuous revision and reformulation of existing concepts, methods and theories is what gives to scientific enquiry its distinctive orientation. There is a difference, however, between the piecemeal revision and reformulation that is a part of everyday scientific practice and the call to set aside the entire stock of existing tools in order to start with a whole new orientation and approach. There can be several critiques of the existing and established framework of enquiry, and several proposals for alternatives to it. Here I shall examine that kind of radical critique which is directed against alien approaches to the study of Indian society and, in the concluding part, attempt an appraisal of the underlying promise of an alternative sociology more in tune with the Indian tradition.

* * *

Before proceeding further with questions of method, I would like to survey briefly some of the main substantive issues. Tradition has been viewed as an attribute of types of action and of authority, of institutions and of whole societies. It has been viewed positively as ensuring stability and continuity in society and culture, and negatively as providing resistance to development and change. The concepts of tradition used by sociologists are shaped by their theories of social structure and social change, but those theories are more often implicit than explicit.

In a study of the subject published some time ago, the sociologist Edward Shils (1981) drew attention to the lack of any systematic discussion of the concept even among its habitual users. If it is a characteristic of tradition that it is largely taken for granted by those who are in its grip, it may be said that the concept of it too has been more generally accepted as given than critically examined, at least by sociologists in the last fifty years. Significantly, that period witnessed the rise and fall of the dichotomous division of the world into societies labelled 'traditional' and 'modern'.

Tradition is, or at least was until recently, an important subject in the study of history, particularly the history of ideas and the history of art. Students of art and literature have always had to deal with the relationship between tradition and individual talent. More recently, those dealing with the history and sociology of science have drawn attention to the important part played by tradition in the development of scientific research. In neither art nor science is it reasonable to view tradition as simply an obstacle to creativity and innovation. Today, few scientists can hope to contribute effectively to science without being socialized into the traditions of the laboratory, and paradoxically this appears to be more true of scientific work at the end of the twentieth century than it was at the end of the eighteenth.

In its broadest usage, the idea of tradition is almost coterminous with that of culture which, in Tylor's famous definition, is 'that complex whole which includes knowledge, belief, art, morals, law, custom and any other capabilities and habits acquired by man as a member of society' (Beattie 1964: 20). Tradition, like culture, is both a facility and a constraint; it provides the individual with resources he would be incapable of creating by his own unaided effort, but it also confines his actions within a given framework of rules and practices. Both refer to things that exist independently of their individual bearers and outlive the individuals through whom they are transmitted from generation to generation. In both cases, the attention is on the past in the present.

What distinguishes tradition in the specific sense from culture in general is its conscious, not to say self-conscious, orientation to the past. The past is valued for its own sake and is invoked as a model for present practice. As Edward Shils has put it, 'Recurrence or identity through time is not, as such, the decisive criterion of traditional belief or action. It is not the intertemporal identity of beliefs or actions which constitutes a tradition; it is the intertemporal *filiation* of beliefs which is constitutive' (Shils 1975: 187, emphasis in original). Tradition is not simply the 'dead hand of custom'; traditions are consciously maintained, revived and even invented.

Nevertheless, tradition is not all that there is to social practice. A large part of the inspiration for the study of tradition in contemporary sociology derives, directly or indirectly, from the work of Max Weber. There it figures as only one of the components of social life, and not necessarily the most important one.

Weber's general sociology begins with a consideration of the nature and types of social action. As is well known, there are, according to him, three main types of action, defined in terms of their orientation. These are: traditional action, affectual or emotional action, and rational action. Weber's emphasis is by conscious choice on rational action rather than the two other types of action. As such, rational action is itself differentiated into two important sub-types, namely, instrumentally-rational (Zweckrational) and value-rational (Wertrational) action. The author's intention was to formulate as sharply as possible the contrasts between the types of action; they were, in his scheme, ideal or pure types, and not average types.

The treatment of the pure type of traditional action is sketchy, not to say casual. Traditional action serves (along with affectual action) as a foil for setting off the distinctive features of rational action, particularly instrumentally-rational action. It is described as being governed by 'the habituation of long practice', and to that extent appears as unreflective. Weber realizes that by stressing the habits of the past, he pushes traditional action to the borderline between meaningful action and mere behaviour. As he puts it, 'Strictly traditional behaviour, like the reactive type of imitation discussed above, lies very close to the borderline of what can justifiably be called meaningfully oriented action, and often on the other side' (Weber 1978: 25). As we have seen, to be oriented towards a tradition is not necessarily to be ruled by the dead hand of custom.

Weber sees that there is at the other end too an affinity between traditional action and action that is rationally oriented towards an absolute value, in other words, value-rational action. As he points out, 'attachment to habitual forms can be upheld with varying degrees of self-consciousness and in a variety of senses. In this case the type may shade into value rationality (Wertrationalität)' (Ibid.). The willed and conscious revival, not to say invention, of tradition by a religious or political movement need not be more mechanical or unreflective than the routine of everyday practice in a scientific laboratory. It will be hard indeed to argue that people can never act within the framework of tradition in a rational way.

It should be obvious that most ongoing social arrangements manifest actions of all the principal types, ranging from the purely habitual to the purely calculative. This makes it difficult to move directly from the types of social action to the types of institutional arrangement. The latter show a mixture of components and can be distinguished from each other at best only in terms of the degrees to which the basic components are present.

We get a clearer insight into the place of tradition in social arrangements through a consideration of the nature and types of legitimate domination. Weber repeatedly drew attention to the distinction between traditional and modern law, between the traditional state and the constitutional state and, above all, between traditional and rational-legal principles of administration. There is a significant difference between institutions that have existed since time immemorial and derive their legitimacy from their antiquity and those that are created, modified and reconstituted by human beings in a deliberate and methodical manner. The continuous effort to improve upon existing social arrangements and to create new ones is a specific feature of the modern as against the traditional orientation to life. In India, the constitutional state is the prime exemplar of the departure from all traditional forms of governance.

Crucial to the continuity of any kind of social arrangement is its legitimacy. The sources of legitimacy are diverse and they combine in various ways to provide different kinds of unity and coherence to particular social arrangements. Here there is a striking contrast between traditional and rational-legal forms of legitimacy. As Weber puts it, 'The validity of a social order by virtue of the sacredness of tradition is the oldest and most universal type of legitimacy'. And again, 'Today the most common form of legitimacy is the belief in legality, the compliance with enactments which are *formally* correct and which have been made in the accustomed manner' (Weber 1978: 37).

An examination of contemporary Indian society—as of any large and complex society today—reveals the coexistence of a great variety of institutional arrangements. In addition to the institutions of kinship, caste and religion inherited from the past, there are many new ones devoted to a variety of specialized tasks in the fields of administration, finance, health, education, communication, research, and so on. These modern institutions are open and secular institutions, and they provide indispensable linkages between the citizen and the state. The success of civil society in India will depend to a large extent on the health and well-being of these new open and secular institutions (Béteille 1996).

Modern institutions such as hospitals, laboratories and universities differ in form and function from the traditional institutions of village, caste and joint family. Their principles of recruitment are different and the rules for their internal regulation are also different. As a social arrangement, an institution has not only a certain form and function, but also a certain legitimacy and meaning for its individual members. Its form and function are what may be observed from outside; but viewed from within and by its members, what count for as much, if not more, are its meaning and legitimacy.

Today, there is much disquiet about the health and well-being of the modern institutions on which much of our public life depends. In their outward form, they resemble similar institutions that work successfully, or more or less successfully, in the western world. Fifty years ago, it was believed that they would work successfully here as well once their teething troubles were over. But in many respects, these institutions—municipal corporations, universities, public hospitals, political parties, and so on— are in worse shape than they were fifty years ago. For, irrespective of their outward form, they have failed to maintain among their members the meaning and legitimacy indispensable for their effective functioning. The norms by which their activities are expected to be regulated yield too readily before the many traditional values that seep into them from the outer environment and disrupt their internal life.

There are those who say that our public institutions—legislatures, municipal corporations, political parties, universities and colleges—do not work well, and indeed cannot work well, on our soil because they are all alien to the Indian tradition, and hence should be replaced by alternative institutions that are more in tune with that tradition. But the appeal to tradition as a guide for building alternatives to existing institutions, whether in administration or commerce or even education, has hardly led to any concrete results. So far it has been more a matter of rhetoric than of sober consideration of available alternatives. Open and secular institutions are an innovation of the modern world, and it is difficult to see how we can dispense with them on the ground that they are out of tune with traditional values. Once we accept the ideal of the constitutional state and the principle of equal citizenship for all irrespective of caste, creed and gender, certain traditional options become automatically closed.

What has been said above should not be taken to mean that all the institutions of modern India, or of any modern society, must be cast in one and the same mould. To say that our public institutions should by and large be open and secular institutions in contrast to what largely prevailed in the past is not to propose that religion, family and kinship should be abolished or deprived of their legitimacy. It is obvious that institutions that have little to do with instrumental rationality have an important place not only in Indian society but in all human societies. Moreover, in western countries, institutions such as the English universities have retained many traditional components while adapting themselves successfully to changing legal, economic and political requirements.

Enough has been said to show that traditional and other components of social action and social relations are closely intertwined in most, if not all, human societies. The construction and use of ideal types helps to sort these components out from each other, but only up to a point. Beyond that point, the use of contrastive categories becomes misleading and counterproductive. It is one thing to construct ideal types of social action or social relations or even social institutions, but quite another to apply ideal types for contrasting whole societies and even whole continents.

With the beginning of the process of decolonization about fifty years ago, the relationship between tradition and modernity acquired a new focus in sociological enquiry. The examination of that relationship was seen to have both a theoretical and a practical value. The societies of Asia and Africa were all seen to be traditional societies and those of western Europe and northern America as modern ones. Tradition became an important topic, and for some time the most important one, in sociological studies of Turkey, Iran, India and other countries in Asia and Africa. It figured hardly at all in studies of contemporary France, Germany and the United States, and it is in this light that we have to view Shils's disquiet over the absence of any serious discussion of the concept in the sociological literature. For a certain period of time, sociologists and other social scientists came to view tradition not as something to take pride in but as something to be got rid of in the interest of modernity and modernization.

A landmark in this new perspective on traditional societies was a joint project of the MIT and Columbia University for the study of a number of countries in the Middle East, including Turkey, Iran and

Egypt. The results of the study were published in an influential book by Daniel Lerner entitled *The Passing of Traditional Society* (1958). Lerner observed, 'The direction of change is the same in all the Middle East lands. Everywhere the passing of traditional life is visible; the secular trend is toward mobility—physical, social and psychic mobility' (1958: 83). He dwelt in particular on the emergence of a new personality type and the part played in it by education, communication and the media.

The churning process observed—and welcomed—by Lerner and his associates in the Middle East was taking place elsewhere as well. In India, in the wake of independence, there was a marked enthusiasm for the transformation of society through rational legislative enactment and rational economic planning. Economic development was seen as the necessary precondition for every kind of desirable change. A major concern among all social scientists, and not economists alone, was with achieving faster rates of growth. This concern made traditional habits, practices and attitudes a major target of attack. Tradition was viewed as the source and foundation of underdevelopment, and modernization was advocated in the name of both economic growth and social justice.

The negative attitude towards tradition encouraged by theories of modernization did not go unchallenged and it did not last very long. For one thing, modernity and modernization came under increasingly critical scrutiny. The actual experience of modernization gave people a better sense of its social and human costs than they at first had. Moreover, the United States, the prime exemplar of modernity, rapidly lost its glamour in the eyes of the intelligentsia throughout Asia and Africa. The journey to modernity seemed excessively arduous, and what lay at the end of it was both uncertain and uninspiring. The abandonment of tradition lock, stock and barrel seemed too high a price to pay for such a venture. The attention soon shifted from tradition as an obstacle to modernity to tradition as a guarantor of national identity.

* * *

The noisy disparagement of tradition as a source merely of obstacles to the realization of a better and fuller life can hardly be regarded as reasonable. At the same time, the obsession with national tradition as the only guarantor of a meaningful social existence is not without its costs. In what follows, I shall examine some of the hazards that accompany the attempt to mobilize national tradition in the service of sociological enquiry.

Sociology has been practised in India for not more than seventy-five years, but then, as I have already pointed out, as an academic discipline, it is hardly more than a hundred years old anywhere. We are dealing with a relatively new discipline that in fact entered our academic practice not very long after it first became established in the west. To be sure, the real expansion of the discipline took place only after independence. Today, it is not only taught in a large number of colleges and universities also but has found a place in institutes of research outside the university system. It has its own professional associations, national and regional, and its own professional journals. The volume of research and publication in the subject is now not inconsiderable.

There are two sides to sociology as a discipline which we may describe in short as the empirical and the theoretical sides, including in the latter not just theories in the strict sense but also approaches, methods, concepts, procedures and techniques. Ideally speaking, the two sides should grow together and roughly at the same pace. But when we look at the actual development of sociology, we find that Indian sociologists have produced a very large body of empirical material, sometimes very competently analysed and interpreted, on virtually every aspect of their society; but there has been very little innovation by them of concepts, methods and theories. For the latter, they have relied by and large on the stock of ideas produced by sociologists in Europe and America for the common use of all.

People point out that there is a French, a German and even an American tradition of sociology, and ask why there is no corresponding Indian tradition. Several questions arise out of this. Is it necessary for every nation to have its own tradition of sociology? Are national traditions the only significant ones in all fields of intellectual endeavour? And finally, if a national tradition has not emerged on its own, what should be done, and by whom, to bring it into being?

The question still remains as to why Indian sociologists have shown so little innovation in the practice of their discipline. Many would say that this is because they have depended too heavily on borrowed theories, borrowed concepts and borrowed methods of enquiry. The practice began as a matter of convenience, and then became established in the routines of teaching and research so that now it has become difficult to dislodge. When the social sciences began to be taught in our universities, there were very few books written by Indian scholars who depended by and large on books written in the west. The practice continues to this day, and it affects not only the content of teaching but also the nature and direction of research.

It is not easy to set oneself free from habits of the mind that have become established over several generations through continuous practice. Some years ago, a distinguished Indian economist complained about the demoralizing effects of the dependence on western textbooks and more generally of the preoccupation with catching up with the west (Chakravarty 1986). The same kind of complaint is persistently made by Indian sociologists about the work of their colleagues. It is not that Indian social scientists have never tried to write their own textbooks. But these are for the most part either unabashed imitations of western products, or they are of very poor quality. Finding little to choose between them, most sociologists who are serious about teaching and research return sooner or later to the mainstream of their discipline.

Most working sociologists in India, as elsewhere, act in the implicit belief that their work moves forward mainly through borrowing and creative adaptation. After all, what we call western sociology is not all of one piece, and American sociology, which is in the ascendant today, would not be what it is but for extensive borrowing from French and German sociology. Perhaps the majority believe that we should use such tools as are already available, adapt them to our uses as well as we can, and improvise to the extent possible. Whether we engage in participant-observation or in survey research, the basic procedures have to be broadly the same, so why should we agonize over where and by whom they were first devised? A large body of concepts and methods, suited to a variety of tastes, is already available for the study of virtually every substantive problem, and the principle of economy demands that we first try out what is available.

But the discontent with the passive and dependent status of Indian social science is not easily removed. Critics of the existing state of affairs argue that the poverty of our social theory follows from our own unreflective adherence to a framework of enquiry and analysis that is alien in origin and inappropriate to our needs. Working within the framework leads to its further entrenchment and to a continuing dissipation of intellectual energy. They point out that the analogy between the natural sciences and the human sciences is misconceived and misleading. In the latter, there is far greater risk of even observation and description being vitiated by the use of concepts and procedures that have emerged in response to a different and alien cultural and historical tradition.

If we set aside the existing framework of sociology used more or less throughout the world on the ground that it is of alien provenance and hence out of tune with the Indian reality, what shall we put in its place? The prospect of an alternative sociology of India or even an alternative to the sociology of India has attracted some scholars almost from the time when the subject was introduced into India. Among the early exponents of the view were Benoy Kumar Sarkar in Calcutta and D.P. Mukerji in Lucknow, each of whom had a considerable following in his lifetime (Bhattacharyya 1990; Madan 1994).

In his presidential address to the Indian Sociological Conference in 1955, D.P. Mukerji took issue with his colleagues for their abject dependence on imported knowledge. 'It pains me to observe,' he said, 'how our Indian scholars succumb to the lure of modern "scientific" techniques imported from outside as a part of technical aid and "know-how", without resistance and dignity.' He wished Indian sociologists to take greater pride in their own tradition. 'Thus it is that it is not enough for the Indian sociologist to be a sociologist. He must be an Indian first, that is, he is to share in the folk-ways, mores, customs and traditions for the purpose of understanding his social system and what lies beneath it and beyond it' (Mukerji 1958: 232–3). Few Indians can resist the appeal to national dignity when it is made at a public gathering.

Professor Mukerji spoke about the kind of training he considered appropriate for the formation of the sociologist in India. He observed, 'Unless sociological training is grounded on Sanskrit or any such language in which the traditions have been embodied as symbols, social research in India will be a pale imitation of what others are doing' (1958: 233). The bias for Sanskrit is evident but the grounds for it are not altogether clear, for surely there cannot be any language in which traditions are not embodied as symbols.

It is difficult from the sociological point of view to see why Indian traditions have to be recovered through Sanskrit rather than living languages such as Tamil or Bengali that have been in continuous use for centuries. Perhaps we feel that the resources of our modern languages cannot measure up to those of English, French and German, and that only our classical languages can meet the test. Or we assume that the classical tradition, being sufficiently remote from the present reality, offers the safest refuge from the plague of imitation. In either case, the adulation of classical and the implicit denigration of modern languages does not augur well for the serious pursuit of sociological enquiry, whose point of departure is the present and not the past.

Views such as the above find echoes in the minds of many Indian sociologists. They are important, but at the same time difficult to engage with. For one thing, the arguments are rarely developed in a sustained manner. For another, they are expressed in speech more often than in writing—at conferences, in discussions, and in between formal presentations. When they are set down in writing, they are generally hedged in with qualifications that make it extremely difficult to determine the exact role that is being assigned to tradition in sociological enquiry. Mukerji's writings, for example, present a melange of methodological, substantive and ethical recommendations. Nobody would deny the need for the interpretation of symbols, or the advantage of doing so through the native language, but whether that in itself amounts to an alternative approach and an alternative methodology is a different question.

The point around which the debate seems to turn is that of the penetrability of particular traditions to general methods of social enquiry. Some would say that such methods cannot reach into the inner core of meaning constitutive of every tradition, and others that they can, at least in principle. The issue is not of the complete adequacy of the general methods at present available, but of the possibility of making such methods more adequate through comparative study. Here I would place the greatest emphasis on the role of fair and objective comparisons, for I believe, with Durkheim, that comparative sociology is not a special branch of sociology, it is sociology itself.

The obdurate fact about the world in which we live is that there are very many, and not just two or three, national traditions. The promise of comparative sociology, which it has fulfilled in some measure though by no means in full measure, is that it will enable us to detach ourselves, at least to some extent, from these particular traditions in order to reach towards a general understanding of social action, social relations and social institutions in their entire range and variety. How can we move forward if we turn our backs on what has been done so far on the ground that the whole framework of enquiry was alien and hence distorting, and that we will be better served by our own particular sociology? Why should the clock stop with the inception of an Indian sociology, and other people elsewhere not set about developing a Korean sociology, an Indonesian sociology, a Turkish sociology, a Nigerian sociology and a Peruvian sociology?

The matter will not rest there, for if we examine it a little more closely, we will encounter the same problem of the plurality of traditions within

India. Even if we begin by speaking of one single Indian tradition, there is no reason why everyone should stop there. Within India there is a Hindu tradition and an Islamic tradition; north Indian and south Indian languages and traditions; and numerous sub-traditions within and outside these. When people speak of the replacement of the alien western framework of enquiry by one more in tune with the Indian tradition, they almost invariably have in mind the Brahminical Hindu tradition, although only some make this explicit and others do not. The plea for recasting the categories of sociological enquiry from English into Sanskrit is symptomatic of this.

I have yet to see a proposal for an Indian alternative to the existing framework of sociological enquiry presented through categories other than those of Brahminical Hinduism. To be sure, what prevails today as the framework of general and comparative sociology is not free from its own biases, its own distortions and its own constraints. But not all Indians may feel the same enthusiasm for having those constraints replaced by the constraints of Sanskritic Hindu categories. Many, if not most of them, are likely to find more room for intellectual manoeuvre in the former than in the latter.

The bias for the categories of Brahminical Hinduism is most explicit in the approach to sociology advocated by Kewal Motwani, a contemporary of Benoy Sarkar and D.P. Mukerji, though perhaps never as influential as them. Professor Motwani (1961: 19) maintained that Dharmashastra was the Sanskrit word for sociology. The sociology that he recommended was to be based on the Dharmashastra in general and the Manu Dharmashastra in particular (Motwani 1934; 1961). His views were apparently well received abroad and by some scientists in India in the forties and fifties (Hallen and Prasad 1970). But we can well imagine how this presentation of Indian sociology as Manuvad is likely to be received today by those who speak for the Backward Classes. Professor Motwani published a very great deal, and his arguments have a peculiar insistence and consistency. It is not necessary to decide whether he should be blamed for being ingenuous or praised for being candid. His work has an exemplary value if only because it brings fully into view the biases that other proponents of an Indian alternative to mainstream sociology can only mask but never really escape.

The search for an Indian way of doing sociology appears on balance to be both half-hearted and disingenuous. I call it half-hearted because the intention, though never abandoned, has not led to any cumulative progression of effort. In terms of the development of an alternative framework for the sociology of India, we are no further today than we were in the thirties and forties with B.K. Sarkar and D.P. Mukerji. People speak at conferences and write the occasional paper about an Indian approach to the sociology of India, but then they seem to lose concentration and go about their work in much the same way as the others do. What we have as a result is a completely static dialectic in which the same or similar formulas are repeated without any forward movement. If it is generally true that every Indian sociologist begins as if there has been no work done by Indians before, this is particularly true of those who set out to take the Indian tradition as their point of departure.

This is accompanied by an orientation to tradition that places it not only in the past, but by preference in the distant and remote past. Some refer back to Manu and others to Panini, but few care for their own immediate predecessors who we may assume to have been closer to them in outlook and sensibility. There is a large and yawning gap in time and context between the tradition that is invoked and the purpose for which it is invoked, rendering largely fictitious that sense of filiation which is an essential part of tradition as an active principle. The desire to connect with the remote past without any regard for the nearer links of filiation hardly betokens a sincere engagement with tradition. It is obvious that the appeal to tradition serves a rhetorical purpose; but it is doubtful that it contributes anything of value to the method of sociological enquiry.

References

Beattie, John. 1964. *Other Cultures: Aims, Methods and Achievements in Social Anthropology*. London: Cohen & West.

Béteille, André. 1996. *Civil Society and Its Institutions* (The First Fulbright Memorial Lecture). Calcutta: USEFI.

Bhattacharyya, Swapan Kumar. 1990. *Indian Sociology: The Role of Benoy Kumar Sarkar*. Burdwan: The University of Burdwan.

Chakravarty, Sukhamoy. 1986. 'The Teaching of Economics in India'. *Economic and Political Weekly*. Vol. 21. No. 7, pp. 1165–8.

Hallen, G.C. and Rajeshwar Prasad (eds). 1970. *Towards a Global Sociology: Essays in Honour of Professor Kewal Motwani*. Agra: Satish Book Enterprise.

Lerner, Daniel. 1958. *The Passing of Traditional Society: Modernizing the Middle East*. New York: The Free Press.

Madan, T.N. 1994. *Pathways: Approaches to the Study of Society in India*. Delhi: Oxford University Press.

Mannheim, Karl. 1953. *Essays in Sociology and Social Psychology*. London: Routledge & Kegan Paul.

Motwani, Kewal. 1934. *Manu: A Study in Hindu Social Theory*. Madras: Ganesh & Co.

————. 1961. *Integration: A Programme of Education*. Madras: Ganesh & Co.

Mukerji, D.P. 1958. *Diversities: Essays in Economics, Sociology and Other Social Problems*. New Delhi: People's Publishing House.

Shils, Edward. 1975. *Center and Periphery: Essays in Macro-sociology*. Chicago: University of Chicago Press.

————. 1981. *Tradition*. Chicago: University of Chicago Press.

Weber, Max. 1978. *Economy and Society: An Outline of Interpretive Sociology*. Berkeley: University of California Press.

Chapter

11

Science and Tradition*

Both science and tradition are large subjects, and each has been conceived in a variety of ways. I have to explain very briefly what I mean by these terms if my observations are to have some semblance of clarity and cogency.

The concept of science may be used in a broad or a narrow sense, and I would like to indicate very briefly the sense in which I will use it. The term tends to be used more narrowly in English than in French or German, for even though we speak of the social sciences or the behavioural sciences in English, the term 'science' without qualification stands in- variably for such disciplines as physics, chemistry, botany and zoology, and not for sociology, politics or economics. The cognate word 'science' in French has a wider connotation so that Durkheim had no hesitation in appropriating it, without qualification, for sociology. The term 'Wissenschaft' has also a broad connotation in German; and when Max Weber gave his celebrated address on 'Wissenschaft als Beruf' or 'Science as a Vocation', he spoke mainly of such disciplines as economics, politics and sociology, although he also kept what are called the hard sciences in mind.

In the popular mind, science is associated with precision and meas- urement, so that sociology is not a science whereas mathematics is. Of course, measurement is an important part of science but it is not the defining feature of science as I understand the term. What is decisive is

*This is a revised version of the inaugural address given at a seminar on Science and Tradition at IIT Kanpur on 22 December 1997.

a certain kind of engagement with empirical reality, central to which is the careful and methodical observation and description of facts. There are many kinds of intellectual exercises in which facts 'do not affect the question'. Some of these are of very great importance, but they are outside the province of science as I understand it. I have surprised generations of my own students by saying that in my judgement mathematics is not a science but geology is. The issue is not of exactitude but of a particular orientation to facts.

No individual can go through life without any regard for facts. But some pay more attention to facts and treat them with greater respect than do others. I have known brilliant intellectuals who can construct bold and ingenious arguments from first principles but are bored by facts and are impervious to empirical evidence that goes against their arguments. What is true of individuals is also true to some extent of intellectual traditions. Some traditions value abstract ideas and formal principles while others cultivate the disciplined practice of empirical enquiry. The pursuit of science, as I understand the term, is not in tune with every kind of intellectual tradition.

I have now come to the point where I must clarify, however briefly, where I stand on the question of tradition. Tradition is what links present practices with past ones: it is the past in the present. No society is created *ex nihilo* by its present members. Ideas, beliefs and values are carried over, with additions, modifications and deletions, by successive generations from the past to the present and onto the future. But this transmission is not a uniformly self-conscious process; very often it occurs without reflection or deliberation. The past as a thing in itself is not equally valued in every social milieu. We can speak of a tradition only when a positive value is placed on the past as something to serve as a guide to everyday thought and practice in the present.

Tradition and innovation should not be viewed as antithetical. A living tradition is more or less accommodative of new elements, although it is naturally mistrustful of novelty for its own sake. All traditions make additions and deletions to a greater or lesser extent, acquiring in some cases a greater expanse and in others a sharper focus. A tradition that seeks to shut out all innovation becomes atrophied and lifeless in course of time.

Tradition in the sense I would like to give the term, involves not only a distinct value being placed on the past but actual links of filiation between the present exponents of ideas and practices and their forebears. These links may be more or less active, and there may be gaps and breaches, but without some kind of filiation, tradition would be a lifeless thing. There is a class of cosmopolitan Indians who decorate their homes with artefacts bought at great expense from the Cottage Industries Emporium; this does not necessarily betoken any active engagement with tradition on their part or even any great respect for it. Paradoxical as it may sound, tradition can also become a fashion, but that is of little present interest.

Those who invoke tradition tend to stress its antiquity. How old does a tradition have to be in order to establish its legitimacy? A tradition need not go back to the remote past in order to be counted as one. Some intellectual traditions are in fact relatively recent in origin and their historical beginnings may be traced with reasonable exactitude. What is important to a tradition, as I understand it, is not so much its antiquity as the intertemporal filiation of the beliefs and practices constitutive of it.

I find it convenient to speak of traditions in the plural, particularly in the context of Indian society and culture. I do not ignore the existence of national traditions, but a strong national tradition may sometimes act against the growth of traditions in science and scholarship. Even in a small country like France, one may speak separately of the tradition of wine growing, the tradition of medical science and the tradition of historiography; the French tradition of historiography, which has had great influence on scholarship, is in fact of relatively recent origin. The plurality of traditions has always been valued in Indian society, and many scholars have commented on it.

The various traditions in any large national society are no doubt linked to each other in some way. But these links are complex, tenuous and fluid, and often difficult to identify in any exact way. A strong national tradition exerts pressure on distinct and separate traditions to recast themselves in its own mould. In various fields of activity, a search begins for lost traditions in the name of authenticity and national dignity. Where a tradition cannot be recovered, it is sometimes invented. The self-conscious search in science and scholarship for antecedents in the remote past may act against the traditions specific to those fields.

When we look back on India's intellectual achievement, we are struck as much by its strength as by its one-sidedness. For a hundred years and more, that achievement was persistently denigrated by the country's colonial rulers. It can certainly be argued that they are still undervalued in the western world. There is no major entry in the current edition of the *Encyclopaedia Britannica* on Aryabhata, Bhaskara or Panini, even though there are many such entries on western scholars of a lesser stature. The edition of 1929 gave even shorter shrift to Indian contributions to knowledge. Even today, Indian thinkers who receive the greatest attention in the west are religious thinkers.

The unjust denigration of India's past intellectual achievement has left permanent scars on Indian intellectuals with unfortunate consequences for their present attitudes. It has led them to alternate between being subservient and being combative. The combativeness began in the nineteenth century itself with the most extravagant claims about past achievements in science and technology that were either lost or destroyed by foreign invaders. This state of affairs makes it extremely difficult to arrive at a balanced assessment of the legacy of the past.

What I would like to do here is to draw attention not so much to the greatness of India's past intellectual achievement as to its peculiar orientation. This is manifested in a continuous emphasis on formal intellectual disciplines and a corresponding neglect of empirical knowledge. There are great, not to say spectacular, achievements in mathematics, grammar, logic and metaphysics, but hardly any contribution to or interest in such subjects as history and geography, if we leave aside the little that came in with the Muslims.

This peculiar emphasis might have had something to do with the social framework of the cultivation and transmission of knowledge in past times. The brahminical Hindu intellectual tradition was elitist in more than one sense. All intellectual traditions are exclusive, more or less, but this was exclusive to an unusual extent. Its bearers belonged to a particular caste, the Brahmins, and other members of society had a small part to play in the cultivation and transmission of systematic knowledge. Obviously others also pursued knowledge and contributed to its growth in one way or another. But the traditional Hindu literati, who were the repositories of systematic theoretical knowledge, were by all accounts socially far more exclusive than their European or Chinese or Islamic counterparts.

A striking feature of the Indian in comparison to other intellectual traditions was the heavy reliance on the spoken as against the written word in the transmission of systematic knowledge. This may have had something to do with the socially closed nature of the bearers of knowledge in the past. Reading and writing have been known and practised in India for well over two thousand years: ancient or medieval India was by no means a pre-literate society. Nevertheless, down to modern times, writing has been used far less extensively in the transmission of knowledge than in other civilizations. In my experience of academic cultures in the social sciences,

Indians tend to value what they say rather more than what they write. This is a large and fascinating subject into which I cannot, unfortunately, enter here.

A tightly-closed intellectual stratum, acutely conscious of the continuity of its own tradition, develops its own intellectual style. Observers through the ages have commented on the inward-looking character of the bearers of the Indian intellectual tradition and on their overweening conceit. The Arab scholar al-Biruni who was in India in the early part of the eleventh century was baffled by his encounter with the local pundits. They were supremely self-confident and treated him with great condescension. When he tried to bring some of his own knowledge to their notice, they refused to believe that he could have acquired that knowledge on his own or from anyone but a Brahmin pundit.

What appears to others as overweening conceit may in fact be the expression of a characteristic intellectual stance in which theoretical knowledge or knowledge acquired through ratiocination is valued immensely above empirical knowledge or knowledge acquired through observation. The overvaluation of theoretical knowledge at the expense of empirical knowledge remains a feature of brahminical culture to this day. This may be illustrated with an example from my own fieldwork in a village in Tanjore district with a community of Brahmins. After spending some months recording observations on the domestic rituals of the Brahmins, I decided to turn my attention to the non-Brahmins in the village. I mentioned the matter to an influential Brahmin resident of the village who had helped me much in my work and whose counsel I valued. He told me coolly that I need not seek out non-Brahmin informants for he would himself tell me whatever I needed to know about their religious observances; and if that did not satisfy me, he would ask the most knowledgeable Brahmins in the *agraharam* to answer whatever questions remained. Since he had taken some interest in my research, I explained to him that I wished to make my observations and to secure my information at first hand. He said that he knew all that very well, but the non-Brahmins, being peasants, not only did not understand their own rituals but would lack the capacity to describe them to me in a coherent way. Not only that, he had the same view of the facts relating to agriculture. The non-Brahmins might practice agriculture but the Brahmins alone knew the theory of it, and it was the theory that counted and not the practice.

I recognize the difficulty of relating long-standing patterns and tendencies to the current practices of science and scholarship in our universities and research institutes today. The evidence is scattered and not always consistent. My impressions are based on the observation of professional life in the last forty years and relate mainly to the social sciences in India, and especially to sociology and a few related disciplines. There I have been struck again and again by the tendency among the best practitioners to seek out the arcane and to neglect the commonplace. This tendency has not led to any great advances in theory for, at least in the social sciences, attempts to develop theory cannot bear fruit unless they are grounded in the careful and reliable observation and description of the commonplace facts of existence.

The methodical pursuit of social enquiry is relatively new in India. This point is often made in defence of the weaknesses of current social science practices in the country. But we should not forget that the practice of sociology and social anthropology as systematic academic disciplines is not very much older in the western countries. Our beginnings in many cases were not much more than forty to fifty years behind theirs. Yet we have failed to make the advances that they made in comparable periods of development. I would suggest that one significant reason for this is that our social scientists have to act against the current of the Indian intellectual culture which has a marked tendency to neglect the observation and description of the external world.

I should hasten to add that the obstacles that Indian social scientists face in developing their disciplines may be great, but they are not insurmountable. There have been outstanding individuals who have contributed much to the development of their disciplines. I myself have had the good fortune to have worked with two of them, N.K. Bose and M.N. Srinivas, and their achievements appear all the more remarkable when we recognize how hard they had to work against the prevailing tendencies of their intellectual environment.

Knowledge can advance only when it is driven by individual curiosity; where curiosity is at a low ebb or where it is discouraged by the social environment, there cannot be any significant advance of knowledge. But the curiosity of the mathematician about numbers or the curiosity of the grammarian about words is not the same thing as the curiosity of the naturalist about observable external reality.

A whole new tradition of enquiry began in the second half of the nineteenth century when scholars sought to examine variations among human beings with the eyes of the naturalist. It is no accident that many of the first anthropologists had started as biologists; even those who had not were significantly influenced in their work by such great naturalists as Alexander von Humboldt and Charles Darwin. They took an interest in all aspects of human beings everywhere: their physical characteristics, their habitat, their material artefacts, their religious observances and their social arrangements. To be sure, they were interested in theory, but that interest was driven by their desire to observe, record and represent the varieties of human existence.

Although a large body of data on societies and cultures of every kind had accumulated by the beginning of the twentieth century, these data were highly uneven. Anthropologists and sociologists soon began to be concerned about the quality, the reliability and the accuracy of their data. From the 1920s onwards, there was a sustained development in the methods of data collection through participant-observation, through survey research and by other means. Generations of students have been trained in the techniques of data collection and analysis. It is through this kind of systematic training that anthropology and sociology have been transformed from amateur and speculative pursuits into specialized scholarly and, if the phrase be permitted, scientific disciplines.

In India, anthropology and sociology were already established as specialized academic disciplines when the country became independent fifty years ago. Since then, there has been a great expansion in these disciplines with the opening of new university departments, new universities and new institutes of social science research. Despite perennial complaints about financial constraints, the funds now available for social science research are enormously greater than what was available fifty years ago. Yet in the last two or three decades, the quality of social science research has not shown any great improvement. Empirical research in any branch of systematic enquiry is costly, and social scientists no less than natural scientists complain about the paucity of funds. I cannot at all judge the situation in the natural sciences, but I am not convinced that the lacklustre quality of empirical research in the social sciences is solely, or even mainly, due to the paucity of funds. Indeed, there may be some ground for saying that empirical work is now somewhat poorer in quality than when the funds were far more meagre.

I would now like to return to the remark I made earlier that I prefer to speak of traditions in the plural rather than in the singular. There is a tradition of empirical research in the social sciences whose course of development may be traced with some degree of exactitude. It is not an old tradition, but it is a tradition nevertheless. How well has this tradition become established in India? Has it acquired any distinctive features in its Indian environment?

In speaking of traditions in the plural, we risk our view of tradition being fragmented; this of course is anathema to some, although others might be prepared to live with the prospect. The traditions of sociology have not grown in exactly the same way in Germany, France and the US, although there has been much cross-fertilization. One may undoubtedly speak of a French tradition in sociology, and it is true that the growth of this tradition can be related to certain aspects of the French intellectual environment and also to certain tendencies of French social and political life. But if there are distinctive features in the French practice of the discipline, it is doubtful that they all owe their existence to any deliberate effort by Durkheim, Mauss and others to create a discipline that would be distinctly French.

I would like to stress the importance of cross-fertilization in the growth of science and scholarship in the contemporary world. I will do so by pursuing examples from my own discipline, sociology. One of the foremost exemplars of French sociology in the preceding generation was Raymond Aron. But he drew his inspiration much more from the work of Max Weber who was a German than from that of the Frenchman Émile Durkheim. It is well known that American sociologists drew much of their inspiration in the 1930s and 1940s from the works of the European masters, but today American sociology is a significant influence in the work of many European sociologists.

Traditions in science and scholarship are shaped by the continuing practices through which methods, procedures, techniques, and habits of work and of life are elaborated, systematized and transmitted over time. To repeat an observation made earlier, what is important here is continuity and filiation and not antiquity. Again, it is not altogether clear whether the search for pedigrees in a nation's ancient and medieval past is a help or a hindrance in the development of every type of social and intellectual practice. Disciplined intellectual pursuit requires continuous reference to both contemporary and antecedent practices. An overzealous preoccupation with the national past tends to divert attention away from directly relevant contemporary and near-contemporary practices in other geographical settings, and that is not healthy for the development of science and scholarship. A tradition becomes atrophied when its bearers wilfully turn their backs on other related traditions.

Traditions emerge and develop in unforeseen ways. To paraphrase a remark made by Edward Shils some time ago, the growth of significant knowledge is never an orderly movement. It rarely happens that a tradition emerges because a determined individual or a band of determined individuals decides to bring it into being. That can lead at best to the invention or the fabrication of tradition. Now it is a truism that a tradition—any tradition—is a product of shared collective experience. Traditions differ greatly in the extent to which they are consciously articulated and elaborated. The traditions of science and scholarship are consciously articulated to a greater extent than other traditions.

The building of a tradition is a slow and laborious process whose results show only in the long run. There is always the temptation to abandon the effort and to pursue some grandiose project that will transform everything overnight. In order to understand how traditions of scholarship take root and develop—or fail to develop—one has to examine the details of everyday practice. In the scholarly disciplines, professional associations, conferences, learned journals, and so on play a significant part in the extension, reformulation and transmission of specialized knowledge. All this takes place through the spoken as well as the written word. The written word is of very great importance in the transmission of knowledge not only between proximate generations but also between the living and the dead. In a way, it enables bygone generations to address present ones directly.

Traditions of scholarship are sustained and carried forward through critical reviews by scholars of the work of other scholars in their immediate environment as well as across vast geographical distances. This is a continuing process, and where it is undertaken fitfully or half-heartedly, this is a clear sign that the tradition of scholarship is infirm. Certain aspects of the writing and publication of reviews in my own discipline have struck my attention. Firstly, in our scholarly periodicals, the writing of reviews is left generally to young persons, and established scholars publish reviews very sparingly. Secondly, senior scholars rarely, if ever review the publications of their juniors. This betokens the hold of the hierarchical mentality in our professional life. It also restricts the impersonal learning process essential to the continuity of modern traditions of knowledge.

Intellectual traditions grow and crystallize within defined social milieus. In the modern world, the growth of the scientific tradition has been indissolubly linked with the growth of specific institutions such as universities, research institutes, laboratories, professional associations, and so on. Here, from the beginning of the nineteenth century, the great universities, with their design for the unity of teaching and research, have provided the most congenial social environment for integrating different disciplinary practices within larger traditions. One can discern certain common patterns in the natural as well as the social sciences in practically every part of the world.

The institutions of contemporary science first emerged in western countries, in Britain, France and Germany, and then spread their influence throughout the world. In the last two hundred years, the growth, first of the natural sciences and then of the social sciences has been closely associated with the growth of these institutions. Today, the success of science depends as much on their vitality as on the creativity of individual scientists. Individual talent certainly counts, but no individual can contribute effectively to science today by his sole unaided effort; this appears to be even more true of the natural than of the social sciences. Therefore, in considering the traditions of science and scholarship, it is difficult to discuss them in isolation from their institutional settings.

It will be difficult to exaggerate the changes that have taken place in the practices of science in the course of the last two hundred years. Till the end of the eighteenth century, it was possible for the individual scientist to do his work largely on his own. This is no longer possible. From the sociological point of view, the decisive change has been the institutionalization of science. In the eighteenth century, Henry Cavendish did his pioneering scientific work in the seclusion of his home, supporting himself and his research from his private fortune. Benjamin Franklin conducted his experiments in his own backyard, combining his scientific work with many other pursuits. The scientist of today has to go through a long period of apprenticeship in a research laboratory where he must first be socialized into the traditions of his craft.

We take it for granted now that the social scientist will work in universities and research institutes in association with his senior and junior colleagues, and his students in an institutional location with a certain infrastructure. But this was the exception rather than the rule in the nineteenth century. Most of the builders of the social sciences in the nineteenth century—Alexis de Tocqueville, John Stuart Mill, Karl Marx, Herbert Spencer and many others—worked largely on their own, outside the university system, laying the groundwork for the traditions of their disciplines which then became institutionalized in universities and other centres of learning.

Although the term 'sociology' was coined by Auguste Comte and given wide currency by his writing in the first half of the nineteenth century, it became established in France as a systematic intellectual discipline after his time. Here Émile Durkheim played a crucial role in giving the discipline an institutional focus. He became the first professor of sociology in a French university, roughly a hundred years ago and set about training a band of able and dedicated scholars who worked in close association with him. He wrote a manual, *The Rules of Sociological Method,* for their guidance in 1895, and in 1898 began the publication of the influential periodical *L'Année sociologique,* in which he and his colleagues published their own writings and reviewed the writings of other scholars working on related topics elsewhere. Similar developments were taking place at the turn of the nineteenth century in other European countries and in the US.

The same process was initiated in India with the establishment of the first universities in Calcutta, Bombay and Madras in 1857. Teaching and research in the natural and the social sciences grew with the expansion, first of the universities, and after independence, of specialized institutes for advanced study and research. If we are to consider the traditions of science and scholarship in India, it is in the light of these institutions that we have to consider them today. Many able, dedicated and distinguished scientists and scholars have worked in them now for about a hundred years. What is the legacy that they have left behind, and in what way and to what extent does that legacy act upon the work being done there today?

It will be an understatement to say that things are not well with our universities today. I believe that a very distinguished scientist said not long ago that the science departments in our universities have become the slums of the scientific world. There are many outstanding Indian physicists, but they rarely speak well of what is being done by way of physics in Indian universities. The physicists I know all say that the work done in the university in Calcutta compares very poorly with the work done in the 1920s, 1930s and 1940s under Raman, Bose and Saha; and that the work done in Delhi in the 1950s and 1960s under Kothari and Majumdar was superior to the work being done there today. There was substantial forward movement then but somewhere along the way the momentum was lost. More persons are working now and more money is being spent, but scientists complain one and all that the atmosphere in our universities is no longer conducive to scientific research or even to teaching science.

There has been a similar decline in the social sciences in Indian universities; perhaps one can say that there the decline began before disciplined habits of work had found the time to become properly established. The decline in both cases is partly due to the flight of talent away from the universities, some of which has moved into specialized institutes of research, which are now many in the social as well as the natural sciences. I can say nothing of the state of affairs in the natural sciences, but from what little personal knowledge I have of the 27 institutes supported by the Indian Council of Social Science Research, the work being done there is not perceptibly superior to the work in the universities.

If the tradition of scientific work has secured a foothold in India, it is at best an insecure one. This is not because individual talent is lacking but because science has so far failed to find a proper institutional focus; or, having found one for a brief span, lost it before long. It is true that there is a massive flight of individual talent to the west, particularly in the natural sciences. But this flight of talent is as much a cause as a consequence of institutional failure within the country. Lack of adequate material resources is one side of the story, wanton misuse of resources is another. Whatever the ultimate reason, our record of sustaining the institutions of science and scholarship in the fifty years since independence has been poor and unsatisfactory.

We have to take serious note of the poor record of our institutions of science and scholarship which is but a part of the poor record of our public institutions in general. Outstanding contributions to science have been made by Indians in the recent past. They are still being made, but now mainly outside India. If the traditions of science are to be revitalized within India, the institutions of teaching and research in the sciences have to be renovated. There is no simple recipe for that. But it is doubtful that the search for glorious antecedents in India's ancient or medieval past will provide any concrete or usable results. That search can and does distract attention from the everyday tasks through whose disciplined and methodical pursuit alone do traditions grow and develop.

Newness in Sociological Enquiry*

M any of those who entered the profession of sociology in the last decade, as also those who are entering it today, are dissatisfied with the existing state of the subject. They are eager to explore new ways of undertaking their work. The search for newness is of course central to science and scholarship, and an essential condition of their progress and even their continuing vitality. At the same time, nothing new emerges in the world of ideas out of a sheer desire for novelty. Newness would amount to little if it did not arise from a careful, detailed and methodical scrutiny of existing knowledge—its concepts, methods and theories. It speaks well of a profession when its new entrants are out of sympathy with the mere mechanical reproduction of existing and available knowledge in their field. But that cannot justify the frantic search for novelty for its own sake. And if it be said that those who hunger for newness do not do so aimlessly, it can also be said that those who transmit accepted knowledge need not do so mechanically.

On an occasion like this, it is not enough to ask: How does newness begin? One must also ask how it becomes integrated into the practice of a discipline. This, I should stress, is a difficult issue, particularly in the early phase of a discipline's career when it may not at all be clear that what seems to have become established is going to last and must therefore

*This is a revised version of the inaugural lecture given at the seminar on 'Recasting Sociology' at the Jawaharlal Nehru University on 20 March 1997.

provide a yardstick for the inclusion of exclusion of new components. At the same time, it will be unrealistic to expect that everything that is new, even if it appears sound, will be automatically accepted and accommodated. The established practice of a discipline is itself a social fact, and I hardly need to remind this audience that social facts exercise their own constraints. It is well to remember that practices that are taken for granted in the discipline today did not get automatically incorporated into it without facing any resistance; I could give many examples from the work of sociologists of my generation and of the preceding one.

My main interest today is not in individual sociologists and their personal achievements, but in sociology as a discipline and a profession. Individual virtuosity has, and in my view ought to have, a smaller place in scholarship than, let us say, in jazz music. Most sociologists realize this, particularly as they advance in years, but young scholars find it hard to accept it, especially when they are highly talented. I do not wish to devalue the latter but only to point to the need for a proper appreciation of the relation between tradition and individual talent in sociology as in other branches of scholarship.

Sociology in India, as in many parts of the world, is in need of renewal. This much we can all agree upon without having to make dire predictions about the crises that are impending. Much of the work produced in the last two or three decades is of very poor quality. A great many things get published that do not deserve to be published, largely because we have failed to establish an honest, reliable and discriminating system of refereeing. In many colleges and universities, teaching at both undergraduate and post-graduate levels is often perfunctory and sometimes dispensed with altogether. At the same time, some work of quality has been produced continuously in the last fifty years.

The problem with us is not that the small amount of good work done by preceding generations is unjustly criticized by succeeding ones, but that it is ignored and then quickly forgotten. In India, each generation of sociologists seems eager to start its work on a clean slate with little or no attention to the work done before. This amnesia about the work of their predecessors is no less distinctive of Indian sociologists than their failure to innovate. My main argument today is that the amnesia and the failure to innovate are two sides of the same coin; we will not be able to understand the one unless we understand the other. It would be rash for me to point my finger at anyone, for I know very well that someone else can point his finger at me. I simply draw attention to this as an obdurate condition of our discipline and our profession with no intention of singling out any individual sociologist or group of sociologists for blame.

I will now run quickly through some of the work produced by sociologists and social anthropologists in the recent past in India. My broad objective will be to see if any newness was introduced by this work and to ask, incidentally, how this newness came into being. Naturally, my treatment will be selective and illustrative, for it will be impossible—and also inappropriate—to attempt an exhaustive survey of research in the subject in India. Further, I will confine myself to the work done in the last fifty years, that is, since independence, without any judgement on the quality and significance of the work of earlier scholars.

The first thing to note is that there was a tremendous burst of work in the years immediately after independence, associated to some extent with the expansion of institutions of advanced study and research, namely, the universities and the newly-created institutes of research. The sheer volume of work in the first two or three decades after independence far exceeded what had been produced in the entire period before independence. Fifty years ago, sociology was still a young subject, and in retrospect, the scope for innovation appears to have been large. But of course, much of the work produced even then was stereotyped and trivial, and only a small part of it was of lasting value. In research, whether at the level of the individual scholar or the profession as a whole, most of what is done falls by the wayside and only a little endures; it is well to remember that research is in this sense a costly undertaking.

The first two decades after independence may be described as the great age of village studies. I am sure that the work of this period appears dull and uninspiring to those who are entering the profession today, but this is because the very success of that work led to its routinization in the seventies and eighties. That is not at all how it appeared to those of us who were entering the profession in the fifties and sixties before the work became a part of established sociological practice. The first full-length monograph on an Indian village was published in 1955 by S.C. Dube. I was still a student in the Department of Anthropology in Calcutta where everybody or almost everybody studied tribes. The new book, along with the two collections edited by Srinivas (1955) and by Marriott (1955), opened up new possibilities of research. Within a matter of years young social anthropologists, myself included, took up detailed and intensive studies of the Indian village which was at that time a whole new field of enquiry and investigation.

Village studies established not only a new domain of research, but also a new way of looking at Indian society and culture as a whole. Through a series of writings in the fifties and sixties, Srinivas (1962) established the distinction between the 'book-view' and the 'field-view' of Indian society, advocating the primacy of the latter over the former in sociological enquiry. The thrust in these studies was on life in the village as it was actually lived, and not on that life as it had been ideally conceived to be. The concept of the village as a harmonious and integrated unit was found grossly inadequate in the light of careful ethnographic studies. It gave way before accounts of the divisions visible everywhere and the conflicts of interest associated with them. Moreover, the idea of the village as a self-sufficient unit was replaced by one in which the many links of the village with the outside world were carefully examined and recorded.

Village studies were important in another way. They became for many sociologists and social anthropologists the basis for training in the craft of their discipline (Béteille and Madan 1975; Srinivas et al. 1979). Sociology is an empirical discipline in which the observation, description, interpretation and analysis of facts is of central importance. In earlier accounts of Indian society and its institutions, facts were used for apt illustration rather than detailed and methodical enquiry. Village studies established high standards of enquiry through participant-observation. Unfortunately, similar standards were not established as extensively in survey research, the other principal mode of empirical investigation. It may even be argued that the standards of empirical investigation through participant-observation established in the fifties and sixties have tended to become somewhat relaxed over the years. In my own very limited personal experience, the few students from overseas whose research I have supervised have produced better empirical work than the majority of their Indian counterparts.

The field-view of society transformed the study of caste. This had implications for the understanding of caste not only in the present but also in the past. Here, a landmark was the paper published by Srinivas in 1956 on '*Varna* and Caste' (Srinivas 1962: 63–9). Srinivas argued that the operative units of the system were not the four categories of the idealized scheme of *varnas*, but the innumerable *jatis* which provided the real basis of social identity on the ground. Whereas the *varnas* were the same four throughout the country and throughout its history, the *jatis* varied from one region to another, and split, amalgamated, emerged anew or even disappeared over time. By closely examining the dynamics of caste, sociologists in the fifties and sixties were drawing attention to the declining role of caste in religion and ritual and its increasing role in politics. Here I ought to point out that sociologists were in advance of journalists who began to appreciate the great significance of caste in democratic politics only in the eighties and nineties.

One particular aspect of the dynamics of caste drew considerable attention among sociologists at first and then among students of Indian society and culture as a whole. This is the process whereby individual castes change their social rank after a change in their economic and political conditions. If one takes the book-view and sees castes as *varnas*, one gets a picture of a hierarchy that is completely frozen and static. If one takes the field-view and sees castes as *jatis*, one gets a picture of castes continually changing positions, although this is almost always a change in slow motion, not easy to detect in the particular case while it is taking place. This new representation of caste, with its own patterns of mobility, has encouraged historians and Indologists to take a fresh look at their data relating to the past.

I have described two major shifts of perception brought about by sociological studies in the fifties and sixties. But there were also many minor shifts, too inconspicuous for attention in each individual case, whose cumulative effect has been considerable. As a result, our present understanding of family, kinship and marriage, of religious belief and practice, of local-level politics, and of economic arrangements and transactions is both richer and deeper than it was fifty years ago. Thus, newness in our discipline does not come about solely or even generally through a sudden and dramatic breakthrough; more often it is the unforeseen consequence, over a long stretch of time, of collective effort that is at best loosely organized. What I wish to stress here is that someone may in fact contribute to newness in his discipline without himself being aware of it while making his contribution.

The work to which I briefly referred above, and particularly the enthusiasm for village studies and the field-view of society, created something like a community of scholars who actively influenced, if not interacted with, each other. Disciplinary boundaries became porous, and although sociologists and social anthropologists took the lead in village studies, they were joined by political scientists, historians, geographers, economists and others. It is also important to note that the community included western as well as Indian scholars, and it will be false to say that the flow of ideas was only in one direction. Looking back on that experience, it can be said that indigenous and foreign scholars worked in more active and fruitful collaboration, and on nearly equal terms, in the study of society and culture in India than perhaps in any other country in the world. What I would like to stress is that this collaboration, with all its strains and stresses, had become an established fact before the theorists of hegemony had had time to agonize over its moral and political implications.

Thus, it is quite clear that some new ideas, new concepts and new approaches did emerge in the study of Indian society and culture in the last fifty years. But of course all of this was embedded in routines of study and research that were for the most part dull, monotonous and repetitive. Would it not be marvellous if we could henceforward dispense with the dull routine and simply get on with the pursuit of innovation? To someone who has chosen the vocation of scholarship, such a desire must appear both shallow and frivolous. In sociology, whether in India or in the west, we cannot achieve significant innovation if we disregard the routine of scholarship.

If we acknowledge that sociological knowledge is cumulative, it will be clear that the growth of that knowledge cannot be left solely to individual creativity. Every intellectual discipline is at the same time a craft, with its own requirements of training and apprenticeship. The outgoing generation cannot teach the incoming one to be original, and it should not even try; but it does have the responsibility of handing down to it the traditions of its craft. By the traditions of a craft I mean something more than a set of technical procedures, important though they are, that can be acquired directly from the kind of manual that comes with the personal computer. These traditions are assimilated in and through the institutions, such as universities and centres of research, where the vocation of sociology is collectively practised.

It may be useful to pursue the metaphor of the craft a little further. Here I would like to refer very briefly to the work of Meyer Fortes, who was an acknowledged authority in the field of kinship studies and whom I had the good fortune to know personally. Towards the end of his life, he wrote an account of his career which he called 'An Anthropologist's Apprenticeship'. Following the philosopher A.J. Ayer, he divided anthropologists into two types, the 'pontiffs' and the 'journeymen', saying that he himself was of the second and not the first type. The journeyman is devoted to his craft rather than to some grand creative project. Fortes saw his own intellectual career thus:

A journeyman's eyes are on his material, not on higher things. His aim is to turn out a particular product at a time using the best tools at his disposal. What he has by way of skill and technique are directed strictly to the job in hand, to making the most of the material he has to work with in the light of whatever good ideas happen to be appropriate to his task (1978: 1–2).

It was through work done in this spirit that he made his most significant contribution to his discipline; and he did in fact bring much newness into the study of kinship.

I had of course read some of Fortes's writings as a student in Calcutta in the fifties for he was then already an established scholar. When I came to know him many years later, I naturally tried to find out from him what he considered his most significant contribution to social anthropology. But I never got very far. He somehow managed to turn the discussion around to Malinowski and Radcliffe-Brown who had been his teachers or to younger persons who had been his pupils. He was by no means approving of all the work they had done, for as a man and a scholar, he was of a critical, not to say a carping, disposition, but till the end he kept himself informed about the work being done in his field. He read everything, took out whatever little he found to be of value, and attacked the rest relentlessly; in this attack, he spared neither his teachers nor his pupils. He always spoke respectfully of his seniors, even those who had entered the field only a few years ahead of him, but he had an unforgiving hostility towards those who sought to project themselves as pontiffs, *mahants* or creative geniuses.

Like N.K. Bose, my teacher in Calcutta, Meyer Fortes believed that anthropology was a science. What place can tradition have in the work of the scientist? It is easy to be misled by the antithesis between tradition and modernity into the belief that the progress of science must take place wholly outside of tradition. The falsity of this belief becomes immediately apparent if we look at the experimental sciences where no one can hope to achieve significant results without first acquiring the culture or the tradition of the laboratory in which he is initiated into his craft. It is true that this tradition can become a constraint and an obstacle to further progress; it is also true that individuals emerge from time to time who reconstitute the tradition of their science; but today no individual genius can begin to do this without first mastering the existing tradition of his craft.

While no intellectual discipline can dispense with apprenticeship in its craft, the form and duration of this apprenticeship varies from one discipline to another. I am told that in the experimental sciences, a PhD degree is no longer enough, a young scientist has now to do an additional spell as a 'post-doc' in the laboratory of a mature scientist before he can strike out on his own. In our discipline, the conditions of apprenticeship are somewhat different, and sometimes they appear excessively lax and permissive. The requirements of PhD work as a form of apprenticeship are not always taken seriously by either the student or his supervisor. It is natural that a fresh entrant into the PhD programme should be eager to make a breakthrough in his discipline, and so he tends to choose somewhat grandiose topics for his dissertation. It is then his supervisor's responsibility to bring him down to earth, to explain to him that the ground must first be prepared before any significant contribution can be made, and that this preparation is a slow and laborious process. In our universities today, this responsibility is seen more often in its breach than in its observance.

In India, the apprenticeship that is indispensable to the formation of the sociologist is subverted by a variety of factors. Professional standards are not sufficiently well established to discourage work of poor or even very poor quality. There is inadequate attention to detail in the collection and arrangement of empirical material, and the data collected through both participant-observation and survey research are often insubstantial and unreliable. Concepts are not always clearly defined or rigorously applied, and frequently what is presented as a new concept is only a new term. Arguments of the most sweeping kind are dressed up as new arguments, without any firm support of either data or reasoning.

If the craft of sociology had been well developed, there would be some check against this. In its absence, technical requirements are easily set aside in the interest of social relevance. Many sociologists, both young and old, feel that the real problem is not to interpret the world, but to change it. Changing the world is indeed a noble objective, but it is doubtful how many of us have the intellectual tools for making that change. In the first two decades of independence, many sociologists and social anthropologists expected to contribute to social transformation by working through the government in such fields as rural reconstruction, community development, Panchayati Raj, and so on. The Planning Commission was then the mecca for social scientists working for the transformation of society. Then a disenchantment with what could be done through the government set in, and in the eighties and nineties, many found a new appeal in programmes of active intervention through voluntary or non-governmental organizations. There is of course no reason why sociologists should not work with either the government or non-governmental organizations if they are convinced that their work will be made more socially relevant in that way. But they must first ensure that they have, as *sociologists*, the technical equipment required for attending effectively to the problems set before them by the agencies with which they work. Some of this equipment can be improvized on the job, but not all of it.

Someone who values autonomy in intellectual pursuit must be mindful not only of his own individual autonomy but also of the autonomy of his profession. Professor P.C. Mahalanobis, one of the most influential intellectuals of independent India, is reported to have said, on being provoked by Nehru, that 'scientists should be on top, not on tap'. Today most young sociologists will perhaps agree that they should not be on tap for ready use by agencies of the government. But many of the same persons seem to believe that their profession has a tacit obligation to meet the demands of Leninists, feminists, environmentalists, eco-feminists and other promoters of radical social change. Professional integrity requires some measure of autonomy from both government and opposition.

Of those who say that it is desirable, at least initially, to work within a tradition of scholarship, one might well ask whether there is indeed an established tradition of sociological enquiry in India. One might point to certain distinctive features of the tradition in France, in Germany, or in the United States. But if such a tradition exists in India, its essential ingredients are by no means clear to everyone. One might say at best that there are several and diverse traditions, with little or no agreement on their relative merits, so that one has to pick one's way through a thicket of terms, concepts, techniques and procedures, and in the end rely mainly on improvisation. This is by no means a happy state of affairs, but such, according to many, is indeed the current state of sociology in India.

Why have Indian sociologists, despite continuous effort for three quarters of a century, failed to develop firm traditions for the systematic study of society and its institutions? Many would say that this is because they have depended too heavily on borrowed theories, borrowed concepts and borrowed methods of enquiry. This is true to a greater or lesser extent of all branches of modern science and scholarship in India, but it manifests itself in a particularly acute form in the discipline of sociology. For several generations, Indian sociologists have agonized over the mismatch between the concepts and methods, on which they draw from the common pool of their discipline, and the data, to which they seek to apply them. That this mismatch is widespread and pervasive can hardly be denied. Moreover, it is a good thing that we should be troubled and concerned about it, provided that our worry does not lead to paralysis in the practice of our craft.

The fact that most of the basic tools of sociological enquiry and analysis used in the study of Indian society and culture were devised outside India does not disturb all Indian sociologists equally. Some would say that one should use such tools as are available, adapt them to one's use as well as one can, and improvise to the extent possible. Whether we engage in participant-observation or in survey research, the basic procedures have to be broadly the same everywhere, so why worry about where or by whom they were first devised? Again, there are broadly similar concepts and methods for interpreting and analysing social stratification and mobility, family, kinship and marriage, religious belief and practice, political processes, and economic transactions wherever they exist and operate, and we would be foolish to turn our backs on the available concepts and methods in the hope of devising new ones by our own unaided effort. Why, they would ask, try to reinvent the bicycle?

But perhaps the majority continue to be disturbed by the mismatch between the tools available to them and the material on which they have to work, and they seem to oscillate between two alternative courses. The first course is to work within the system, keeping the mind open to the possibility of small, incremental changes in the hope that the cumulative effect of such work by many scholars over several generations will lift the subject to a higher plane theoretically and methodologically. This probably is how most of us work, in the spirit of the journeyman, although few of us can reasonably hope to achieve the success of Meyer Fortes to whose work I earlier referred.

The second response is articulated by a smaller number of persons, but they are more radical and more assertive. Their views raise echoes in the minds of many scholars, particularly in the younger generation, and therefore deserve attention. They assert that the poverty of our social theory follows inevitably from our unreflective adherence to a framework of enquiry and analysis that is altogether inappropriate. Working within the framework leads to its further entrenchment and to a continuing dissipation of intellectual energy. They call for a replacement of the established framework with its entire baggage of concepts, methods and procedures by an alternative sociology, or even an alternative to sociology. In this view, if I were to put it starkly, newness does not emerge bit by bit, it has to be created all at once.

What is to be the shape of this new, alternative sociology? Naturally, there are different voices that seek to express different views and impulses. These voices are more agreed about what is to be set aside than about what is to be put in its place. One source of this call for the rejection of the existing framework is radical Marxism which has trained its guns on 'bourgeois sociology' for nearly a century. Another source of it, more specific to our intellectual climate, is radical nationalism whose target is western, rather than bourgeois, sociology. In our contemporary context, the second source is more potent than the first one, although of course the two may be combined, either consciously or unconsciously.

The search for alternatives to existing theories, concepts, methods, procedures and techniques will no doubt continue, for that search is a part of intellectual life everywhere. It will lead to the opening up of new areas of substantive enquiry, as it has already done in the last couple of decades in gender studies, in environmental sociology and in the sociology of science. The real question is how this search will connect itself with the existing body of knowledge that has already accumulated. I am not convinced that a radical disconnection between what has been done in the past and what is to be done in the future is either feasible or desirable. Those who wish to create a whole new alternative sociology will no doubt go their way, at least for some time, but my instincts tell me that their work too will in due course of time either fall by the wayside or fall in line. Experience shows that the idea of paradigm shift is operationally less useful in the social than in the natural sciences.

The discontent with existing approaches and the search for radically new alternatives has had paradoxical consequences. It has led able scholars into extreme forms of the very weaknesses they attack most mercilessly in others. It is doubtful that we will ever be able to lay to rest the ghosts of 'bourgeois sociology' and 'Western sociology', and the attacks against them are often misdirected, and they backfire with unfailing regularity.

Twenty-five years ago, *Seminar* magazine devoted one of its issues to the discussion of the social sciences, and in particular to the demands of quality and of Relevance within them. In a forceful article on 'The Question of Relevance', P.C. Joshi pointed out that 'the lack of relevance of social sciences constitutes one of the key problems in many underdeveloped countries including India' (1972: 24). He questioned 'the relevance of the entire Western intellectual heritage to the underdeveloped countries', and attacked the 'mere borrowing and transfer of knowledge from the Western to the non-Western world' (Ibid.). However, he then proceeded in the main part of his article to give a vivid exposition of the views of four major thinkers—Gunnar Myrdal, Wassily Leontief, J.K. Galbraith and Simon Kuznets, all acknowledged western authorities. Apart from a brief and passing show of deference to Gandhi and Mao, there was no discussion of any Indian or other Asian social scientist.

These contradictions reveal themselves in discussions not only of research but also of teaching. In a paper on the teaching of economics in India published some ten years ago, Sukhamoy Chakravarty drew attention to the many shortcomings in the existing practice (1986: 1165–68). These he attributed to three main factors: the extensive use of texts written outside India, the pervasive desire among Indian economists to catch up with the West, and the generally lacklustre quality of Indian teachers of the subject. The essay provides a very scholarly exposition of the ideas of the world's leading authorities on the subject, but there is no discussion of the work of any Indian economist. Reading the paper one might justly wonder what there is to teach to students of economics in India other than the works of those European and American authors to whom Chakravarty gives his exclusive attention. He does mention that there are some important exceptions to the generally poor quality of Indian economists, but he does not tell us who they are, or, more importantly, what makes them exceptional. How can we begin to raise the level of the subject in India if we pay such scant regard to even the important exceptions among the four or five generations of economists who have taught and written about the subject in India?

It is evident that the ablest among our social scientists are unable to discuss the works of western authorities without a sense of guilt. That is understandable and not necessarily undesirable, but unfortunately the sense of guilt is almost always overlaid by a thick coat of self-righteousness. We are too quick to throw stones all around without paying any heed to the glass houses we erect for our own habitation.

We have all encountered some advocates of autonomy and self-reliance who quote extensively from the works of western scholars: promoters of new alternatives who are never too shy with their references to Foucault and Derrida. If there is nothing wrong in borrowing from Malinowski and Parsons, there should be nothing wrong in borrowing from Foucault and Derrida; but this must be understood on both sides. The adoption of new ideas can be healthy and fruitful only if it does not lead to a complete disregard of what was going on before. It is here that we find the weakest link in the chain. Every new generation of Indian sociologists acts as if nothing had gone on before; it does not ask what its own fate will be when another new generation takes its place.

Being attentive to what has been done before does not require one to close one's mind to new ideas. One should pursue the search for ideas according to one's interest and inclination, and not be unduly concerned over the intrinsic worth of the places in which others are pursuing their search. One should be prepared to look for new ideas wherever they may be found, and some of the best scholars I have known have been diligent scavengers, retrieving very good ideas from other people's dustbins. But it is not enough to find new material; we must then undertake the slow and laborious effort of finding a place for it in the existing practice of the discipline. Only then will that practice change in a significant way.

References

Béteille, André, and T.N. Madan (eds). 1975. *Encounter and Experience*. New Delhi: Vikas.

Chakravarty, Sukhamoy 1986. 'The Teaching of Economics in India'. *Economic and Political Weekly*. Vol. 21. No. 27, pp. 1165–68.

Dube, S.C. 1955. *Indian Village*. London: Routledge & Kegan Paul.

Fortes, Meyer. 1978. 'An Anthropologist's Apprenticeship'. *Annual Review of Anthropology*, 7: 1–30.

Joshi, P.C. 1972. 'The Question of Relevance'. *Seminar*, 157 (September).

Marriott, Mckim (ed). 1955. *Village India*. Chicago: University of Chicago Press.

Srinivas, M.N. (ed). 1955. *India's Villages*. Bombay: Asia Publishing House.

————. 1962. *Caste in Modern India and Other Essays*. Bombay: Asia Publishing House.

Srinivas, M.N., A.M. Shah and E.A. Ramaswamy (eds). 1979. *The Fieldworker and the Field*. Delhi: Oxford University Press.

Sociology as Critical Understanding: An Interview by Stefan Molund

SM: You are a professor of sociology, but in Scandinavia most people would probably think of you as a social anthropologist. There seems to be some confusion here. What is the relationship between sociology and anthropology in India?

AB: I think it is true that I am regarded mainly as an anthropologist, not just in Scandinavia but also elsewhere in the west. That is partly because of the fact that in the western world the study of society and culture in general is partitioned in the following way: the study of other cultures is anthropology and the study of ourselves in sociology. Anyone who studies India or Africa or Melanesia is an anthropologist, whereas to be a sociologist one has to be a specialist in western industrial societies. I have rejected that point of view. At the conceptual level, much of my work is in fact concerned with problems that are central to what one would regard as the discipline of sociology anywhere—social stratification, social mobility, different conceptions of equality, etc. The one book of mine that has been translated into Swedish, a book on social inequality which I put together as editor, I would regard as an attempt to bridge the gap between sociology and anthropology. I see myself as a sociologist and a social anthropologist in the Radcliffe-Brown tradition. The same is true of M.N. Srinivas, for example, who is regarded as an anthropologist in Sweden, Britain and the United States, but in India is regarded as both.

SM: One very notable thing about your work is its broad comparative perspective. In your general writings on social inequality and stratification, for example, you are careful to include the socialist countries, which is not all that common, even among sociologists.

AB: I am, at least in principle, an inveterate comparativist. I don't think that one can get very far as a sociologist or a social anthropologist, whichever you choose to call it, without using a comparative perspective. Durkheim once wrote that comparative sociology was not a special branch of sociology, but sociology itself; that is something I believe in.

You are right in drawing attention to the socialist countries. I have recently been much concerned with the question of the role of the intelligentsia in Indian society. My interest in this problem was stimulated by an article on the intelligentsia as a ruling class by the economist and statistician Ashok Rudra, one of our leading Marxist intellectuals. Rudra argues, from what he believes is a Marxist perspective, that in order to understand the dynamics of Indian politics today it is not enough to talk about capitalists and landlords; the intelligentsia—in the broad sense of what in the Soviet Union is called mental workers—are also extremely important. I think that since the *locus classicus* of the intelligentsia is not in India, but in the Soviet Union and the east European countries, a great deal is to be learnt about this problem by making a comparative study of the intelligentsia in different kinds of societies. In my view, the socialist countries are tremendously important for our understanding of what is happening in Indian society, as indeed they are for the understanding of human societies everywhere.

SM: Do you share Rudra's view that the Indian intelligentsia have the characteristics of a ruling class? What about capitalists and landlords?

AB: I would put the Soviet Union at one extreme, where the intelligentsia have been the dominant stratum, because there is no capitalist class. The other extreme is the United States, where there is a very powerful capitalist class. India would fall somewhere in between, I don't know whether closer to the Soviet or the American extreme. Certainly there is a capitalist class in India, there is no doubt about that, but I think the intelligentsia, including the extremely important civil service, also play a very large part, particularly in the public sector, and in defining what place that sector should have in the general scheme of things. This whole idea of planning, of creating a new kind of welfare state, of ensuring that distribution is properly achieved is largely their idea. Whether or not they succeed in doing what they say they want to achieve, they certainly have a very important voice in Indian public life.

The Indian capitalist class may be very powerful, but does not have the prestige or the esteem that the capitalist class enjoys in the United States and western Europe. Their self-image is not necessarily that of a dominant class. Talking to members of this class I have been struck by their own perception of the importance of the intelligentsia with their slant towards socialism, towards the public sector, and the control of public life that they are supposed to exercise. I will not agree that the intelligentsia in India have only a minor position.

SM: How would you account for the great importance of the Indian intelligentsia in historical terms? What importance do you give to the fact that the literati had a very prominent position in the precolonial society?

AB: The historical background is crucial and decisive, but how far back we go in history I am not absolutely sure. It is true that India has a very old and continuous intellectual tradition. Intellectual activity has been very highly valued—many people would say overvalued—but I think that the crucial place that the intelligentsia now occupy is of more recent historical origin. What I see as very important here is that it was the intelligentsia who wrested independence for India from the British, not the capitalists who played a minor role in the nationalist movement. The leaders of the nationalist movement were basically intellectuals; they were lawyers, writers, and so on. Look at the number of lawyers among them; it is remembered that Nehru was a lawyer, but Jinnah was also a lawyer, as were Gandhi, Patel and others. When India became independent, these people could claim that it was their inheritance, rather than the inheritance of the capitalists. Whether you look at planning or at social policies in general, they played a very important part, which is not to say that the capitalists were unimportant in real terms. It is the nationalist movement that in many developing countries accounts for the important role of the intelligentsia; the nationalist movement was in a very important sense the creation of the intelligentsia.

SM: The concept of the intelligentsia as you define it is clearly much broader than the concept of intellectuals.

AB: I would describe the intellectuals as those who are concerned with the creation of new knowledge, the criticism of existing knowledge, or with the critical dissemination of existing knowledge. I would then have academic intellectuals as an important component of the category of intellectuals, although not all academicians are intellectuals, since not all of them are concerned in fact with the creation or even the criticism of knowledge. Then I would also include literary writers, poets, novelists, journalists, and scientists, whether in the university or outside it. In India, like in many western countries, much of scientific research is now done outside the university, in specialized research institutions. I myself have been particularly interested in academic intellectuals, but that does not mean that I consider the others less important. Journalists, for example, I regard as an extremely important section of intellectuals. I have been something of a journalist myself, in fact, because I write for newspapers, and regard that as very important.

SM: I have the impression that in recent decades Delhi has become ever more important as a centre of Indian intellectual life, to the detriment of other centres. Yet India is a very large country, and one would still expect the intellectual community to be internally somewhat fragmented, not least by language. To what extent is there a single intellectual community covering India as a whole?

AB: Delhi has certainly achieved a kind of pre-eminence in one particular sector of intellectual life, that of the academic intellectual. The two universities in Delhi, the University of Delhi, where I work, and Jawaharlal Nehru University, would generally be acknowledged to be the pace-setters, and Delhi also has a large number of social scientists in research institutions outside the university. Certainly, scientists, economists, and other social scientists are concentrated in Delhi to a far larger extent than in Calcutta and the other intellectual centres which played a more important role in the latter part of the nineteenth century and the earlier part of the twentieth century. However, poets, writers, novelists, filmmakers and so forth are also intellectuals, and where they are concerned I am not so sure that Calcutta has yielded its supremacy to any other city. The literary life of Calcutta is still very vigorous. But then that raises your other question as to how far these intellectuals are able to reach out to intellectuals in other parts of India. Some of them do, others don't. Works get translated between the regional languages, but I do not think there is enough translation from one Indian language to another. I have done a bit of translation myself but that was from one Indian language, Bengali, into English. Yet the work of translation is sometimes very difficult. It is much easier to translate between one north Indian language and another than between Hindi and Tamil, or between Tamil and Gujarati, which are very different from each other. I don't know what the role of English will be in the future, but I think it will continue to be important. In any case, I don't see it as a question of either, or, of either using English or not using English.

SM: An obvious question with regard to the intellectuals is that concerning their role as social and cultural critics. I have the impression that frequently Indian intellectuals do not think very highly of themselves in this respect, that they tend to describe themselves as opportunistic servants of the system, rather than as independent critics. Do you agree with this negative judgement?

AB: Although it is said, most of all by the Indian intellectuals themselves, that they are a self-serving lot, that they have always been on the side of the government, this is not quite true, especially not nowadays. I would be inclined to say that 1975 to 1977, the period of the Emergency, was something of a watershed in the life of the Indian intellectual. During the Emergency it was the intellectuals, including the academic intellectuals, who publicly protested—as one of the signatories against the Forty-second Amendment of the Constitution. I was personally involved in this. In retrospect, the risk was not very great perhaps, but certainly they took that risk. After 1977, the orientation of the Indian intellectual to the government changed substantially, and during the last decade there has been a very strongly oppositionist strain in the Indian intellectual. Those who have supported the government are mainly the scientists. Scientists, and this would not seem to be uniquely Indian, tend to support the government by their silence, which they justify by saying that they are too busy with their research to get involved in anything else. Social scientists are the ones who tend to be openly critical. Even in the fifties and sixties there were Indian social scientists who were critical of the government. Yet the social sciences were then dominated by the economists, many of whom found themselves working with, if not necessarily for, the government in planning and policy making. The role which the economists defined for themselves was that of social engineering. As the country had become independent, and as it had inherited a terrible legacy, first from its traditional hierarchical past, then from the oppression and exploitation of colonial rule, the economists—and along with them many sociologists—felt that they had a responsibility to help the government to create a new kind of society. I personally feel, and many would probably agree with me today, that their involvement with the government was somewhat short-sighted. They were not self-serving, I believe, but rather excessively optimistic. My view of social science, certainly of sociology, is that it has very little to contribute in the form of social engineering, but much to contribute by way of critical understanding. Yet for me critical understanding does not mean simply bashing the government, it does not mean simply taking an oppositionist stand in relation to the government. In a country like India that is fairly easy to do. Critical understanding, as I use the term, means critical understanding not only of the government but of the people as well, including a very deeply critical attitude towards the people, which does not come easily.

SM: I assume that you are then also critical of the idea of social science as an undertaking basically comparable to natural science. How do you see the role of value commitments in social enquiry?

AB: I think that it is a delusion to regard sociology as a natural science; many very outstanding social scientists have taken that view. For social scientists, particularly when they are studying their own society, or, indeed, when they are studying their own time, some kind of commitment is unavoidable. You may be a Swedish social scientist studying a different society in space, but you are still studying your own time and cannot pretend that you can view the people you study with the same detachment with which an astronomer views stars and planets. Moreover, certain forms of commitment are essential to the pursuit of the social sciences. The commitment to pluralism, to the coexistence of alternative values, for instance, is essential to the sociologist, because in a society committed to one single ideology, whether it is a transcendental religion or a modern 'secular' religion—fundamentalist Islam or Leninism—there is very little room for sociology. As a sociologist, I have a vested interest in pluralism.

SM: In a paper published some years ago, you made a distinction between commitment and partisanship, which would seem to be directly relevant here.

AB: This distinction derives from a more basic one between the pursuit of truth and the pursuit of power, science as a vocation and politics as a vocation. Social scientists have been sharply divided in the attitude they take to the relationship between these two pursuits. There are those, orthodox Marxists not least, who have argued that they are the same, that you cannot pursue the truth very far unless you take some direct part in altering the structure of power in your society. My position is rather that the pursuit of power and the pursuit of truth should be kept separate, since they easily come into conflict with one another. The view that they have to be pursued in conjunction I regard as a delusion which takes one further and further away from the pursuit of truth. By partisanship, I mean a very specific kind of commitment, a commitment to a particular party, to a particular organization, by which the pursuit of the truth is subordinated to the demands of that organization or that party. Partisanship in that sense would not be compatible with my role as a sociologist.

SM: Over the years you have repeatedly stressed the importance of safeguarding the university as an arena of free inquiry and debate.

AB: The universities are going through difficult times, not only in India, but everywhere. I don't know what fate they will have in the years to come, but I do believe that they are extremely important as an institutional area in which the truth can be pursued in different ways in the same place. The political party also has room for intellectuals—all over the world the communist parties have produced important intellectuals—but it has not had room for the pursuit of truth in different ways. This is where it differs from the university.

SM: In one of your most recent papers, you point to democratization as one of the forces threatening the Indian university. Yet elsewhere you have described the Indian universities as 'islands of modernity', where teachers and students, men and women, people of different caste and community are given the opportunity to interact in radically new ways. Could you briefly explain this apparent contradiction?

AB: The contradiction is only apparent. Real democracy cannot be an impediment to the pursuit of scholarship. But one must make a distinction between democracy and populism. I have been somewhat disturbed by the growth of populism among Indian intellectuals, particularly within the universities.

SM: Since you take the view that the major task of the social sciences is critical understanding, you would presumably also regard it as very important that sociologists and social scientists generally are not isolated from the society around them. Do you feel that the social science intellectuals in India have managed to reach out to their surrounding society, or would you rather describe them as a community apart?

AB: This is a very large question. In a country like India, where more than half the population remains illiterate, the intellectuals can only reach a small section of the population, at least through their writings. Still, the intellectuals have a role to play in reaching, directly or indirectly, larger and larger sections of the population. School teachers, some of whom would themselves qualify as intellectuals by my definition, have a very important role in this, and so have journalists. As I mentioned before, I have myself occasionally written for daily newspapers, and I think that Indian intellectuals, Indian social scientists, ought to do far more of that. There are exceptions, of course, like Ashok Rudra, who does a lot of writing for a wider audience, not only through English language newspapers, but also through Bengali ones. That is really my ideal; I wish I could do that kind of thing more extensively.

SM: In one of your articles you mention that while an earlier generation of Indian sociologists used to write in the vernacular as well as in English, Indian sociologists now tend to write more exclusively in English and more exclusively for a professional audience, an audience which is often international. You also indicate that there is something about the reward structure of sociology which tends to favour disciplinary writing rather than writing for a more general public.

AB: My ideal would be someone who is ambidextrous, someone who contributes to the discipline, and also writes in another medium, for a different audience. People used to do this before independence. N.K. Bose, for example, used to write in Bengali as well as in English, and others like Irawati Karve, the distinguished Maharastrian anthropologist, also wrote in the vernacular. In the generation that became professionalized in the fifties and sixties that ambidextrous resource seems to have been lost to some extent, but I see signs of its coming back again; Ashok Rudra writes in Bengali, and Arvind Shah, my colleague at the University of Delhi, has written in Gujarati. Now there is a journal in Gujarati devoted to the social sciences. There are also translations of social science writing in Bengali, and there have even been some social science writing in that language. Much more of this should be done. Yet this is not to say that the trend towards increasing professionalization is itself bad; I don't think that one can or should reverse it. It is very important that Indian sociologists continue to write for an international audience of sociologists. At a certain level, the social sciences are international and they must be international. I don't believe that there is any way of creating a different social science for India, which will be expressed through the medium of Indian languages. I do not accept that position.

SM: You are not in sympathy with those who would like to construct a sociology which in some sense would be distinctively Indian?

AB: I am very sceptical about that idea, and I am also somewhat uneasy about it. To the extent that such a sociology will deal with problems that are specific to Indian society at its present stage of development, it will have a certain distinctive feature, but that distinctive feature will be reflected not only by Indians who write about Indian society but by Swedes, Americans, Frenchmen, Italians, who also write about Indian society. I do not see that Indian society can develop by building walls around itself, and that is why I have always been unhappy with the title of our pre-eminent sociological journal, namely, *Contributions to Indian Sociology*. That is not a very appropriate title; I don't think that I would like to work towards the building of a specifically Indian sociology. Sociology of India, certainly, but it has to include a comparative perspective. In most of my writings, I have tried to carry a comparative perspective and I think that such a perspective is terribly important.

SM: What about the argument, variously developed by people like Srinivas and Merton, that there are often significant differences of perspective between insiders and outsiders in social research? Do you reject the idea that there is a specifically Indian perspective on Indian society?

AB: That argument can easily be taken too far. On many points I find myself much more in agreement with someone like Gerald Berreman, for example, who is an American, than I do with some of my Indian colleagues who work in the same department, and that, I think, is how sociology should develop. I do not think that there is a particular Indian genius, which should express itself differently in the understanding of Indian society from the way in which that understanding is expressed by a Frenchman, or an American, or a Scandinavian. How you approach the subject depends very much on your value commitments, it depends very much on the problems that you select, and probably, as a matter of fact, there will be some differences of emphasis. But I would be unhappy to see the sociology of India as developed by Indian sociologists growing in one way and the sociology of India as developed by western sociologists growing in a different way. In a very important sense, the modern world is one; it is no longer what it was in the nineteenth century; that is extremely important.

SM: One of the arguments of the debate around the concepts of academic colonialism and dependency, an argument that lies behind the plea for a specifically national sociology in many places, is that the asymmetries of the global academic system tend to prevent, or make it very difficult, for the intellectuals at the periphery to be independently creative and critical. More specifically, it is suggested that the structures of centre and periphery are such that through the selection of problems, the choice of theories, and so forth these intellectuals tend to approach the study of their own society in ways that do not reflect their own existential conditions so much as those of their metropolitan colleagues. What do you think about that?

AB: This is a very important issue; the difference between centre and periphery in the development of intellectual orientations is marked, and very important. I would say that when a young Indian sociologist embarks on a career of research the problems that he chooses, the methods that he adopts, the concepts that he uses are determined by two sets of conditions; they are determined by his own experience of the society in which he lives and they are also determined by intellectual influences from the metropolis. Sometimes the balance is not right, sometimes the choices are determined very much more by intellectual influences coming in from outside, to the detriment of the richness of his own experience. The problem is there; the question is how we address ourselves to it. We cannot solve it by pretending that it does not exist, claiming that there is one universal sociology, one universal method, which can be applied anywhere. Nor can we solve it by insulating ourselves from the metropolis; that is not the right way of trying to deal with it. I believe that there is no possible way of ensuring permanent insulation. One can insulate oneself for a certain period of time, but when that period is over, one will have fallen behind a very great deal. One can see this from the experience of east Europe today. East European social science insulated itself substantially from the development of social science, including Marxism, in west Europe, and now they find themselves in the position where they have an enormous amount of backlog to catch up with. I think that this is bound to happen in the modern world; if India tries to insulate itself, it will also have an enormous backlog to catch up with when the insulation breaks down, which is bound to occur some time or other in the future. This is what is happening in China. I think Chinese intellectuals realize this very strongly, from whatever I have been able to gather. They realized this very strongly in the few years before June 1989. Thus the problem, the very real problem, of the disparity between the metropolis and the periphery, which to some extent you face in Sweden as well, cannot be solved by insulating ourselves from the metropolis; we should rather face it head on.

SM: With some reservations, you seem to accept the view that the strong metropolitan influence on Indian sociology has tended to divert the interests of Indian sociologists from questions which might otherwise have been central to them. What do you personally regard as the neglected areas of the study of Indian society?

AB: There are plenty of areas that have not been explored in the sociology of India, although you must realize that a lot of sociology is being done in India. The country is large and while resources are not very abundant, they are nevertheless available. Yet while there is hardly any area of sociology that is not being investigated somewhere in some university or some college, there are large areas that are not receiving the serious attention they deserve. The problem of the intelligentsia, which I have already mentioned, is one such area. It is mainly the economists who have dealt with this problem, but I feel that it is more deeply and more fundamentally a sociological problem, and I would like to see it examined much more seriously than has been done so far. I also think that nationalism requires to be studied more seriously. Another area is the sociology of the professions and the modern occupational structure, including occupational ranking. But I can only point to what I personally find interesting and exciting. This may be partly my commitment to a pluralistic attitude, but I find it very difficult to lay down a charter for all entrants into the sociological profession in India. The Indian Council for Social Science Research has been trying to do that for the last twenty years, but I think that this is not really how an intellectual discipline grows.

SM: I have the impression that by and large Indian sociologists and anthropologists are more concerned with problems of modernity, if not necessarily modernization, than their non-Indian colleagues studying India. Among western anthropologists, at any rate, India is often discussed in a more distant perspective, as a strange cultural specimen making sense mainly in contrast to western society; one of the main preoccupations of western anthropologists seems indeed to be the maximization of the differences between Indian society and western society. Would you recognize this as a genuine difference?

AB: The maximization of differences, as you call it, has become a kind of occupational disease in contemporary anthropology, the anthropology of the eighties. I think that it is very misleading, and I have written against it. Let me put it like this. There were those sociologists and anthropologists of an earlier generation who, under the influence of the theory of evolution and later under the influence of development sociology, regarded India, Latin America, and Africa as being copies of western civilization, except for the fact that they were less developed. The stress on similarity has that danger: they are the same, basically, only they need to try a little harder to catch up with us. What is equally unacceptable, however, is the view of the other, not as a copy of oneself, but as an inversion of oneself. This has been the dominant trend in the anthropology of India in the last twenty years; India as the opposite of the west, *homo hierarchicus* versus *homo equalis*, or code and substance seen in one way in America and in the opposite way in India.

SM: The work of Louis Dumont has been very important in the development of this approach. Your view of that work must be a fairly critical one?

AB: Louis Dumont's is a very powerful mind; there is no doubt about that. His work has stimulated me, as it has stimulated many other people. But I think that the total impact of Dumont's work has been in a sense a return to the book-view, as against the field-view of Indian society. I want to be very careful in applying this distinction. I don't mean that Dumont has not done fieldwork; he has done very good fieldwork. Yet the orientation of that fieldwork has been to the past rather than to the present, to the pure structure of traditional Indian society, to ritual and kinship rather than to all the untidy and messy things that are so much a part of the Indian reality today. In that sense, I think that his work has put the sociology of India back one step.

SM: Would it be correct to say that Dumont's work to some extent is a modern restatement of the common nineteenth-century view of India as the spiritual other of the secular, materialistic west?

AB: Let me repeat that Dumont is not a simple-minded intellectual; his is both a very powerful intellect and a very sophisticated one. Still there are very clear echoes of the old distinction in his work. In the nineteenth century, there was a kind of easy relationship worked out between the British, who were governing India, and the Indian intelligentsia. The view was that the Indians had religion and kinship and the Europeans economics and politics. In a way, this gave satisfaction to both parties. It enabled the British to do what they were in India to do, and it also satisfied the vanities of the Indians to think of themselves as a very spiritual people. It made them feel that they might be subordinate in material terms, but that they had a unique spiritual heritage. That is not just intellectually wrong; it is a politically mischievous point of view. Every society has to handle its problem of religion; there is no society which does not have to do that. Religion may take new forms, but the notion of the sacred is part of every society. Likewise every society has to attend to its economic and political problems.

SM: One of your more specific criticisms of Dumont and those who have adopted his approach is that they do not pay sufficient attention to the inequalities of the market, inequalities which are very pronounced in India as well as in the west. How do you think that the increasing acceptance of the market among Indian authorities in recent times and the concomitant decline of Nehru's idea of a socialistic pattern of society will affect the sociology of India? Will there now be a shift towards the study of market inequalities among sociologists and anthropologists?

AB: Even under the socialistic pattern of society, the market was generating all kinds of inequalities, which were there for everybody to see. It is true that the anthropologists did not look at those inequalities by and large; they looked at the inequalities of caste. However, these inequalities were not ignored by the Marxists. One must not forget that over the last forty or fifty years there has been a fairly powerful Marxist intellectual current in India, particularly in Bengal, which is the part of India where I come from. The Marxists have been very much aware of the fact that capitalism generates new inequalities, not only in urban areas, but also in the rural areas. They have been engaged in important discussions about the semi-feudal mode of production, capitalist farming, and so forth. I took this up in the late sixties and early seventies; I worked on agrarian social structure and class formation, and I had students who worked on class formation. The problem with the anthropologists then was that they were preoccupied with the traditional hierarchy. I grew up in the city of Calcutta, and if you walk the streets of that city you cannot miss the inequalities of the market, which are generated on a very different basis from the traditional inequalities.

SM: One very striking aspect of the economy of contemporary India is the juxtaposition, or combination, of a large-scale, largely public and largely urban sector, governed by the protective principles of the modern welfare state, and a small-scale, largely private and largely, but by no means exclusively, rural sector, where people are ruthlessly exposed to the unregulated forces of the market. This structure has been examined in terms of the concepts of the so-called formal and informal sectors, but not so much in the more sociological terms of class and social stratification.

AB: These are problems that have been left to the economists by and large; the sociologists and the anthropologists have not really looked at them; except when they were Marxists. You see, no matter what sort of a welfare state you have in India, no matter how socialistic its ideology, one must not forget the fact that most Indians live in villages and most Indians work in agriculture, where you have private holdings. The pressure of population, new technology, market forces and so forth have transformed Indian agriculture, creating an increasingly larger class of landless agricultural workers. The logic of those inequalities is not the same as the logic of the hierarchy of Brahman, Kshatriya, Vaishya, Shudra, and so forth. It is very difficult for the state to reach into that area. It is not that the state has never tried. To be fair to the state, land reforms have had some effect, but obviously they have not cancelled or even arrested the development of new inequalities. Yet the modern working class has done rather well by itself, and if you can get a foothold into the corporate sector, even as a manual worker, you enjoy a kind of protection which the agricultural labourer, or even the small tenant, does not enjoy in the rural areas. Manual workers in large industry, whether in the public sector or in the private sector, do reasonably well by themselves. That has been partly the result of the welfare state, which has protected the interests of the working class, first in the public sector and then through the demonstration effect in the private sector as well. But this working class comprises only a small section of the disadvantaged in Indian society.

SM: It seems that we have now returned to where we started, to the important role of the intelligentsia in Indian society. One very remarkable thing about India, it has often been pointed out, is that unlike many other so-called developing countries, including most of its neighbours, it has managed to keep a pluralistic political system going. This, I assume, is something for which the Indian intelligentsia must receive much of the credit?

AB: You were very right to point out that the Indian intelligentsia like to think worse of themselves than they really are. They are indeed a very self-deprecatory class of people. Yet I think that if India has had reasonable success with a pluralistic political order, with a free press, a multiparty system, more or less regular elections, and so forth, the role of the intelligentsia, and particularly the intellectuals, cannot be discounted. Yes, I think they have played some part in ensuring that all that works.

Appendix

II

Is there a Marxist Anthropology?

I s there a Marxist anthropology? It may appear capricious to ask this question at a time of unprecedented enthusiasm for Marxism among social anthropologists in Britain, France and America. Yet the question has been asked for more than fifty years in relation to the cognate discipline of sociology, and the answers given to it there have been by no means clear or unequivocal.[1]

Any discussion of the scope or possibility of a Marxist anthropology must begin by recognizing the plurality of conceptions people have of both anthropology and Marxism. I would like to disclaim any pretence at dealing even-handedly with all the available conceptions, or even the most important among them, of either Marxism or anthropology.[2] My attempt will be to confront a particular conception of the one with a particular conception of the other. I hope that my choice will not appear altogether arbitrary in either case, although such a choice is bound by its nature to be personal. It should be said at the outset that I make no claim to being a Marxist and that my credentials as an anthropologist are easily open to question.

The two conceptions that I would like to bring face to face are of anthropology as 'the study of other cultures' and of Marxism as 'the philosophy of praxis'. I would like to argue that these are both valid and authentic conceptions, the first of anthropology and the second of Marxism. What exactly are the problems in establishing and maintaining a working relationship between the study of other cultures and the philosophy of praxis?

This seems to me to be the fundamental question to be asked in a discussion of Marxist anthropology, and I am struck by the facility with which it is evaded by anthropologists who are keen to see their discipline enriched by its association with Marxism.[3]

The problem on which I am trying to focus attention will vanish to a large extent if we represent Marxism as a positive science and social anthropology as the comparative study of human societies in general. Indeed, it may be argued that the aim of social anthropology as defined by some of its ablest exponents has been to establish nothing less than a fully comparative sociology. On the other side, there have been Marxists who have claimed with considerable authority that their theoretical objective has been to establish an empirical science of society on a level with the natural sciences. Why should there be any problem in bringing together two approaches to the study of society that are both empirical, general and scientific?

Very little will be gained by making the problem of the relationship between Marxism and anthropology vanish by a choice of convenient definitions. It is a fact of recent intellectual history—in the west as well as outside—that Marxism and sociology have been at odds with each other to such an extent that a British sociologist, well known for his sympathy with Marxism, has said that we should perhaps speak not so much of a Marxist sociology as of a 'Marxist anti-sociology'.[4] The tensions between Marxism and anthropology lie even deeper and are perhaps for that reason less readily visible. The advantages in creating a closer relationship between anthropology and Marxism may be both real and obvious, but the difficulties in maintaining such a relationship are no less real, although they may not be equally obvious.

Anthropology as the Study of Other Cultures

What do we mean when we describe anthropology as the study of other cultures? It is important to distinguish between the aims, including the scope and method, of anthropology and the work actually done by anthropologists. Both have changed over time and there has always been some disparity between the two. Anthropologists have of course been aware of this disparity but they have not all responded to it in the same way. On the whole, anthropologists have been less concerned with what anthropology is than Marxists have been with what Marxism is, the question of orthodoxy being very differently considered in the two cases.

It is well known that disagreement on even fundamental questions of scope and method has not prevented anthropologists from working in close association with each other.[5]

In order to avoid going too far back into history I would like to begin with a consideration of the conception of anthropology characteristic of the work of Radcliffe-Brown. There are several advantages in doing this. Firstly, Radcliffe-Brown occupied a commanding position among anthropologists in his own country and throughout the Commonwealth at a time not very remote from our own. Secondly, he was tireless in his effort to define the scope and method of anthropology, expressing himself with great force and clarity on the subject.[6] And thirdly, Radcliffe-Brown came close to establishing a conception of anthropology which is in some ways the opposite of the one which I wish to explore here.[7]

As is well known, Radcliffe-Brown sought to develop anthropology into a natural science of society. He was a tireless advocate of the comparative method, and he argued that a natural science of society which was truly general and comparative could be created only by applying the same rules of procedure to the study of all human societies, from the simplest to the most complex. Such an approach cannot accommodate a radical separation between either primitive and advanced societies or other societies and one's own society. It is not surprising that for Radcliffe-Brown social anthropology and comparative sociology were one and the same thing, not in practice perhaps but certainly in principle.

It is forgotten how great Radcliffe-Brown's influence on anthropology was in Britain at a time when the subject was rapidly expanding there. His influence extended outside Britain as well. An anthropology freed from the taint of its historical association with 'primitive', 'savage' or 'uncivilized' societies has an immediate appeal in countries outside Europe and America. Indeed, it is difficult to see what students of society in Africa and Asia are to do with an anthropology which is tied to the study of 'primitive' societies. In India, a social anthropologist would rather call himself a sociologist and I believe that this is even more the case in Africa.

One cannot see how anthropology can establish itself as a general, comparative science of society without merging with sociology or displacing it. Radcliffe-Brown's claims on behalf of anthropology acquired some force in Britain precisely because sociology had not found a place for itself there. With the rapid expansion of sociology in Britain after his death, those claims began to lose much of their force.

In any case, the claims Radcliffe-Brown made in theory on behalf of social anthropology were never pursued very far in practice. Radcliffe-Brown's own specialized work was on the Australian Aborigines and the Andaman Islanders, types of society chosen for their simplicity, if not their remoteness from modern civilization.[8] The two collections of studies, one on political systems and the other on kinship and marriage, which became landmarks in British social anthropology and which both drew their inspiration from Radcliffe-Brown, were devoted to tribal or at least small-scale societies.[9] The title chosen for the collection of Radcliffe-Brown's own papers published towards the close of his life was *Structure and Function in Primitive Society*.[10]

Although Radcliffe-Brown made far-reaching claims for social anthropology as the theoretical natural science of society, he was always aware that it was in fact concerned mainly with the study of primitive or pre-literate societies. On the one hand he saw that if there was to be a general and comparative science of human societies, there could be only one such science and not two, one for primitive and the other for civilized societies.[11] On the other hand, the division of labour between students of the two kinds of society was too well established in Europe and America to be ignored or wished out of existence. In a textbook on which he began work after retirement from Oxford, he wrote, 'Social anthropology may be defined as the investigation of the nature of human society by the systematic comparison of societies of diverse types, with particular reference to the simpler forms of society of primitive, savage or non-literate peoples'.[12]

It is no accident that Radcliffe-Brown sought to establish his natural science of society by promoting the idea of social structure—or social morphology[13]—at the expense of culture. 'Culture' for him represented 'content', what was particular, whereas his interest was in the general. 'You cannot have a science of culture', he wrote. 'You can study culture only as a characteristic of a social system. Therefore, if you are going to have a science, it must be a science of social systems'.[14] He declared that it would be good if the concept of culture could be banished from anthropological discourse.

But culture, which to Radcliffe-Brown appeared an embarrassment, is in a very important sense what anthropological study is actually about. At the height of Radcliffe-Brown's influence in Britain, the belief was created that the study of culture was both unscientific and un-British, that it was a charactersitic of the American approach to anthropology.[15] Even in Radcliffe-Brown's lifetime this belief had very little basis.

Malinowski, who was Radcliffe-Brown's principal adversary in Britain, contributed as much as any other anthropologist to the understanding of culture; and Evans-Pritchard, who was Radcliffe-Brown's successor at Oxford, devoted himself primarily to the humanistic understanding of the ideas, beliefs and values of people lacking the resources of literacy.[16]

It is Evans-Pritchard's rather than Radcliffe-Brown's conception of anthropology that is embodied in a textbook published twenty years ago by another Oxford anthropologist, John Beattie. This book, entitled *Other Cultures*,[17] was widely acclaimed on publication and is used as a text in introductory courses on anthropology throughout Britain and elsewhere. In it Beattie maintains that, although closely related to sociology, social anthropology is also different from it, for social anthropologists study 'other people's belief systems not simply from a sociological point of view, but also as being worthy of investigation in their own right'.[18]

Both Radcliffe-Brown and Evans-Pritchard emphasized fieldwork as a central part of anthropology, but their attitudes to fieldwork were nevertheless different. Radcliffe-Brown regarded fieldwork in the spirit of a natural scientist: for him the field was a kind of substitute for the laboratory. For Evans-Pritchard fieldwork was much more of a total experience with emotional as well as intellectual implications. It was like a journey into another world whose moral categories were exciting precisely because they were different. For Evans-Pritchard—and countless others— it was the challenge of coming to terms with an unfamiliar moral universe that gave zest to fieldwork and hence to anthropology.[19]

Evans-Pritchard has written memorably about his own fieldwork among the Nuer. 'I was a *ger*, what they call a *rul*, an alien sojourner, among them for only a year, but it was a year's relationship of great intensity, and the quality of a relationship counts for more than its duration.' It was, he said, 'an experience which has greatly influenced my life'.[20] One carries back something of the culture one experiences in the field but, of course, one leaves the people behind. It will be difficult to exaggerate the value placed by anthropologists like Evans-Pritchard on leaving unchanged—perhaps 'unspoilt' would be a better phrase—the people whose experiences they have shared during fieldwork.

The intellectual task to which primacy is assigned in the approach described above is the 'effort at translation'.[21] It is not enough to penetrate the moral universe of another culture. One must travel back into one's own universe and illuminate it with the insight gained by looking at the human condition from a different angle. This kind of anthropology presumes the unity of human beings, but it combines that presumption with a respect for their differences.

The same conception of anthropology as the study of other cultures, even remote cultures, has been articulated by its most celebrated living exponent, Claude Lévi-Strauss. '*The anthropologist*', he has said, using a striking phrase, '*is the astronomer of the social sciences*'.[22] The point of emphasis in this conception is that the societies studied by anthropologists are chosen not for their simplicity or even their primitiveness, but for their distance, their remoteness from the social universe of the anthropologist.[23]

Lévi-Strauss has claimed for the study of primitive societies a privileged status among the sciences of man.[24] This privileged status is claimed not by virtue of any intrinsic property of these societies but by virtue of their position in relation to the observer: it is, as he puts it, 'the privilege of being distant'.[25] Distance not only gives enchantment to fieldwork, it provides a genuine advantage in the construction of theory. It is on this basis that Lévi-Strauss has repeatedly stressed the distinction between anthropology and sociology, and between anthropology and history.

The view from a distance has moral as well as scientific implications. The moral predicament of the anthropologist is different from that of the sociologist since the former studies societies other than his own whereas the latter studies his own society.

The sociologist objectifies for fear of being misled. The ethnologist does not experience this fear since the distant society he studies *is nothing to him*, and since he is not compelled in advance to extract all its nuances, all its details, and even its values; in a word, all that in which the observer of his own society risks being implicated.[26]

It is difficult to believe that the statement that the distant society the anthropologist studies 'is nothing to him' was meant to be taken literally. This was hardly Evans-Pritchard's sentiment about the Nuer, and I doubt if many anthropologists will subscribe to such a statement. On the contrary, they are inclined to stress the depth and intensity of their involvement with the people they have studied. If this appears at times to be a little strained, there is an element of generosity in it which it would be wrong to overlook.

While it is not generally true that the society studied by the anthropologist 'is nothing to him', it is nevertheless the case that anthropologists are on the whole reluctant to pass judgement on the societies they study. The moral attitude favoured by the anthropologist is not of the judge but of the witness. But this is an aspect of the relationship between the social scientist and the subject he studies that has received far less attention than it deserves. There has not been among anthropologists anything comparable to the debate among sociologists on the possibility of a value-free science of society. Perhaps there is, at this level, a genuine difference between those who study their own society and those who study other cultures.

Marxism as the Philosophy of Praxis

It is not necessary to argue at length that there are several versions of Marxism, indeed, several versions of orthodox Marxism.[27] Marxism has been presented as positive science and as revolutionary dialectic, as historical materialism and as philosophy of praxis. It is not my intention here either to attempt to reconcile these or other versions of Marxism or to argue that such an attempt at reconciliation is bound to fail. My aim is to discover where the points of tension between Marxism and anthropology lie, and if I choose to dwell on a particular version of Marxism, I do so with that aim in view.

All Marxists have assigned some importance to the connection between Marxism as an intellectual system with its own concepts and categories and Marxism as a political movement with its own aims and objectives.[28] After pointing to the fact that the founding of the First International and the publication of the first volume of *Capital* took place within three years of each other, Karl Korsch wrote, 'Within one single period of history, in the 1860s, both aspects of Marxism attained their full realization: the new autonomous science of the working class attained its developed theoretical form in literature at the same time as the new autonomous movement of the proletariat achieved its practical form in history'.[29] Marxists like Korsch and Lukács insisted that this connection was necessary and not contingent, and they saw in it the real foundation of their own method—the dialectical method—as against the methods of bourgeois social science.

If we speak today of a Marxist economics, a Marxist sociology, and even a Marxist anthropology, this is because Marxism has had a strong sense of its identity as an alternative to and not merely a critique of 'bourgeois' social science. This sense of Marxism as a radical alternative— a completely new departure—has not been equally strong everywhere or at all times, but it has given a distinctive orientation to Marxism as an intellectual system. We must proceed with some awareness of this if we are to explore the possibility of bringing together Marxism and anthropology, a discipline which has grown largely since Marx's time and outside the framework of his thought.

Marx presented his own principal work as a 'critique of political economy', intending it as a critique of both a given order of reality and a given body of theory. The theory was in some sense a reflection of the reality and its limitation lay precisely in its inability to see the contradictions in the reality of which it was a reflection. The categories of bourgeois thought were the categories of bourgeois society, and political economists from Petty to Ricardo had assumed these categories to be absolute, eternal and unchanging. Therefore, the critique of political economy could be made from only a particular standpoint, the standpoint of 'the class whose vocation in history is the overthrow of the capitalist mode of production and the final abolition of all classes—the proletariat'.[30]

The view of Marxism as an alternative to bourgeois social science, if not a negation of it, gained ground after Marx's death, especially after the great success of the Bolshevik revolution. Such a view was for a time sought to be extended to all branches of learning, although it could not be pressed equally far in the physical as in the historical sciences. It is not surprising that sociology was virtually supplanted during the whole of Stalin's regime; ethnography, however, was allowed to function within its particular sphere.

Marx's penetrating insights into the complex relationship between categories of thought and modes of social existence became codified into somewhat mechanical formulas in the hands of Soviet Marxists.[31] One such formula related to the 'class character of the social sciences'. In an influential work first published in 1921, N.I. Bukharin, then in the front rank of Soviet Marxist intellectuals, wrote, 'it is not difficult to see that bourgeois practice will demand one thing, and proletarian practice another; that the bourgeoisie will have one view of things and the working class another; that the social science of the bourgeoisie will be of one type and that of the proletariat unquestionably of a different type'.[32] Bukharin's didactic style is characteristic; what is unusual, for at least that phase in Soviet intellectual life, is his attempt to develop a system of sociology within the framework of historical materialism.[33]

While all social knowledge was believed in principle to have a class basis, not all the social sciences were viewed as being governed equally by class. For a variety of historical reasons, sociology was singled out as representing the standpoint of the bourgeoisie.[34] Economics and ethnography were viewed in a somewhat different light, the former because it was thought to have some of the properties of the natural sciences, and the latter because it was thought to be not directly involved in the interests of either of the two basic classes. The distinction between sociology and anthropology (or ethnography, to use the Soviet phrase) in Soviet social science is rooted in the distinction, fundamental to Soviet Marxism, between 'class societies' and 'classless societies'.

The view that social theory is or ought to be rooted in practical activity became quickly stereotyped within Soviet Marxism. But the same view served to breathe new life into Marxism outside the Soviet Union, particularly in the writings of Korsch, Lukács and Gramsci who were all contemporaries of Bukharin. All three writers had been deeply impressed by the Bolshevik revolution and they all sought, against the orthodoxy of the Second International, to present a version of Marxism that would acknowledge its profound significance for theory as well as practice.

Korsch and Lukács stressed the inherently revolutionary character of Marxism as both scientific theory and political movement: 'The philosophers have only *interpreted* the world, in various ways; the point is to *change* it'.[35] For them Marxism viewed as a positive science whose truth was independent of any political struggle was a contradiction in terms. A certain conception of Marxism as a positive science, more objective, more comprehensive and more accurate than previous forms of it, had become established as a part of the orthodoxy of the Second International. Korsch, Lukács and others attacked this conception as being a denial of the spirit of Marxism which was 'dialectical in theory and revolutionary in practice'.[36]

The link between Marxist theory and the revolutionary movement of the proletariat is an internal one. The theory cannot be fabricated independently of the movement at one place and applied at another place to the creation of such a movement. As Korsch put it, 'The emergence of Marxist theory is, in Hegelian-Marxist terms, only the "other side" of the emergence of the real proletarian movement; it is both sides together that comprise the concrete totality of the historical process'.[37] It is not easy to see how this can accommodate the kind of intellectual endeavour which defines itself as the study of societies at a distance.

Korsch made the mistake of attacking in the name of Marxism both Kautsky and Lenin, and his work soon faded from view. But the idea of Marxism as the theoretical expression of the revolutionary movement of the proletariat lived on in the writings of Georg Lukács, whose towering intellectual personality haunted European Marxists of more than one generation. I must say at once that I am not concerned here with the correct interpretation of Lukács's entire work which underwent many transformations,[38] but only with a particular vision of Marxism which has been expressed over and over again, but never as forcefully, as exactly or as clearly as by him.

As is well known, Lukács sought to characterize Marxism not by its results but by its method. He refused to make any concession to the criticisms of the revisionists and he rejected at the same time the orthodoxy of the Second International. He castigated those Marxists, whether 'revisionist' or 'orthodox', who 'seek refuge in the methods of natural science, in the way in which science distills 'pure' facts and places them in the relevant contexts by means of observation, abstraction and experiment'.[39] Thus, 'method' for Lukács meant something quite different from the methods of fact-finding developed by bourgeois social scientists in imitation of the natural sciences.[40]

The method characteristic of Marxism is the dialectic which is a movement towards unity of subject and object. Thought must change, but so must reality: 'It is not enough that thought should seek to realise itself; reality must also strive towards thought'.[41] Again, as Lukács puts it, 'for the dialectical method the central problem is to *change reality*'.[42] The dialectic is the appropriate method in the human sciences because the understanding of reality can be achieved only in the process of changing it.

The dialectical method is defined by Lukács in the sharpest opposition to the method of contemplation. Much of what passes for science in the bourgeois world, including natural science with its experimental method, is pure contemplation, for it accepts the structure of the world as it is given. Marxism rejects the possibility of understanding through pure contemplation. Nor is it a question of rejecting it only in theory. One must change the world through rational practical action; or else accept it blindly, fatalistically and without comprehension. Perhaps few Marxists would carry the argument about the dialectical unity of theory and practice to the point to which it was taken by Lukács; yet it cannot be denied that there is a fundamental antipathy in Marxism of every variety towards a contemplative orientation to the world.

The idea of Marxism as practical activity rather than disinterested pursuit of knowledge finds its most authentic expression in the life and work of Gramsci. Gramsci's description of Marxism as 'philosophy of praxis' was meant to evade the censors, but it was also singularly appropriate to his conception of it. Others have used the phrase 'critical philosophy', but for Gramsci the practical or creative side of Marxism was as important as the critical.

There are certain aspects of Gramsci's approach which the anthropologist is likely to find particularly congenial. These include his deep and continued preoccupation with culture, and his rejection of a one-sided emphasis on economic and material factors. An important reason behind the apathy, if not the hostility, of most anthropologists towards Marxism has been the close historical association of Marxism with economic determinism, and its relative neglect of culture as an important and to some extent autonomous area of collective life. In his effort to free Marxism from the straitjacket of a materialist philosophy, Gramsci appears to give back to culture its due place in human life.

Gramsci's concern, however, was not with culture at a distance but with culture at close quarters. The philosophy of praxis would cease to be itself if it became absorbed in a detached contemplation of distant cultures without any practical aim in relation to those cultures. Gramsci believed that a new culture representing the life and aspirations of a new class was taking birth and that the philosophy of praxis had a part to play in understanding it and, above all, in creating it.

Gramsci maintained that capitalism exercised pre-eminence not only in politics but also in thought. Capitalism could be displaced only by a new civilization which could not be called into being by a mere change in the distribution of power. What was required above all was a new way of looking at the world, new ideas and beliefs, in short, a new culture. It is here that the philosophy of praxis had a pre-eminent role 'as a modern popular reformation'.[43] The philosophy of praxis has aims and objectives that are distinct from those of any of the specialized social sciences.

The intellectual content, and not merely the intellectual function, of the philosophy of praxis is inseparable from the life of the class and party which are its characteristic bearers. Marxism not only expresses and creates the world-view of the working class, it can grow as an intellectual system only within the framework of the working-class party. The party rather than the detached or independent scholar was to provide intellectual leadership to the people. Marxism as the philosophy of praxis would reduce itself to nullity in isolating itself from the working-class movement and its political organ.

The distinctiveness of Marxism lies not so much in its rejection of a value-neutral science of society and culture as in the way in which its intellectual enterprise has been linked, in Marx's own writings, with the working-class movement, and, since Lenin's time, with the working-class party. Perhaps Marxism itself is now entering a new phase, as it did in 1889 with the establishment of the Second International, when these concerns were to some extent displaced by other ones. But even under the Second International they were only displaced and never repudiated or rejected.

Soviet and Western Anthropology

The fact that the philosophy of praxis may not go very well with the study of society at a distance does not necessarily mean that Marxists must neglect anthropology or that anthropologists should be indifferent to Marxism. Various kinds of accommodation have in fact been achieved and maintained between anthropology and Marxism at different times and in different places. It will be impossible to assess fully the relationship between Marxism and anthropology without considering some of the attempts so far made to develop a Marxist anthropology.[44]

Marxism had made very little impact on western anthropology until about twenty years ago. Maurice Godelier says, 'Marxism only made its appearance in anthropological research in France some time around the 1960s'.[45] In Britain, there were occasional attempts to apply the materialist interpretation of history to primitive societies as in Peter Worsley's ill-fated Curle Bequest Prize Essay,[46] but these were few and far between.[47] The situation was not very different in the United States, although there the work of Leslie White and his associates created some interest in what came to be known later as 'cultural materialism'.[48] Otherwise, if anthropologists from these countries ever referred to Marx and Engels, it was generally to show that almost everything the latter had written in *The Origin of the Family, Private Property and the State* was factually wrong and theoretically unsound.

When we turn to the Soviet Union we get a different picture. Soviet ethnography and western anthropology developed along somewhat different paths, and while Marxism is only now beginning to find adherents in the west, it has provided an intellectual background for ethnographic studies in the Soviet Union from the very beginning. Soviet scholars have maintained the distinction between sociology and ethnography (that is, anthropology) even more clearly than their western counterparts, and while sociology suffered long neglect, ethnography was able to follow a more even course of development. In no sense did ethnography seek to present itself as an alternative to Marxism, as bourgeois sociology might appear to have done.

Soviet ethnographers, like western anthropologists, began with the study of primitive, pre-literate or simple societies. The ethnographers were the first experts on the races, languages and cultures of the simpler peoples, but for various historical reasons the distinction between the study of other cultures and of one's own society did not acquire the same form in the Soviet Union as it did in America and Europe. Soviet ethnography is now extending its scope to cover all social formations from the simplest to the most complex;[49] but even here its subject matter, the study of ethnos and ethnicos,[50] reflects strikingly its basic pre-occupation with pre-class societies.

To the extent that Soviet ethnography has grown within the climate of Soviet Marxism, it has been marked by its emphasis on materialism and on progress, of which the cause as well as the symptom is material progress. In this sense, Soviet ethnography has retained much more of the original flavour of anthropology as it was in the nineteenth century than its counterparts in Europe and America. The link with the nineteenth century goes through Engels to Morgan and the beginnings of anthropology. Nineteenth-century anthropology, including the anthropology of Morgan, was evolutionary rather than revolutionary. The connection between what Engels wrote about primitive societies and any kind of revolutionary praxis was at best indirect and implicit.

The two outstanding features of Soviet ethnography as I see it are its historicist concern and its concern with the problems of ethnos.[51] Both these have been fitted into the framework of Marxism which in the Soviet Union is viewed above all as the materialist interpretation of history. If Soviet ethnographers show greater unity in their theoretical framework than their western counterparts, this is partly because of the high degree of consistency characteristic of Soviet Marxism. This is not to say that there are no disagreements among Soviet ethnographers, but these disagreements centre around certain basic issues whose significance is widely, if not universally, acknowledged.

A statement by a Soviet ethnographer declares; 'The leading principle of ethnographic research in the USSR is historicism', and further, 'The Marxist materialistic view of history underlies this approach'.[52] Soviet ethnography has, in keeping with the spirit of Soviet Marxism, served to reinforce the view that human history is an extension of natural history. Not only is progress ineluctable, but the stages of progress are also determinate, and one of the tasks of ethnography is to identify the succession of stages in the development of society.[53]

The concept of ethnos has provided Soviet ethnographers with their basic organizing principle for studying the contemporary world. Indeed, it is through the development of this concept and its application to the contemporary world that Soviet ethnography has made its most significant advances. The concept of ethnos has enabled Soviet ethnographers to study all social formations from the most archaic to the most progressive within a single theoretical framework. It has enabled them to reach towards a universal human problem while articulating at the same time a distinctively Soviet preoccupation. Soviet ethnography has not only had greater continuity than Soviet sociology, it has also been more innovative.

It would, however, be a mistake to overlook the fact that the concern for ethnos derives from the historical association between ethnography and the study of archaic or simple societies. Thus, while the division of labour between ethnography and sociology no longer rests on the simple distinction between archaic and progressive societies, a division of labour nevertheless exists. This division of labour rests on the distinction between 'ethnic' phenomena and 'social' phenomena in the strict sense of the term. As a leading Soviet ethnographer has put it, 'It is necessary to note the conventional delimitation of ethnic phenomena proper and social phenomena proper; by the latter we understand essentially class and professional relations and corresponding institutions'.[54] In other words, the study of class is put outside the reach of ethnography by confining the latter to the study of either 'pre-class' societies in their totality or ethnos and ethnicos in 'class' and 'post-class' societies.

In fairness to Soviet social science, it must be pointed out that the concerns of Soviet Marxism, at least since the death of Lenin, have never been the same as the concerns of Occidental Marxism.[55] Soviet Marxism has presented itself as dialectical materialism rather than as philosophy of praxis, and its concerns have been those of a post-Revolutionary society, that is, one in which the working-class revolution has already been made. Hence the kinds of tension on which I have earlier dwelt are likely to be least marked in Soviet ethnography, especially since Soviet ethnographers have never ventured on field expeditions outside their own society extensively enough to have felt the need to claim a separate scientific status for the study of other cultures.

When we turn to the west, we are struck by the diversity of both western anthropology and western Marxism. The conception of Marxism as a philosophy of praxis and of anthropology as the study of other cultures are both distinctively western conceptions, but this does not mean that either conception has held its ground without any rival. Indeed, most western anthropologists who have thought of themselves as Marxists have thought of Marxism somewhat differently from the way in which Lukács or Gramsci might represent it. For them, the main lesson to be drawn form Marxism has been materialism rather than the unity of theory and practice. They have, with a few exceptions, fought shy of the problem of relating their theoretical enterprise to any kind of political practice within a Marxist framework.

In discussing the interface between Marxism and western anthropology I shall speak first of American anthropology and then of British and French anthropology. American anthropology had for a long time a place for a few Marxists, although it was a subordinate place. The mainstream of American anthropology has at least since the time of Boas been either unsympathetic or indifferent to most, if not all, of the concerns of Marxism. Until the 1960s and 1970s Marxist anthropologists in America were a small minority, sharing perhaps a certain sense of being victims of the academic establishment.[56]

The mainstream of American anthropology has been dominated at least in the twentieth century by its anti-evolutionist bias and by its concern for culture viewed as the superorganic. The former may be traced back to Boas[57] and the latter was given currency by Kroeber.[58] On both these counts, Marxist anthropologists came into conflict with established positions in their discipline. For some time it was mainly the Marxists who were prepared to champion the theory of evolution although, of course, there is no necessary connection between Marxism and evolutionism, the concept of evolution fitting better in most ways with a liberal than a radical theory of history.[59] Further, it became a hallmark of the Marxist approach to primitive societies to stress the primacy of material factors over beliefs and values, although, again, material culture had at one time been a subject of general interest for all anthropologists.

The American anthropologist known best for his Marxist sympathies was Leslie White, who exercised considerable influence through his own work and the work of his younger colleagues and pupils at the University of Michigan. Leslie White was an evolutionist and a materialist, perhaps best known for his 'energy theory of culture', according to which the evolution of culture may be measured by the amount of energy harnessed per capita per annum.[60]

It was Leslie White who developed the viewpoint known as 'cultural materialism', although the term itself was given currency by Marvin Harris who became best known among White's successors for his Marxist sympathies.[61] But cultural materialism, whether in White's conception of it or in the form given to it by Harris, is Marxism in only a very special sense. Both White and Harris reject the dialectic as an unnecessary obstacle to the development of a scientific cultural anthropology. Harris in particular has argued for a value-neutral anthropology, maintaining that cultural materialism has no implications for political practice.

British anthropology had until the 1970s maintained a comfortable distance from Marxism, although some might detect a Marxist aroma in the work of Gluckman and more recently in that of Goody. A notable exception in the fifties was the ambitious paper by P.M. Worsley which sought to recast Fortes's Tallensi material within a Marxist framework.[62] This framework had at that time appeared fairly simple and straightforward in that it was based on a recognition of the primacy of the relations of production (meaning the economic structure) over the superstructure (including kinship). Worsley took his stand on the argument that the primacy of economics over kinship, which had been established in the study of advanced societies, was in fact valid for all societies. Although he was a committed Marxist when he wrote his paper, Worsley did not spell out the political implications for the Tallensi of his new theoretical insight into their social structure.

There is today much greater interest among British social anthropologists in modes of production.[63] This interest has impelled them to take a closer look at the entire corpus of Marx's writings rather than at only those which Marx, and more particularly Engels, devoted to non-western societies.[64] Though central to the Marxist approach, an interest in modes of production does not of course commit an anthropologist to Marxism as a system. One may well consider a society's mode of production to be only one among its several fundamental features, and an interest in modes of production may or may not be accompanied by a commitment to any specific programme of action. All that can be said perhaps is that anthropologists in Britain have shed some of their inhibitions about appropriating concepts believed earlier to have been tainted by their association with Marxism.

The interest among British anthropologists in modes of production owes much to influences from France which is the only country outside the USSR where serious attempts are being made to establish a fully-formed Marxist anthropology. French anthropology differs from Soviet ethnography as much as French Marxism does from Soviet Marxism, but beyond that it is not easy to say much more. French anthropology has attained international standing relatively recently and French Marxist anthropology even more recently, and it is still marked by something of the effervescence of a new intellectual movement. Almost from its very birth Marxist anthropology in France has been divided, and this very division reveals some of the fundamental problems that arise in bringing Marxism and anthropology face to face.

Maurice Godelier has listed the principal issues that divide Marxist anthropologists in France.[65] These include issues of both theory and practice, but while he has dwelt at some length on questions of theory, he has barely touched upon the political issues involved. We learn that some French Marxist anthropologists are or were Trotskyist activists and others Communist Party activists, but we do not learn what implications this has for the communities they investigate.[66] Anthropological investigation, of no matter what kind, obviously has some direct implications for the investigators; one presumes that a truly Marxist investigation would also have some implications for the investigated.

We get some indication of the way in which Marxist anthropology can relate to the political concerns of the people under investigation in the work of Claude Meillassoux.[67] Beginning with studies in West Africa, he has tried to show how capitalism sucks the tribal domestic community into its orbit of influence. Deprived of hearth and home, the West African tribesman or peasant becomes a migrant labourer in France where he has to work under severely exploitative conditions. The peasant-proletarian from West Africa lives in two worlds without security in either. Meillassoux's work on tribal migrants moving between West Africa and France is as yet tentative and exploratory, but it seems to me to be based on an implicit rejection of the idea that anthropology is the study of other cultures and that the anthropologist is the astronomer of the social sciences.

Marxism as a theory of knowledge is concerned in a fundamental way with the practical implications of that knowledge for the people whose lives it seeks to illuminate. Knowledge about the Nuer is not just for the anthropologist; it is, or should be, above all, for the Nuer: to compromise on this would be to repudiate the spirit of Marxism. It seems to me that although many western anthropologists are today captivated by Marxism, few have given serious thought to the part that may be played by the knowledge they generate in transforming the lives of the people among whom they live and work as anthropologists. Their political concerns, if any, have been mainly with the implications for themselves of political divisions in their home environment.

A question on which Marxists and non-Marxists are often divided in the related field of sociology is that of a value-neutral science of society.[68] At least in western countries today the idea of a value-neutral sociology is associated more with a non-Marxist or bourgeois point of view, whereas most Marxists would maintain that such a sociology is neither possible nor desirable.[69] The place of values in the study of culture and society has not been discussed in quite the same terms in anthropology as in sociology, although the question is as important in the one case as in the other. The possibility of a distinctively Marxist anthropology will, in my opinion, turn much more around this question than around questions about modes of production or the relationship between infrastructure and superstructure.

Those with a liberal conscience are perhaps inclined to feel that, while a case may be made for passing judgement on one's own society, it might be unethical or at least ungenerous to do the same for another society. A person is bound to his own society in a way in which he never is to a remote or a distant society. A recommendation for political intervention is never without a price. A person pays at least part of the price of his recommendation for his own society; who pays the price of one's recommendation for another society?

As is well known, the assessment among Marxists of the revolutionary potential of the different parts of the world has altered vastly between the time of Marx's death and the present. Marx and his immediate successors thought of the advanced societies of the west—England, France and Germany—when they thought of a revolutionary transformation through the class struggle. The countries of Asia, Latin America and Africa did not figure very prominently in their consideration of the centres of revolutionary movements. If they thought of hunters, gatherers and shifting cultivators, they thought of them as objects rather than as subjects of history.

All of this has changed in the hundred years since the death of Marx. The Bolshevik and the Chinese revolutions revealed the part that revolutionary consciousness could play in economically-backward societies. The withdrawal of the established imperial powers—Britain, France, the Netherlands—from their colonies was accompanied by revolutionary, militant and insurgent movements in Asia, Africa and Latin America. Precisely at that historical moment, when the working-class movement in the west faced the threat of embourgeoisement, the Third World was waking to new life, opening up unprecedented vistas of revolutionary possibility.

It is well known that in the 1960s radical movements in the west under the inspiration of writers ranging from Marcuse to Fanon, turned their attention away from the established working class in search of revolutionary potential among new classes and strata. These included students, but also minorities, 'ethnics' and triabls—the very people whose study had been the anthropologist's vocation. It is difficult to believe that the appearance of Marxism in anthropological research in the 1960s, of which Godelier has spoken, was unrelated to the appearance at the same time of new possibilities of political mobilization. Needless to say, all of this made little or no impact on Marxist ethnography in the Soviet Union.

It is not surprising that anthropologists who leave their homes in Europe and North America to do fieldwork in distant places in Asia, Africa and Latin America are often struck by the material and moral impoverishment of the people among whom they live and work. Imperialism, capitalism and neo-colonialism have left very few parts of the world untouched, and 'the destruction of aboriginal society' has become a commonplace of anthropological writing. The same Lévi-Strauss who has called the anthropologist the 'astronomer of the social sciences' has also described anthropology as 'daughter of an era of violence'.[70]

More than any other social scientist from the west, it is the anthropologist who encounters at close quarters people of small resources whose very survival is threatened by the advance of civilization. The experience of fieldwork, which has become the hallmark of anthropological research, particularly in Britain, gives the anthropologist a kind of privileged access to the inner lives of the people he studies. As has been stressed by so many practitioners of the craft, fieldwork is as much a moral as an intellectual experience. Whatever may be their general intellectual orientations, few anthropologists find it easy to adopt a morally-neutral position towards the people whose lives have, however briefly, touched their own.

Although the anthropologist seeks out an alien culture, he does so with the conscious intention of establishing a point of intimate contact with another human community. Anthropologists have written at length about the human aspects of their fieldwork experiences in distant places. Graduate seminars in Departments of Anthropology, at least in the English-speaking world, are full of personal accounts of each member's experience of his own fieldwork. It is almost a point of honour with the anthropologist to speak well and perhaps also to think well of his chosen people.[71]

Even where the anthropologist defines his theoretical task as the study of other cultures, it does not necessarily mean that he practises detachment from the community he actually studies. Anthropologists of every persuasion develop some kind of commitment to the well-being of these communities. It is not surprising that at least some of them should seek to translate this commitment into a programme of social transformation based on a definite ideology. Perhaps this urge to generate a total political transformation has grown with the growing awareness of the misery and squalor that are the common lot of tribesmen and peasants in Asia, Africa and Latin America. Viewed in this light, Marxism appeals to something generous in the anthropologist as a person with a concern for the human condition.

But after all this has been said, it must also be admitted that there is an element of make-believe in the intimacy between the anthropologist and his chosen people. Nothing is more difficult than to establish true reciprocity between unequals; and having for twenty-five years watched western anthropologists come to do fieldwork in India, I am not sure that all of them have even a genuine desire for reciprocity. The anthropologist comes with gifts which his informants covet even when they suspect that they may not be of much value. It is true that the anthropologist has to endure many of the hardships of a life of meagre resources. But his hardships are the hardships of camp life; the hardships of the natives are permanent and without visible escape.

Even where the moral concern of the anthropologist for the people he studies is deep and authentic, it does not follow that this concern will be expressed in a political programme. The lack of a definite political programme is no evidence of absence of concern, particularly where it is a question of another society. It will not be difficult to find examples where anthropologists have felt and expressed, at some risk to themselves, deep moral concern for the people they have studied without engaging in political action that might put at risk the people whose trust they have enjoyed.

Advocates of a Marxist anthropology must accept the full implications of the distinction between the anthropologist as witness and as partisan. Nothing much is required to be said about the anthropologist as witness because that has been his conventional role as a student of other cultures, at least since the profession differentiated itself from the activities of explorers, missionaries and administrators. It is true that some anthropologists have in the past played a sort of political role as agents of the colonial government, but this is an aspect of their past of which liberal anthropologists are not very proud. If there are anthropologists today who continue to play such a role, they do so furtively and under cover of some other activity.

For a hundred years and more Marxists in Germany, France, Italy and other western countries have debated and explored the possibilities of creating a scientific understanding of their own society in conjunction with the working-class movement. They have spoken of a new kind of intellectual—the 'organic' intellectual—and of a new milieu for intellectual activity—the working-class party—as bearers of a new understanding of society. Marxist anthropologists have not so far provided any significant clues as to how they expect to achieve the unity of theory and practice in their encounters with distant societies.

The Marxist anthropologist, if he is true to his political vocation, will resist the delimitation of anthropology to the study of other cultures. Those of us who have sought to resist this delimitation on other grounds have come to realize how difficult it is in practice to do so. Linking the study of man to a political project brings out another dimension of this difficulty. The anthropologist does not stand in the same relationship to the tribesmen he studies as the sociologist does to the working class in his own society. The man who combines science and politics in his own society accepts a lifelong commitment, exposing himself to all the risks of such a commitment. The anthropologist who goes to work in a distant community is by contrast a transient, what the French call a *passager:* he can give only a small part of himself and therefore his claims will always remain suspect. In this sense, a Marxist anthropology appears to be even more problematic than a Marxist sociology.

Notes and References

1. For a provocative response, going back to the fifties, see Lucien Goldmann, 'Y a-t-il une sociologie marxiste?'. *Les temps modernes*, No. 140, October 1957, pp. 729–51.

2. I exclude from consideration anthropology in the special sense of 'philosophical anthropology' as developed within the German intellectual tradition. For a consideration of the place of Marxism in anthropology in this sense, see George Markus, *Marxism and Anthropology*, Van Gorcum, 1978.

3. It is on the whole evaded by Maurice Bloch in his otherwise excellent recent book, *Marxism and Anthropology. The History of a Relationship*, Clarendon Press, 1983.

4. T.B. Bottomore, 'Marxist Sociology', in *International Encyclopedia of the Social Sciences* (David L. Sills, ed.). Macmillan and Free Press, 1968, Vol. 10, p. 52. See also his *Marxist Sociology*, Macmillan, 1975, especially chapter 3, 'Marxism against Sociology'.

5. An example that immediately comes to mind is the long and I believe cordial relationship between Radcliffe-Brown who sought to make anthropology

into a natural science and Evans-Pritchard who viewed it as a branch of humanistic studies.

6. See A.R. Radcliffe-Brown, *A Natural Science of Society*, Free Press, 1957; also his *Method in Social Anthropology* (ed. M.N. Srinivas), University of Chicago Press, 1958. Radcliffe-Brown was also a very persuasive speaker as has been attested by a somewhat unsympathetic witness, E.R. Leach in his Radcliffe-Brown Lecture: 'Radcliffe-Brown's academic influence depended much more on what he said than on what he wrote. He had a large, imposing physical presence, he was very fluent, and he was superficially knowledgeable about a great variety of subjects' (Edmund Leach, 'Social Anthropology: A Natural Science of Society?' *Proceedings of the British Academy*, Vol. 62, 1976, p. 8).

7. This conception is most clearly set forward in Radcliffe-Brown, *A Natural Science of Society*.

8. Radcliffe-Brown's work on the Australian Aborigines was published in several papers, notably, 'Three Tribes of Western Australia', *Journal of the Royal Anthropological Institute*, Vol. 43, 1913, pp. 143–94; and 'The Social Organization of Australian Tribes', *Oceania*, Vol. 1, pp. 34–63, 206–46, 322–41, 426–56, 1930–1. His work on the Andaman Islanders was published in a monograph, *The Andaman Islanders*, Cambridge University Press, 1922.

9. M. Fortes and E.E. Evans-Pritchard (eds.), *African Political Systems*, Oxford University Press, 1940 (with a Preface by A.R. Radcliffe-Brown); and A.R. Radcliffe-Brown and C. Daryll Forde (eds.), *African Systems of Kinship and Marriage*, Oxford University Press, 1950.

10. A.R. Radcliffe-Brown, *Structure and Function in Primitive Society*, Cohen and West, 1952.

11. Radcliffe-Brown, *Method in Social Anthropology*, p. 39.

12. Ibid., p. 111.

13. In this Radcliffe-Brown was a follower of Durkheim. See E. Durkheim, *The Rules of Sociological Method*, Free Press, 1966, especially chapter 4, 'Rules for the Classification of Social Types'.

14. Radcliffe-Brown, *A Natural Science of Society*, p. 106.

15. For the British point of view see R. Firth, 'Contemporary British Social Anthropology', *American Anthropologist*, Vol. 53, 1951, pp. 474–90; for the American point of view see G.P. Murdock, 'British Social Anthropology', *American Anthropologist*, Vol. 53, 1951, pp. 465–73.

16. Meyer Fortes has given a more differentiated account of the influences that contributed to the formation of British social anthropology: 'two distinct lines of descent are represented in the intellectual heritage of modern social anthropology. I see one as going back through Radcliffe-Brown, Lowie, and Rivers, to Morgan and Maine in particular, and the other as going back through Kroeber, Malinowski, and Frazer, to Tylor and to some extent Boas. I see the

first one as the source of our structural concepts and theories, the second as the source of our speciality in the study of the facts of custom, or culture' (M. Fortes, *Kinship and the Social Order*, Routledge and Kegan Paul, 1970, p. 14). See also his *Social Anthropology in Cambridge since 1900*, Cambridge University Press, 1953.

17. John Beattie, *Other Cultures*, Cohen and West, 1964.

18. Ibid., p. 29.

19. The problems posed by an unfamiliar moral and intellectual universe are vividly documented in the first major study published by Evans-Pritchard, *Witchcraft, Oracles and Magic among the Azande*, Clarendon Press, 1937.

20. E.E. Evans-Pritchard, *Nuer Religion*, Clarendon Press, 1956, p. ix.

21. E.E. Evans-Pritchard, *Social Anthropology*, Cohen and West, 1951; see also Beattie, *Other Cultures*.

22. C. Lévi-Strauss, *Structural Anthropology*, Penguin Books, 1977, p. 25.

23. Ibid., p. 347.

24. C. Lévi-Strauss, *Structural Anthropology 2*, Penguin Books, 1978, p. 25.

25. Ibid., p. 28.

26. Ibid., p. 26, emphasis added.

27. See my 'Marxism, Pluralism and Orthodoxy' in A. Béteille, *Antinomies of Society*, Oxford University Press, 2000, pp. 34–56.

28. Firth's distinction between 'gut-Marxists' and 'cerebral Marxists' might appeal to a certain kind of common sense, but it is not likely to be acceptable to Marxists themselves. See Raymond Firth, *The Sceptical Anthropologist? Social Anthropology and Marxist Views on Society*, The British Academy, 1972.

29. Karl Korsch, *Marxism and Philosophy*, Monthly Review, 1970, p. 171.

30. Karl Marx, *Capital*, Progress Publishers, 1954, Vol. 1, pp. 25–6.

31. See my 'Marxism, Pluralism and Orthodoxy'; see n. 27 above.

32. Nikolai Bukharin, *Historical Materialism, A System of Sociology*, University of Michigan Press, 1969, p. 11.

33. Soviet Marxism remained indifferent, not to say hostile, to sociology until the mid-1950s.

34. The roots of this go back to Plekhanov's antipathy to Mikhailovsky and, beyond that, to Marx's dismissive attitude to Comte.

35. The eleventh and last of Marx's celebrated *Theses on Feuerbach*.

36. Korsch, *Marxism and Philosophy*, p. 69. It was precisely from this point of view that Goldmann had questioned the possibility of a Marxist sociology in 'Y a-t-il une sociologie marxiste?'

37. Korsch, *Marxism and Philosophy*, p. 45.

38. The changes of position adopted by Lukács have been written about by many, including Lukács himself. For a brief summary, see George Lichtheim,

Lukács, Fontana/Collins, 1970. See also his own 'Preface to the New Edition (1967)' in Georg Lukács, *History and Class Consciousness*, Merlin Press, 1971.

39. Ibid., p. 5.

40. Ibid. See also Jean-Paul Sartre, *The Problem of Method*, Methuen, 1963.

41. Karl Marx, *The Critique of Hegel's Philosophy of Right*, in T.B. Bottomore (ed.), *Karl Marx: Early Writings*, C.A. Watts, 1963, p. 54.

42. Lukács, *History and Class Consciousness*, p. 3.

43. Antonio Gramsci, *Selections from Prison Notebooks*, Lawrence and Wishart, 1971, p. 395.

44. See, for instance, Maurice Bloch (ed.), *Marxist Analyses and Social Anthropology*, Malaby Press, 1975; see also his *Marxism and Anthropology*.

45. Maurice Godelier, 'The Emergence and Development of Marxism in Anthropology in France' in Ernest Gellner (ed.), *Soviet and Western Anthropology*, Columbia University Press, 1980, p. 3. See also his *Perspectives in Marxist Anthropology*, Cambridge University Press, 1977 (first published in French, 1973).

46. P.M. Worsley, 'The Kinship System of the Tallensi: a Revaluation', *Journal of the Royal Anthropological Institute*, Vol. 86, 1956, pp. 37–75; see also n. 62 below.

47. M.N. Srinivas has pointed out in a personal communication the interest taken in the 1940s by both Gluckman and Fortes in some of the ideas of Marx, but even Gluckman's approach to these ideas was eclectic. The first recent attempt by a major British anthropologist to review the relationship between the two was in Raymond Firth's Inaugural Radcliffe-Brown Lecture in 1972; see n. 28 above.

48. See Marvin Harris, *Cultural Materialism, The Struggle for a Science of Culture*, Random House, 1979.

49. See Gellner (ed.), *Soviet and Western Anthropology*, part 3, especially the contributions by Y. Bromley and L. Drobizheva.

50. Ibid.

51. Ibid., especially the articles by Y. Petrova-Averikieva and by Y. Bromley.

52. Y. Petrova-Averikieva, 'Historicism in Soviet Ethnographic Science,' in Gellner (ed.), *Soviet and Western Anthropology*, p. 19.

53. See in particular the contributions by Y.I. Semenov and E. Gellner in Gellner (ed.), *Soviet and Western Anthropology*.

54. Y. Bromely, 'The Object and the Subject-matter of Ethnography' in Gellner (ed.), *Soviet and Western Anthropology*, p. 155.

55. I have discussed the hiatus between Soviet and Occidental Marxism in my M.N. Roy Memorial Lecture cited above (n. 27). But there is a vast literature on the subject to which a recent contribution has been made by Perry Anderson, *Considerations on Western Marxism*, New Left Books, 1976. For a more extended discussion, see Leszek Kolakowski, *Main Currents of Marxism*, Clarendon Press, 1978, 3 Vols., especially Vol. 3.

56. This sense is very clearly expressed by Marvin Harris in his massive work, *The Rise of Anthropological Theory*, Crowell, 1968, although it is not very easy to assess the objective basis of this feeling of persecution.

57. The anti-evolutionist bias in Boas is well known. For an assessment of his work by a leading American evolutionist, see Leslie A. White, *The Ethnography and Ethnology of Franz Boas*, Bulletin of the Texas Memorial Museum, no. 6, 1963.

58. A.L. Kroeber, *The Nature of Culture*, University of Chicago Press, 1952. The phrase itself goes back to Herbert Spencer.

59. The connexion between evolutionism and the liberal view of history was traced by Mannheim in several of his writings. See Karl Mannheim, *Ideology and Utopia*, Routledge and Kegan Paul, 1936; also his *Essays on Sociology and Social Psychology*, Routledge and Kegan Paul, 1953.

60. Leslie A. White, *The Science of Culture*, Farrar, Strauss, 1969.

61. Harris, *The Rise of Anthropological Theory*.

62. P.M. Worsley, 'The Kinship System of the Tallensi: A Revaluation.' Fortes has disposed of Worsley's argument in his outstanding work, *Kinship and the Social Order*, pp. 220 ff. But see also Marshall Sahlins, *Culture and Practical Reason*, University of Chicago Press, 1976, pp. 4–18.

63. See, for instance, Bloch (ed.), *Marxist Analyses and Social Anthropology*; also his *Marxism and Anthropology*, especially chapter 6.

64. Bloch, *Marxism and Anthropology*.

65. See n. 45.

66. Ibid., p. 3–5.

67. Claude Meillassoux, *Maidens, Meal and Money*, Cambridge University Press, 1981 (first published in French in 1975); see also his *Anthropologie economique des Gouro de Cote d'Ivoire*, Mouton, 1964.

68. I have discussed some of these questions in my *Ideologies and Intellectuals*, Oxford University Press, 1980.

69. I do not wish to overdraw the contrast. The influential group of Marxists, known as Austro-Marxists, acknowledged the possibility of a value-free science of society—and were duly attacked by Korsch, Goldmann, etc. For the Austro-Marxist viewpoint, see Otto Neurath, *Empiricism and Sociology*, Reidel, 1973, see also T. Bottomore and P. Goode (eds), *Austro-Marxism*, Clarendon Press, 1978. On the other side, not all non-Marxists have or claim to have a value-free approach to the study of society and culture.

70. C. Lévi-Strauss, 'Anthropology: Its Achievements and Future', *Current Anthropology*, Vol. 7, no. 2, 1966, p. 126.

71. There are no doubt exceptions. Among the ones better known are R.F. Fortune, *Sorcerers of Dobu*, Routledge and Kegan Paul, 1932, and Cora Dubois, *The People of Alor*, Harvard University Press, 1960.

Name Index

Subject Index